MAKER OF HEAVEN AND EARTH

LANGDON GILKEY is a professor of theology at the University of Chicago Divinity School. Before he turned to theology, he studied philosophy at Harvard College and went to China in 1940 to teach English at Yenching University, Peking. In 1943 the Japanese sent him to an internment camp for "enemy nationals" where he was confined for the remainder of World War II. After his liberation and return to the United States, Dr. Gilkey decided to become a theologian and studied at Union Theological Seminary, Columbia University and, under a Fulbright scholarship, at Cambridge University in England. He taught religion at Vassar College and, after he received his Ph.D. in 1954, at Vanderbilt University Divinity School.

MAKER OF HEAVEN AND EARTH

The Christian Doctrine of Creation in the Light of Modern Knowledge

Langdon Gilkey

UNIVERSITY
PRESS OF
AMERICA

LANHAM • NEW YORK • LONDON

Copyright © 1959 by

Langdon Gilkey

University Press of America,® Inc.

4720 Boston Way
Lanham, MD 20706

This edition published in 1985 by University Press of America, Inc.
by arrangement with Doubleday & Company, Inc.

Library of Congress Cataloging in Publication Data

Gilkey, Langdon Brown, 1919-
   Maker of heaven and earth.

   Reprint. Originally published: Garden City, N.Y. :
Doubleday, 1959.
   Bibliography: p.
   Includes index.
   1. Creation.   I. Title
BT695.G5   1985   231.7'65   85-22607
ISBN 0-8191-4976-4 (pbk. : alk. paper)

PREFACE

This book brings to a close several years of study. Since the doctoral thesis of the author was concerned with the relation of *creatio ex nihilo* to process philosophy, the work for that thesis can fairly be said to be preparation for this volume on the idea of creation. Consequently in expressing my gratitude to others for their help in this writing, I find that my indebtedness stretches far back into my graduate-school days, and includes all those persons who in so many ways helped me to complete my studies.

First of all I wish to thank my two teachers at Union Theological Seminary, Reinhold Niebuhr and Paul Tillich, who have laid the theological foundations for so many of us who were their students and are their friends. To Dr. Niebuhr especially I owe my own first interest in theology as well as the fundamental bent of my thought. My indebtedness, both personal and intellectual, to each of these men is better revealed by these chapters than by inadequate words of preface. And I cannot recall my student days without expressing gratitude for the help and encouragement of John Bennett, of the late David Roberts, and of Horace Friess. I wish also to acknowledge at long last my debt to the American Council of Learned Societies, whose generous fellowships for two successive years made possible the study that led to the thesis that lies behind this book. Research on this topic was completed in Cambridge University with the aid of a Fulbright fellowship to Jesus College. While there, I enjoyed the great privilege of leisurely and stimulating discussions on philosophy and theology with my tutor, Canon I. T. Ramsey, then of Christ College, now of Oriel College, Oxford. Finally, I wish to thank Mrs. David Adams, Mrs.

Lawrence Hay, and Mrs. John McMahon for their un-complaining and accurate typing, and retyping, of this manuscript.

Langdon B. Gilkey

Vanderbilt Divinity School
September 20, 1958

CONTENTS

MAKER OF HEAVEN AND EARTH

Chapter 1

INTRODUCTION TO THE PROBLEM

Were anyone to ask "What is the first thing Christians say when they begin to state their beliefs?", he might quite reasonably conclude that this primary role was filled by the idea of creation. For when he opened the Scriptures, he would find the first line stating this belief: "In the beginning God created the heavens and the earth." And if he listened to the most universally repeated Christian creed, he would hear in its opening words: "I believe in God the Father Almighty, Maker of heaven and earth." Apparently the initial confession Christians make about the God they worship is that He is the Creator of the entire universe.

When, moreover, the inquirer delved more deeply into biblical religion to discover its conception of salvation, he would find himself again confronting the idea of creation. In the culminating points of biblical thought, the God who saves is understood to be the same as He who created all things. No conjunction of ideas is more important for biblical faith than this continued affirmation that God is not only Redeemer but Creator as well. For example, the great salvation passages of the Second Isaiah read:

Hast thou not known? Hast thou not heard?
That the everlasting God, the Lord,
The Creator of the ends of the earth,
Fainteth not, neither is weary? . . .
Even the youths shall faint and be weary,

And the young men shall utterly fall:
But they that wait upon the Lord shall renew their
    strength . . .[1]

Thus saith the Lord, thy redeemer,
And he that formed thee from the womb,
I am the Lord that maketh all things;
That stretcheth forth the heavens alone;
That spreadeth abroad the earth by myself; . . .
That saith to Jerusalem, Thou shalt be inhabited;
And to the cities of Judah, Ye shall be built,
And I will raise up the decayed places thereof . . .[2]

The Psalms as well reflect this tremendous conjunction
of ideas: He to whom we look for strength and salvation is
He who has created all that is:

The heavens are thine, the earth also is thine:
As for the world and the fulness thereof, thou hast
    founded them . . .
Thou hast a mighty arm:
Strong is thy hand, and high is thy right hand.
Justice and judgment are the habitation of thy throne:
Mercy and truth shall go before thy face.
Blessed is the people that know the joyful sound:
They shall walk, O Lord, in the light of thy counte-
    nance.[3]

Lord, thou hast been our dwelling place in all genera-
    tions.
Before the mountains were brought forth,
Or even thou hadst formed the earth and the world,
Even from everlasting to everlasting, thou art God.[4]

[1] Isaiah 40: 28–31. See also Isaiah 43: 1–13. (Unless otherwise
specified, all quotations from the Bible are from the King James
version.)
[2] Isaiah 44: 24–26.
[3] Psalm 89: 11–15.
[4] Psalm 90: 1–2.

Happy is he that hath the God of Jacob for his help,
Whose hope is in the Lord his God:
Which made heaven, and earth,
The sea, and all that therein is:
Which keepeth truth forever:
Which executeth judgment for the oppressed:
Which giveth food to the hungry. . . .
The Lord shall reign for ever,
Even thy God, O Zion, unto all generations.
Praise ye the Lord.[5]

When the inquirer turned to the New Testament, he would find the same essential motif: the Word of God through whom God saves the world is also He through whom God created the world:

In the beginning was the Word, and the Word was with God, and the Word was God. The same was in the beginning with God. All things were made by him; and without him was not anything made that was made. In him was life and the life was the light of men. . . . That was the true Light, which lighteth every man that cometh into the world. He was in the world, and the world was made by him and the world . . . received him not. But as many as received him, to them gave he power to become the sons of God . . .[6]

Finally, in the last book of the Scriptures, the same theme is repeated: the God whose saving power and glory we worship is He who is before all and after all, and who is the Creator of all things:

[5] Psalm 146: 5–6, 10. See also Psalms 90, 104, 136, 139, 147, 148.
[6] John 1: 1–12. In Colossians 1:16 ff. the same point is made: "For by him were all things created, that are in heaven and that are in earth, visible and invisible . . . all things were created by him and for him: And he is before all things, and by him all things consist. And he is the head of the body, the church: who is the beginning, the firstborn from the dead . . ." See also Hebrews 1:2.

. . . I am Alpha and Omega, the first and the last . . .
Holy, holy, holy, Lord God Almighty,
Which was, and is, and is to come. . . .
Thou art worthy, O Lord, to receive glory and honour
and power: for thou hast created all things, and for
thy pleasure they are and are created.[7]

The Fundamental Question

In the idea that God is the Creator, therefore, we find
one of the affirmations about God which the biblical
writers, and Christians after them, have regarded as of
primary importance to the Christian faith. And it is no
surprise that this is so: the idea that God is the Creator of
all things is the indispensable foundation on which the
other beliefs of the Christian faith are based. It affirms
what the Christian believes about the status of God in the
whole realm of reality: He is the Creator of everything
else. On this affirmation logically depends all that Christians say about God, about the world they live in, and
about their own history, destiny, and hope. The most
fundamental question of religious thought is: who is God
—He in whom we put our trust? And the primary answer
in both Bible and creed is: "He is the maker of the heavens and the earth." Of course this fundamental assertion
about God is accompanied by others of equal importance:
that God has redeemed Israel, that He has sent His son
into the world to reconcile the world to Himself, that He
loves His children and promises them eternal life if they
return to Him, and so on. These are the crucially significant actions God has undertaken for us, and so they are
the center of the devoted concern of Christians. But we
learn *who* has done these things through the all-important
affirmation that the Creator of all has done them.

In this sense the doctrine of creation provides that primary definition of God which gives meaning and signifi-

[7] Revelation 1:11, 4:8, 11.

cance to all else that is said about God. That God is a righteous judge, a loving savior, and the promiser of an eternal destiny, is certainly the central message of the Gospel. But the importance and meaning of these very affirmations depend on the belief that this judgment, this saving love, and this promise come to us from our Creator —He who has brought us and all else into being, and so He who claims us and rules over us with an essential and eternal power. For there are many judges, many "lovers," many promisers in life; each of them may have importance to us, some more and some less, but none of them has an ultimate claim on us, an ultimate power over us, and so an ultimate significance for us. The good news of the Gospel is not just that we are judged and loved. It is rather that He who is "the maker of the ends of the earth," and therefore He on whom we are totally dependent, judges and loves us. In this way the idea of creation gives meaning and significance to all else in the Christian faith.

The idea has further importance because it lays the foundation for the unique biblical understanding of our finite, historical life. The Gospel of God's saving love presupposes that men are children of God but "fallen" from Him, dependent on God and yet free, lost in life and yet essentially capable of rebirth through His power. It assumes, moreover, that men exist in a natural and historical environment which, while needing redemption, nevertheless has the potentiality of such transformation. All these ideas about man, his world, and his history are essential to the Gospel; and they are all grounded in the idea that God created the world "and saw that it was good." Thus without the idea of God's creation of the world, of history, and of man, the Gospel of the redemption of man's life from sin becomes meaningless, self-contradictory, and vain. The idea of creation expresses that fundamental relation between God and the world within which the Gospel of redemption is both important and viable, and so this conception provides the indispensable framework within which the Christian faith speaks its message of love.

— Finally, the Christian faith has always claimed that within its scope is the healing answer for all the most fundamental problems of man's life. Centrally, of course, this Gospel addresses itself to our problems of "conscience," to the disease of sin with its symptoms and effects in our moral unrighteousness. These are, however, not the only burdens of our existence: men are also deeply troubled by anxious fears arising from their weakness as creatures. The feeling of dependence and contingency, of being subject to uncontrollable forces, forms the content of one of these anxieties. The experience of temporality and mortality, of an approaching "deadline to one's powers and life," forms the frightening content of the other. These experiences of our "creaturehood" foster an undertone of anxiety in our lives; from this dread, too, we need rescue if we would be whole. To these anxieties of our finitude, the Christian faith in the creative and providential power of God provides the only sufficient answer. The idea of creation is, therefore, the concept in theology which answers the problems of our "creatureliness," namely our dependence and our temporality. It is more than the background of the Gospel of salvation: it is itself one of Christianity's most healing affirmations.

In Christian theology the affirmation that "God created the heavens and the earth" was from the earliest times formulated as the doctrine that God created all things out of nothing, *creatio ex nihilo.* Generally speaking, Christian thinkers until our day have regarded the first chapter of Genesis as both the classical scriptural source of this doctrine and the revealed description of how this originating event took place. With the meaning and validity of this doctrine we shall be concerned in this book. Some of the questions we shall ask are: 1) What really does it mean to say "God created all things out of nothing"? Does this mean an acceptance of the "creation story" in Genesis as a valid description of the beginning of our world? 2) Is it really essential to make this affirmation that God is our Creator, if we are also to affirm the other things which Christian faith says about God and about Christian salvation? 3) If it is thus essential to our faith, as biblical writers and churchmen alike have thought, how are we to understand its relation to the rest of our important ideas, especially to modern physical science and to metaphysical philosophy?

Scientific Objections

One would never guess from modern comments on the idea of creation that it contains such an essential and significant cluster of meanings as we have just described. Although most intelligent persons might dimly sense an important religious meaning inherent in this idea, still their immediate reaction would almost certainly be that the idea of creation "out of nothing" was an old, even primitive conception, made completely obsolete by modern science and philosophy. If this feeling represents a rather serious misunderstanding of the doctrine, it is nevertheless true that there are good historical reasons for its popularity. For the idea of creation came out of an ancient past into the modern world something like Don Quixote, a gallant knight unhappily clothed in outdated armor. Let us see, then, the connotations of this idea as it entered our modern scene, connotations that made it vulnerable to the "acids of modernity."

To the Christian of the eighteenth and nineteenth centuries the biblical idea of creation probably meant something like this: "Not so very long ago (4004 B.C., in fact), God, having dwelt in splendid isolation for eternity, suddenly created in one series of momentous, instantaneous acts the whole present world. In this single miraculous series of events, centering somewhere in Mesopotamia, the Lord made in their present form all the kinds and species of things that were ever to be: the sun, the moon, and stars were given their places, our present seas, mountains, and valleys were formed by His direct power, the present species of plants and animals were made by His hand. Thus the whole world as we know it came to be, not by an age-long process of gradual development, but by the fiat of a fabulous artificer in six days of furious activity." According to this view, a child could reasonably be asked in a typical fundamentalist examination on the Scriptures: "On what day were the crocodiles created?"

So expressed, it is small wonder that this doctrine had hard going in the rough and tumble of the scientific and skeptical modern world. For here the idea of creation carries not only a religious understanding of the ultimate relation between God and the world, but also semi-scientific information about the date, order, and method of the process of creation. The inevitable result was that *creatio ex nihilo* seemed to many intelligent Christians, as well as to secularists generally, to be one of those early mythological notions which the Hebrews expressed with their usual poetic and religious sensitivity, but which had no real value or validity for a modern man. Let us, therefore, look briefly at some of the objections, scientific, philosophical, and religious, which the modern mind feels toward this idea. Perhaps we shall find that, far from being justly tried and found wanting at the bar of our Western science and understanding of life, the belief in God's creation of the world is one of the essential bases for that science and that view of life.

1. The first objection comes, as we have indicated, from science. The later eighteenth and the nineteenth centuries saw the rise of a series of important scientific concepts about the origins of our world and the life upon it, which shook to its core the older biblical view as we have stated it above. The nebular hypothesis concerning the origins of the solar system and its planets, the geological explanations of the development of the characteristics of the earth itself, and the evolutionary hypothesis concerning the emergence of the present forms of life—all these pointed to the undeniable fact that our present world

order came to be by a process of immanent development spanning vast reaches of space and time. Every major scientific hypothesis of origins thus seemed to disprove conclusively the idea of a miraculous, sudden event only a few thousand years ago, in which an external, "personal being" created our present world by fiat. Many people reasoned, therefore, that if there was any one thing that modern science, from Copernicus through Darwin, had established beyond dispute, it was that the creation stories in the first chapters of Genesis were fables and nothing else. In this particular argument about the early history of our world, scientific opinion was surely correct. Nevertheless, the history of ideas in Western culture clearly shows that science itself could have developed only in a cultural environment which understood that the world and all that it contains was created by the will and the wisdom of God.

The Philosophical Objection

2. The second objection came mainly from philosophy. To the speculative philosophers of the nineteenth century the doctrine of *creatio ex nihilo* was an example of primitive mythology, expressing the origin of the world in crudely pictorial language. Did it not speak of the process of becoming in such blatantly anthropomorphic terms as "make" and "create"? Did it not, therefore, picture the development of the universe in concepts that suggest the making of a box or a cabinet? And did it not give, as the only reason for the world, the motivation of a humanlike will, namely that "it was good"? Surely it was necessary for the modern mind to translate this "childish" mythology into the more mature and intelligible language of philosophy. The first rule of philosophy requires us to cease talking of God as a personal being, "separate" from the universe, acting upon it only arbitrarily in terms of sudden whim, and to begin to talk of God and the world as impersonal realities, mutually implying one another and so

essentially related to one another. Thus the nineteenth-century speculative philosophy "rationalized" the idea of creation by stripping from it almost all its anthropomorphic terms, and by viewing God as an impersonal principle either identical with or a factor within the total developing system of the universe. Now this protest against an uncritically anthropomorphic theology was surely valid, as was the attempt to relate a fundamental theological idea to our other conceptions of the universe. But it is ironically true that the rejected idea of creation was, in the end, less anthropomorphic than most of its philosophical replacements. Deeply understood, it provides a more secure foundation than does speculative philosophy for that very order, coherence, and meaning which the philosopher seeks to understand and express.

The Liberal Protest

3. Even religious voices joined this scientific and philosophical chorus of protest. By and large, nineteenth- and early twentieth-century liberal theology accepted without drastic emendation the current philosophical and scientific understanding of reality as a creative process generating values out of its own development. For liberal religion, values "come up out of" the development of natural and cultural life; whatever power of goodness there is in existence is not "external" to the world, but immanent within the ongoing process. Understandably, therefore, many liberal religious leaders objected to the "dualism" of the idea of *creatio ex nihilo*. For in that idea, God, as the external, self-sufficient and eternal Artificer, is separated by an impassable gulf from the temporal, finite world He creates. How, they ask, can such a transcendent God be the source of the obvious values which have appeared with the development of process? Is it not better to think of God as the immanent creative spirit that has brought a world of order out of prehistoric chaos? Such a religious concept is

much more harmonious with the scientific understanding of creation as gradual development, and such a concept locates God's creative power where man actually has experienced it, in the natural and historical process which has brought forth so much good. Therefore, they said, let us dispense with the dualism of a transcendent, eternal Creator and a dependent, temporal creation! Let us rather think of God as within process, continually working out His purposes from within it, rather than suddenly acting supernaturally upon it from the outside. As one prominent liberal theologian put it:

> Nature and the supernatural are not two different kinds of reality, but two different aspects of one and the same reality. Nature expresses the law in the process, the supernatural the end to which it tends.

> God is not thought of as separate from the universe, but rather as its immanent law. He is not a transcendent being living in a distant heaven whence from time to time he intervenes in the affairs of earth. He is an ever-present spirit guiding all that happens to a wise and holy end.[8]

This liberal emphasis was much needed. The idea of the immanence of God had all but disappeared in Protestant orthodoxy, and the belief that God's creative activity was not just "once upon a time" in the remote past, but a continuing factor in the ongoing life of nature and of culture, has been an extremely valuable theological contribution. That present-day religious thought is so deeply concerned with culture, its problems and its hopes, is largely due to the emphasis liberalism placed on the immanent, creative activity of God in our cultural life. But it is also ironically true that those same convictions about

8 William Adams Brown, "The Old Theology and the New," *The Harvard Theological Review*, Volume IV, No. 1., January 1911, pp. 15–16. My thanks are due to my friend, Kenneth Cauthen, for these references.

the value of man's individual, cultural, and historical life, which the liberals sought to emphasize, depended more than they guessed on the very notion they abhorred: namely the "dualism" of a transcendent Creator and a dependent creation.

4. Finally, an old but powerful argument against the idea of creation gained immeasurable force in the minds of men in the eighteenth and nineteenth centuries. This argument centers around the problem of evil. It was not that these centuries were more conscious of evil in their world; on the whole, they seem to us sublimely unaware of its pervasive power. Rather it is that one of the major effects of the Enlightenment of the eighteenth century was to encourage every intelligent man to rethink even his most cherished beliefs solely in terms of the available evidence. Thus many fundamental ideas which had been long accepted on traditional authority, ecclesiastical or scriptural, were subjected to the cold light of critical reason for really the first time by ordinary Christian laymen.

One of the first of the traditional doctrines to fall victim to the rational test was that of creation, and this because of the baffling presence of evil within the world. For, as Hume remarked in the eighteenth century, while reason cannot disprove the idea of creation, it certainly cannot establish it in the face of evil. As he wisely pointed out, if it is already firmly believed to be true that an almighty and loving God created this dubious world, the presence of evil in the world is not sufficient "to subvert this principle," i.e., the idea if believed on other grounds can be squared with the ugly facts. But if, on the other hand, we seek by rational argument to establish in the first instance the creation of the world by an infinite and loving God from the facts of a world characterized by evil, we cannot at all succeed. Given a world in which evil occurs, it is logically impossible to derive therefrom the basic Christian idea of creation: "Is He [God] willing to prevent evil, but not able? Then He is impotent. Is He able, but not willing? Then He is malevolent. Is He both able and willing? Whence then is evil?"[9] Thus when, in the eighteenth and nineteenth centuries, men thought themselves increasingly free from the power of traditional ideas, and consequently able to think out for themselves what they believed about God, one of the ideas which seemed to have the least sanction in reason and in experience was the traditional idea of creation.

To many it appeared evident that if they did accept the reality of God's love (and why else should they remain Christian at all?), they must on religious grounds relinquish belief in His almighty power. For could a God who is called loving have created a world of sickness and death, and then called it "good"? It seemed actually to be a demand of religion that God's power be denied in order that His love be maintained. And so again the conception of God was transformed from that of a transcendent, eternal, and almighty Creator, into that of an immanent, finite Spirit who helps to develop the world in the face of difficult conditions, and so who is not responsible for the evil there is in the world. Surely this determination to rethink traditional theology in the face of all the evidence was a most creative and courageous resolve. What was not realized then perhaps as clearly as in our own day was that the "power of God" as the source of all existence is an essential condition for the goodness of God as Christians know and understand it. The Christian promise of redemption, of which God's love is one basis, has as its other foundation the supremacy of God over all that exists.

These, then, are some of the objections to the idea of creation which our age has felt and still feels. This volume will be an attempt so to understand this idea that its basic validity becomes manifest, and these objections lose their force to the modern man. We shall try to reinterpret the idea of creation so that it is not just an irrelevant dogma inherited from a prescientific and prephilosophical past, but a symbol which points to the profoundest understand-

[9] David Hume, *Dialogues Concerning Natural Religion*, Parts X and XI.

ing of the dimensions, the tragedy, and the potentialities of human life, a symbol essential not only to the Christian faith, but also to a full apprehension by any man of the meaning of human existence. In the next chapter, then, we shall open our discussion with an attempt to answer some of the objections from science and from speculative philosophy.

Chapter 2

WHAT THE IDEA OF CREATION IS ABOUT

In this chapter we shall begin our rethinking of the doctrine of creation by attempting to provide an initial answer to the objections of science and philosophy. As we recall, these forceful protests were roughly as follows: 1) The idea of creation is merely an example of primitive science, an attempt on the part of early man to satisfy his curiosity about how the present world came to be. Since it is, like other folk myths, not good science at all, it must be discarded and replaced by reputable, tested scientific hypotheses about our origins. 2) The idea of creation is merely an example of primitive philosophy, an effort by early man to express in childishly pictorial and anthropomorphic language the ultimate reality that lies behind and within things. For both these reasons this idea is a typical product of an outdated cultural period and should be discarded by any enlightened mind.

If these strong objections from science and philosophy reveal one thing about the idea of creation as it was understood at the beginning of the modern period, it is that there was a great deal of confusion among Christians and non-Christians alike as to what this idea was *about*. Some critics apparently thought it concerned the subject matter of science, and sought to discard it because it was untrue science. Others clearly considered it to deal with the subject matter of philosophy, and urged its rejection because it was unintelligible philosophy. And many Christians were no clearer. They, too, thought it was *about* science, since they heatedly denied the validity of any scientific hypothesis that seemed to conflict with the literal interpretation of Genesis. Obviously, then, if we are going to deal with conflict between *creatio ex nihilo* on the one hand, and science and philosophy on the other, we must first ask what the subject matter of this idea is. For if it is true, as most people in the nineteenth century thought, that it is concerned with what science is about, then surely it should be dispensed with when it fails to meet the test of scientific method. But if it is concerned with an entirely different subject matter, then science can have no valid objection.

The best way to understand what is the subject matter of the doctrine of creation is to distinguish between certain basic kinds of questions that men ask. People ask many kinds of questions about the origin of things, and these are often radically different from each other in meaning and intention. Consequently the answers to these questions can be in quite distinct realms of discourse. It is, therefore, in terms of the differences in kinds of questions men ask that we can most easily see the distinction between scientific, philosophical, and theological answers, and can most easily apprehend the different kinds and levels of truth that each one seeks.

First of all there is the scientific question about origins. Here we are inquiring about "causes" or developments preceding a "state of affairs" in nature that we may now know something about. We are pushing our inquiry further back in time by asking about the factors which brought about the state where our last inquiry left us. Thus we can in scientific knowledge move back beyond the formation of the seas and the mountains to the cooling of the earth, back from there to the whirling gases which formed the earth, and back beyond there to the nebular hypothesis, and so on. The question of origins here asks merely about the character of the preceding "state of affairs," about the circumstances among finite things that brought about our present situation, about the unknown finite "causes" that produced the known effects. Scientific hypotheses and statements are thus by definition *about* relations between finite things in space and time. They assume that the process of events in space and time is already going on, and they ask about their character and the laws of their interrelationships. They cannot and do not wish to ask questions about the origins of the whole system of finite things. Therefore, while science may be able to push its inquiry back *toward* an "ultimate origin of things," if there be one, clearly it can never find or even inquire about such an ultimate origin. For the question of an *ultimate* origin asks, if it asks anything at all, about the cause of every finite state of affairs, including each preceding one. It is the question of the origin of the whole system of finite relations, and thus can never be found by an inquiry that restricts itself to the relations within that system. In science there is nothing that corresponds to or can conceivably conflict with either a metaphysical understanding of origins or with the theological doctrine of creation.

Another kind of question people ask about "origins" is more strictly philosophical or metaphysical in character. It goes something like this: "In or behind the changing things that make up existence as we find it (trees, rocks, stars, people, ideas, sensations, etc.) is there any sort of thing (or substance or principle) which is always there, which always has been there, and so from which all these things can be said (by analogy) 'to come'? Is there any basic, fundamental, permanent substance, being, or set of principles which underlies them and so which gives them all the reality they possess? Is there a Really Real at the origin of things, and if so what is it?"[1]

[1] An attempt has been made to phrase these basic "metaphysical" questions without prejudice for any particular kind of systematic answer. Although the phrasing may seem to imply a transcendent monism as the "Really Real," nevertheless, in theory these questions are such that they could be the starting point for an immanent, naturalistic pluralism such as has been formulated by Whitehead.

This is the question that tantalized the early Greek and Indian philosophers and so incited the great tradition of speculative philosophy. It is the question of what it means for anything "to be," of what must be there if something is to exist at all, and so the question of that upon which changing existences ultimately depend—it is the "ontological" question of "being" or "existence." And the answers have been fascinatingly various in the history of thought: there are the water, air, and fire principles of the earliest Greek thinkers; there are the Boundless, the Unmoving Being, and the atoms of more sophisticated thinkers; the Ideas of Plato, the One of Plotinus, the transcendent, unnamable Brahman of Hinduism—and so on to the *Natura Naturans* of Spinoza, the Monads of Leibnitz, the elaborate categorial factors of Whitehead, and the "Nature" of contemporary naturalistic philosophy. In each case, in order to find the "origin" or foundation of experienced existence, the mind asks about an underlying level of reality beyond and yet within sensible experience. This is the metaphysical question of origins.

Now as one can easily see, this is a very different sort of question from the scientific question we noted above. Here we are not asking about the finite "causes" out of which a given state of affairs arose. And the reason is that the metaphysical question would apply with equal cogency to that preceding set of circumstances. In fact, as philosophy quickly realized, our question is not really concerned with what happened "beforehand" at all. Rather we are asking: "Assuming *all* the various 'states of affairs' that have characterized the universe of finite things, on what fundamental structure of relationships or substance or being do they all depend 'for their existence and reality? What is the source and 'origin' of their total being?" Thus even substantial changes in the answers to scientific questions about origins need not have a fundamental effect on metaphysical viewpoints. A man can remain a positivist, a naturalist, an idealist, a pluralist, or monist, whatever the present status of the nebular hypothesis or the idea of evolution.

The Ultimate Question

Finally there is another kind of question that involves the issue of "origins." This is a much more burning, personal sort of question than the scientific or metaphysical ones, which are rightly motivated by a serene curiosity about the universe we live in. Here we ask an ultimate question with a distinctly personal reference. We are raising the question of "origins" because we are asking about the ultimate security, the meaning and the destiny of our own existence. It is the metaphysical question of being in an "existential" form, a question about the ultimate origins of our *own* being, and so a question in which we ourselves are deeply involved. For when we ask about the security and meaning of our own life, we are not asking about something else (a nebula, or even a first substance) outside of us; our question is about ourselves as we are caught within the mighty forces that impinge on us, determine our life, and mete out to us our fate. Consequently, we can never back off from these issues and gaze at them objectively. Rather they come to us in the midst of our involvement within them. Thus we experience them not as spectators but as participants—and so the problems of security, meaning, and destiny, partly engulfing us, become something we can never completely conquer and reduce to intelligible size. They are, as Marcel points out, "mysteries" and not "problems"[2]—something we must think about, but not something we can control, dissect, measure, test, or even contemplate objectively and define clearly. They elude our easy intellectual grasp because they grasp us.

This kind of question comes to us all at certain times. We are aware of them especially when our security has

[2] Marcel, Gabriel. *The Ontological Mystery.*

been somehow rudely shaken, as in a sudden brush with death on the highway, and we realize the arbitrary and precarious hold each of us has on existence and life. We suddenly sense our own creaturely dependence on things and events beyond our control, or we feel with a shudder our own life span slipping away from us—and, wondering how long we will be here, we ask if there is anything that is truly dependable and secure, not to be removed by anything, upon which our own existence depends. Or this kind of question can come when we can find no apparent purpose or meaning making coherent our existence amidst the baffling events of life, and we wonder why we are here. Then we ask (with Pascal) "Who has put me here?" What is the meaning behind my own being at this concrete moment and place? Have I merely been hurled into existence at random by blind forces of parentage and environment as the planets were hurled off into space by the whirling sun? Is there no Creator who has placed me here and given my concrete life a purpose, a destiny, and a ground for hope? Or again, we may ask: "What ultimately determines my life—who or what is in charge here? I see my life determined by powerful, often meaningless, and surely blind forces: outside of me there are floods, wars, conquests, and economic cycles; within me are hereditary weaknesses, neuroses, fatal flaws, and the corrosion of the years. Are these, then, the Lords of my existence? Am I dependent solely on them, and on my own strength to defeat or control them, in order to find a purpose and direction in all I do? Am I merely a cork tossed about on mighty waves, since so clearly I am not able to be captain of my own destiny? Is there no sovereign Lord of all, who is Creator and Ruler over all these powers that rule over me?"

Such questions about the ground of our contingent being, about a transcendent purpose for our short life, and about the Lords of our destiny, are a part of the life of us all. Here we ask why *we* exist, and on what power that existence depends. This is not a speculative question for us, but a deeply personal question about the meaning and security of *our* existence. Such questions, therefore, do not spring from intellectual curiosity so much as they come from anxiety about the mystery of the existence in which our whole being is involved. And they must be answered somehow, if any human being is to live free of insecurity and frustration. Sometimes they are answered superficially in terms of immediate securities and small "meanings"— such as a new car, a paid-up mortgage and an insurance policy. But when these little supports are shaken by some shattering natural, psychological, or historical event, the ultimate questions of the origin, the meaning and destiny of life itself, rush powerfully to the fore and seem to blot out all our other questions. We live in such a time today.

Two things should be said further about questions of this sort. First of all, they are peculiarly "religious" in character. That is, they ask about the ultimate ground and meaning of our existence, they search for a faithful and healing answer to our deepest problems, and they are answered in terms of affirmation and trust, rather than in terms of proof and demonstration. Let us look at this last point for a moment; we shall return to it often again. As we have pointed out, these questions represent "mysteries" and not "problems." What brings these questions on us pell-mell is not usually an intellectual problem which arouses our curiosity and calls for an intellectual solution.[3] Rather they rush up within us because we find ourselves in some personal crisis that has created inner anxiety and a sense of utter lostness. It is our anxiety, our frustration, our futility, our guilt—not our curiosity—that must be assuaged and satisfied. In such a situation an intellectual solution, or even demonstration, may be quite irrelevant. An academic proof of God's existence will not help a man

[3] "The question 'Why should anything exist at all?' . . . does not present itself to us as a conceptual question: our motives for trying to answer it are not those of logical tidiness." Flew, A., and Macintyre, A., eds. *New Essays in Philosophical Theology*, New York, The Macmillan Co., 1955, p. 19.

who is overcome with futility or guilt. His problem is not ignorance or unclarity of mind, so much as it is turbulence and anxiety of spirit. What he needs, therefore, is not a demonstrated concept of deity in his mind, so much as an experienced encounter with Almighty God. For only in such an encounter, and the living relation that flows from it, can a man find the courage and conviction, the purpose and inner strength to accept and to conquer the "mysteries" of existence. Certainly our answers to these questions must satisfy the mind with regard to validity. But because they stem from transforming experiences that are deeper than proof and demonstration, real answers to existential questions primarily tend to promote confidence and serenity in facing life, rather than intellectual satisfaction at resolving a "curiosity" problem. When, therefore, an answer to these questions is received, we speak more meaningfully of faith and trust than we do of knowledge or complete understanding;[4] and so we call these "religious" questions and answers.

Secondly, although these religious questions are centered upon immediate problems of meaning in our contemporary personal or group life, nevertheless inevitably they too imply the question of ultimate origins. The question of the meaning and destiny of our present life can only be answered if we can have confidence in the fundamental goodness of life as promising fulfillment; and such confidence in the promise of life is possible only if we have some basis for trust in the source of all being. The religious question of the meaning of our being drives us to the religious question of the origin of all being in God. To the anxious question: why are we, and on what do we ultimately depend? The Christian faith gives the answer: We are creatures of God dependent utterly upon His sovereign power and love. Thus in asking the religious

---

[4] "Whence we conclude, that the knowledge of faith consists more in certainty than in comprehension." Calvin, J., *Institutes of the Christian Religion*, Book III, Chapter 2, Section XIV. All quotations from the *Institutes* are from Allen's translation.

question "Who created the world?" men are not so curious about how or when the universe came to be as they are deeply concerned about the goodness and meaning of their life, and so about the character of the ultimate source and ruler of their life. The religious affirmation that God created the world is, therefore, fundamentally concerned to give a positive answer to the baffling mystery of the meaning of our life here and now as finite, transient creatures. For it asserts above all that our present existence is in the hands of the One Almighty Lord whom we know as love. The theological idea of creation is first of all an answer to the religious question of the meaning and destiny of man's historical life.[5]

[5] This connection between the "existential" question, "Who rules our destiny?" and the religious doctrine of creation is clearly brought out in the three following quotations:

"The doctrine of creation is not a speculative cosmogony, but a confession of faith, of faith in God as Lord. The world belongs to Him, and He upholds it by His power. He sustains human life, and man owes Him obedience."
Quoted from Bultmann, R., *Primitive Christianity*, New York, Meridian Books, Ltd., 1956, p. 15.

"In the last analysis, the Old Testament doctrine of creation expresses a sense of the present situation of man. He is hedged in by the incomprehensible power of Almighty God. The real purpose of the creation story is to indicate what God is doing all the time."
Ibid. p. 18.

"God rules. He exercises control in every part of this visible universe, and particularly in the affairs of men. If this is true, how does it come about? What is that relationship between God and the world, between the spiritual and the material, which makes such control possible?

"The Hebrew answer is simplicity itself. God can rule the world because He made it. 'The sea is His and He made it, and His hands prepared the dry land.' 'By the word of the Lord were the heavens made, and all the host of them by the breath of His mouth.' God is not dependent on the world; the world is wholly dependent upon Him."
Neill, S. C., *Christian Faith Today*, Penguin Books, Inc., 1955, pp. 72–73.
By associating these ideas or doctrines with human religious

Now if there is anything upon which contemporary theology agrees, it is that the biblical belief in creation derives from an answer to this "religious" question, rather than from an answer either to a scientific or a metaphysical question. The Israelites, who expressed this doctrine in Psalms, history, and prophecy, were not prompted by a scientific curiosity about the exact series of events, or the set of relations and circumstances which accompanied the origin of the world. Nor were they concerned with the speculative question of an underlying substance which would explain the world of changing things. They were overwhelmingly interested in the mystery of the purpose and meaning of their history as a people, and so with the nature of the Ruler of all history. Correspondingly, they sought, in calling God "Creator," to affirm the total sovereignty and the almighty power of the God who had revealed Himself as the author of Israel's destiny and the executor of Israel's fulfillment. They, and the Christians who followed them, confessed God to be the Creator and Ruler of all things, because each had received a vivid answer to fundamental religious questions: Who has put us here; who has fashioned us and for what purpose; who is the ultimate power over our existence; and who claims us as the Lord and Ruler of our life and destiny?

Their doctrine of creation, then, is an affirmation of faith that despite the mystery and anxiety of their creaturely dependence and temporality, they, as biblical people, have found God revealed to them as the Almighty Power who created them and all that seemed to threaten them, and created them for such a purpose that they might through Him have confidence and trust in life and in its meaning.

---

questions, we do not mean at all to imply that "religious truth" is merely a matter of human questions and human answers. Religious truth is first and foremost a matter of divine revelation. Our point is that revelation is always received and understood as the answer to the specifically religious, and not the scientific or even the philosophical, questions a man asks about his life.

The Christian doctrine of creation, therefore, expresses in theoretical language those positive religious affirmations which biblical faith in God makes in response to the mystery of the meaning and destiny of our creaturely finitude. These affirmations are: 1) That the world has come to be from the transcendent holiness and power of God, who because He is the ultimate origin is the ultimate Ruler of all created things. 2) That because of God's creative and ruling power our finite life and the events in which we live have, despite their bewildering mystery and their frequently tragic character, a meaning, a purpose, and a destiny beyond any immediate and apparent futility. 3) That man's life, and therefore *my* life, is not my own to "do with" merely as I please, but is claimed for—because it is upheld and guided by—a power and a will beyond my will. This is what the Christian means when he says, "I believe in God the Father Almighty, Maker of heaven and earth." This is what the idea of *creatio ex nihilo* is essentially "about."

Conflicts with Science

If this is the basic meaning of the doctrine of creation, then we might well ask ourselves, "Why is it that this doctrine has been the center of so many painful conflicts with science?" If the doctrine is merely stating the ultimate dependence of all finite existence on God, its Maker and Lord, why should the theologians have quarreled with scientific theories about the events and developments through which our present age of the world came about? Are not the theories about finite processes quite irrelevant to the very different question of the ultimate origin and destiny of the whole process? Could not the Creator have "made" a cosmos by a process of slow, immanent development over a million years as easily as He "made" the smaller universe six thousand years ago? Almost all contemporary theologians would concur with the implications of these questions, and agree that any scientific hypotheses about *how* the universe developed to its present state, and *how long* these remote processes took, are equally compatible with this theological affirmation. Science and religion are not in real conflict on the question of origins, for the hypotheses of the one are dealing with vastly different questions than the affirmations of the other.

Why, then, all these past conflicts? The answer lies, at least partially, in the fact that the various kinds and levels of truth—scientific, philosophical and religious—have become self-consciously and explicitly distinguished from one another only slowly in the history of culture. All that early man felt to be "truth" he expressed in unified form as his religious myths or "stories of the gods." These myths combined answers to all three types of questions we have discussed: they are at once the prescientific "science," the prerational "philosophy," and the primitive theology of ancient man. Each early myth of origins reflects man's curiosity about how the world came about; it reflects his questions about the great reality on which existence depends; and it answers his anxious wondering about who is sovereign Lord of all and so whom he must obey and worship. Primitive myths are "untrue," not so much because they are religious, although their "religion" may be dubious in character, as because they attempted to combine with the religious wisdom of piety knowledge about the world which could only be gained by scientific inquiry. The religious affirmations enshrined in "myth" have, therefore, become "truer," and certainly more believable, when, in the process of cultural self-understanding, men have separated what is early science from what may be valid religious truth. The separation of philosophy from myth was first achieved in Greece, but science as a self-conscious method, as a level of truth clearly delineated from philosophy, did not achieve autonomy until the sixteenth and seventeenth centuries of our era. It is, therefore, not so strange that only within the past one hundred and fifty years theology has made this important separation of its mode of truth from those of science and metaphysics.

As we have noted, the Hebrew religious mind was almost entirely concerned with the religious questions of meaning and destiny, while seemingly quite indifferent to the questions which scientists and philosophers raised. To them the important meaning of the creation story was the glory and sovereignty of God, the goodness of creation, and the intimate relation between God and men. The other "meanings" of the Genesis story, scientific and philosophical, were almost certainly insignificant to their minds and fundamentally irrelevant to the point they wished to establish. Nevertheless, the early Babylonian and Canaanite creation myths that the Hebrews adopted and transformed to express their faith in God contained a great deal of prescientific and prephilosophical material. Taken as an answer to our scientific questions about origins, the first chapter of Genesis with its six-day creation reflects the prescientific speculation of the Babylonian and Canaanite cultures, which speculation has been rendered invalid by our subsequent knowledge. Taken as an answer to the religious question of origins, the same chapter is as true for us as for the Hebrews, expressing a faith that all things come from God, on Whom they absolutely depend for existence and meaning.

It has certainly been an added complication that the Scriptures which contain this early story of creation were regarded as verbally inspired. Thus every literal statement of the story, whether the content of the statement concerned "scientific" subjects or religious affirmations, was regarded as unequivocally true. Babylonian science as well as Hebrew belief were accorded the same unquestioning credence. The majority of Christians now agree that this understanding of the validity and authority of Holy Scripture is neither religiously helpful nor intellectually satisfactory. God's revelation to men has come in and through the historical events to which the Bible witnesses; it has not come through all the various words, stories, and statements of which the Bible as a book is composed. It is in the event of the Exodus from Egypt, in the events of the history of Israel and the prophetic response to them, and in the life, death, and resurrection of Jesus Christ, that God has revealed Himself. The writings which constitute the Bible are a precious and indispensable witness to this revelation in and through historical events. The words of the Bible, therefore, point us to the revelation which begins in the life of the Hebrew people and culminates in the event of Christ; they are not themselves the revelation. Consequently the stories of which the Old Testament is filled are not "revealed stories"; what is revealed is the divine activity within history to which these stories witness. In the case of our subject, therefore, while the knowledge that God created the world is a response to divine revelation, the early account in Genesis of how it was done has no status as "revealed truth," even though it was the form in which the revelation was enshrined by the Hebrew mind.

Before the nineteenth century, however, this important distinction was not clearly understood. Consequently generations of Christians accepted the scientific "error" of the creation "myth" as revelation in the same sense as the religious truth which it contains. Throughout Christian history, prescientific science and profound theology were woven together into the one Christian belief that God created the world. The inevitable result was that when valid scientific accounts of the earlier history of our universe began to appear in the late eighteenth and nineteenth centuries, they seemed to many churchmen to be a challenge, not only to the detailed description of creation in Genesis, but also to the more important religious affirmations that Scripture contained divine revelation and that the world comes from and depends upon God. Science was actually, and rightly, in conflict with biblical "pre-science"; but it was believed to be in conflict with biblical religion.

It has taken more than a hundred years of theological reconstruction to resolve this problem, so threatening to the minds of the nineteenth century. Mainly as a result of the creative and courageous efforts of the liberal theologians, the "prescientific science" of the biblical account of creation has at last been separated out from the profound religious affirmation contained in that account. The inquiries of the physical sciences and those of theology are now seen to be asking fundamentally different kinds of questions, in totally different areas of thought and experience. Consequently the answers to these questions, the hypotheses of science, and the affirmations or doctrines of theology, cannot and do not conflict. Religious myth has finally become that for which it was most aptly fitted: a symbolic story expressing the religious answer to man's ultimate questions. This was always its most significant function. The present theological understanding of "myth" as having no direct relation to scientific theories is, therefore, a continuation of the essential structure of religious myth as "stories about God." Thus to discuss the religious content of the myth of creation is on the one hand to be concerned with the valid and the significant content of scriptural revelation, and also to be disassociated from scientific questions of origins.

Tensions between Metaphysics and Religion

So much, for the moment, for the relations of religious questions to scientific questions. How about the kinds of questions the speculative philosopher, the metaphysician, likes to ask? Here the relations are much more complex, for here no easy separation, as with science and religion, is possible. For the metaphysical and religious questions of origins are in creative tension with one another. Philosophy and theology are much like blood brothers who fight bitterly between themselves, but are utterly unable in the long run to do without one another. At times each one wishes to be free and independent of the other, because they are not by any means identical, and so their very intrinsic closeness drives each of them to try to establish

his own autonomy. But the invisible bonds of mutual dependence soon draw them back together again, and, to the
surprise of each, they find themselves to be stronger together than apart. Shortly, however, one begins to dominate the other, and so the struggle between them recom-
mences. Thus philosophy and theology, "reason" and
"faith," are at once in perpetual partnership and in perpetual conflict. Because this creative tension is nowhere
more clearly illustrated than in the history of our question
about ultimate origins, it will be well for us to look at this
relationship of philosophy and theology more closely.
There seem to be four fundamental facts which affect
their relation to each other.

1. Theology and metaphysics cannot permanently avoid
each other, because basically both are seeking the same
"object." As we saw, the philosopher asks the question:
"What does it mean for a thing to be?" and he is led by
that question to search for that set of factors or underlying
substance through which things *are* at all, through which
they exist in "reality" and in our experience. He looks for
the ultimate "principle of reality in things." He conducts
this search in order to make his whole experience of things
more intelligible by fixing his mind upon that basic principle within and behind all our experience of things. We
have also noted the question the religious person asks:
"Amidst all the helplessness, tragedy, frustration, and waywardness of life, is there One who has set us here, and so
through whose power and purpose we can find a meaning
to our personal and social existence?" Now inevitably these
two quests are interrelated. If the religious person does
find an answer to the question of meaning, he will have
laid hold on the ultimate source of all existence—for, as
we saw, these two questions are deeply involved with one
another. And if he does henceforward speak of a Creator
and Preserver of all, then he is affirming something about
the "principle of reality" for which his philosophical
brother was seeking. The religious question concerning an
Almighty Creator, a Preserver and Savior, is ultimately

about the same "Being" as the metaphysical question concerning that Real from which all existence comes.

Because the object of each of them is the ultimate principle of reality, philosophy and theology are like two teams of climbers struggling up the world's highest mountain by very different routes amidst a difficult terrain covered with impenetrable clouds. If both of them claim to have been on the slopes of that one highest peak, then either one group must be totally wrong or else they must be climbing the same mountain from different sides. For there can be only one *highest* peak, just as there can be only one *ultimate* principle of reality. The mountain they are climbing is necessarily the same if each of them is, in his own way, aiming for the highest peak. Therefore it is far better for the climbers to compare approaches, to use both as far as possible, to see how each supplements the other, and then (the most significant decision) to take the better path to the summit, than to go each his own way muttering that the other is a fool or a liar. Since the goals of philosophy and theology are likewise ultimately the same, they will, like the climbers, proceed much more successfully in co-operation than in conflict.

2. Further, philosophy is bound invisibly and inevitably to theology, "reason" to "faith," because all philosophy proceeds from experiences and from presuppositions which reveal a surprisingly "religious" character. Any inquiry must make certain assumptions in order to get started. When the inquiry concerns the ultimate nature of things, this means that the assumptions it presupposes cannot be established by any further or higher study. Thus while the ultimate assumptions of scientific inquiry may be debated, evaluated, and undergirded by philosophy, the ultimate presuppositions of philosophy must be upheld by something more like a "decision" than a rational investigation. It is like a sight-seer who must climb up on something to see the view. Significantly, the place on which he stands is not itself a portion of his view, but is

quite hidden from his gaze, since it is the precondition to his seeing at all. It is not an object of his sight, because it is the place from which he looks. Just so, the philosopher, in viewing all experience to ascertain what is essential and permanent therein, must make two basic assumptions which make possible and determine his inquiry, but are not themselves the results of his inquiry. First, he must come to a decision as to what sort of experiences are especially relevant as clues to the essential structure of experience: he must decide what *are* "the facts." And secondly, he must make some decision about the relation between the rules of his thinking and the reality he is trying to understand. These two basic assumptions cannot be "proved" by his inquiry, except very indirectly; for they are the necessary conditions for his inquiring at all. They are the "place" from which he views experience, and thus they are prior to his view. As it would never occur to the sight-seer to make what he stands on a part of his view, so most philosophers have realized clearly they cannot prove their own basic assumptions.[6]

These fundamental points of view that guide and determine philosophical inquiry are assumptions which on the basis of compelling experience the philosopher "believes" to be true, rather than propositions proved to be valid by his objective philosophical inquiry. At its most fundamental level philosophy, like religious thought, is inspired by convictions about the character of reality, derived from deeply personal experiences of illumination

---

[6] As the great metaphysician F. H. Bradley sardonically remarked: "Metaphysics is the finding of bad reasons for what we believe upon instinct, but to find these reasons is no less an instinct." Bradley, F. H., *Appearance and Reality*, London, Oxford University Press, 1946, p. xii. And Russell agrees: "All knowledge must be built on our intuitive beliefs; if they are rejected, nothing is left." Russell, B., *The Problems of Philosophy*, New York, Henry Holt & Co., Inc., 1912, p. 39, quoted in Herberg, W., *Judaism and Modern Man*, New York, Farrar, Straus & Young, Inc., 1952, p. 38.

and release.[7] For this reason it is possible to say that "every creative philosopher is a hidden theologian,"[8] in the sense that every philosophy depends essentially on certain unproved assertions, based on some aspect of the philosopher's "faith" rather than on objective "reason." Try as it will, philosophy can never escape this origin in crucial experiences, nor its own attachment to the existential "stance" of the philosopher himself. It seeks to understand all experience as objectively and as dispassionately as it can—and this is its greatness. But it always understands experience from some position adopted in faith, and it is this common origin with theology that gives to philosophy its passion, its seriousness, and its significance for life.

3. Theology is equally bound to philosophy if it is to be most fully itself. However we may believe that theological ideas or concepts come to us, whether from revelation or from religious experience, still we cannot deny that theology is composed of "ideas." As its name (*theologos*) indicates, theology is intelligible thought or speech about God. Thus theology is like philosophy in two respects: its content is conceptual, and the faculty which produces it is the thinking mind. Try as it may, therefore, theology can never escape the fact that its own primary tools are ideas meaningful to the mind and the rules of valid and coherent thinking—and these, after all, are the essential concerns of philosophy. Furthermore, the theo-

---

[7] The philosopher Whitehead explicitly states the foundation of philosophy in "faith":

"Faith in reason is the trust that the ultimate natures of things lie together in a harmony which excludes mere arbitrariness. It is the faith that at the base of things we shall not find mere arbitrary mystery . . . This faith cannot be justified by any inductive generalization. It springs from direct inspection of the nature of things as disclosed in our own immediate present experience." Whitehead, A. N., *Science and the Modern World*, New York, The Macmillan Co., 1925, p. 26.

[8] Tillich, P., *Systematic Theology*, University of Chicago Press, 1951, Volume 1, Part 1, p. 25.

logian cannot utter an intelligible sentence derived from
revelation without copying, borrowing, or transforming for
his own use words, ideas, and concepts with a cultural,
and so philosophical, origin. And he cannot say of any
religious doctrine "That is true" without involving himself in philosophical questions, as, for example, the relation between that "truth" and other things he holds to be
true, such as that $2+2=4$, and that water is H_2O. Most
of all, if he claims that the God who reveals himself is the
"Creator of all existence," he is obliged to ask himself
what he thinks that word "existence" means and how he
is to understand God's relation to it—questions which are
remarkably similar to the metaphysical questions we have
already discussed. Thus theology, too, cannot escape philosophy. As religious *thought* it can be neither intelligible
nor valid unless it takes account of philosophy, which is
the study of valid concepts and consistent thought. And
as thought about God, it cannot be true to its "object"
unless it includes within its scope much that philosophy
seeks to know about the structure and source of the existence in which we live. One of the themes which will
concern us in this book is this problem of how theology
can deal creatively with those inescapable elements of
philosophy within its own life. For the doctrine of creation, which concerns the *existence* of finite things in and
through God, cannot but relate itself to philosophy's
search for ultimate reality.

4. In discussing the baffling question of the relation of
metaphysics to theology, we have pointed out those things
that hold them together willy-nilly. Now let us conclude
by saying briefly what keeps them continually apart and in
tension. This has to do partly with their method and
partly with their goal. In method the philosopher who
inquires into the structure of existence is committed to
look with equal interest at every kind of experience of
"reality" which human beings have. Since he is searching
for the most essential and pervasive factors in existence,
he must go to all kinds of experience to find those uni-

versal factors.[9] Correspondingly he cannot conclude that
any concept has metaphysical or philosophical significance
unless it is derived from just this sort of universal human
experience: he cannot as a philosopher "believe in God"
unless that "God" be derived from or at least related to
all aspects of experience. Philosophy, to be true philosophy, is based on an analysis of general human experience
and not only on one kind of experience, even "religious
experience."

The religious person, on the other hand, is primarily
concerned with meaning rather than with general structure. That is to say, he asks the question about a purpose
in existence as a whole to which he can "anchor" his own
small purposes, and the question of a resource of power
and of love that can overcome the tragedy, the conflict,
and the guilt that darken his personal and social existence. Now such deeper meanings cannot by their nature
be abstracted from the general, everyday experiences of
ordinary life; they do not reveal themselves in the pervasive coherencies and connections of existence. For it is
precisely the ambiguities *in* the ordinary experiences of
life that have raised the burning personal questions of
religion. If these deeper meanings are known at all, they
are revealed in special moments of crisis, moments of illumination and of response, when some meaning or level
of reality, unseen in the ordinary course of things, breaks
suddenly into our humdrum round and illumines the
whole. Religious thought thus tends to reverse the method
of philosophical inquiry: instead of seeking to uncover the

[9] As Whitehead remarks in a famous passage:
"In order to discover some of the major categories under which
we can classify the infinitely various components of experience,
we must appeal to evidence relating to every variety of occasion.
Nothing can be omitted, experience drunk and experience sober,
experience drowsy and experience awake . . . experience intellectual and experience physical, experience religious and experience skeptical . . ."
Whitehead, A. N., *Adventures of Ideas*, The Macmillan Co.,
1933, pp. 290–1.

basic structure of reality by means of an empirical analysis of its general scope, it seeks to understand the ordinary levels of life in terms of an apprehension of its deepest meaning, discovered in some particular and irreplaceable experience. The method of religion is to see all things in the light of its special knowledge of God; the method of philosophy is to see God in the light of what it knows generally of all things.

It is no wonder, then, that these two can easily be reduced to hurling invective at each other. Theology continually accuses metaphysics of subordinating God to the world, if ever it gets beyond the world at all; and philosophy accuses theology of seeking to force an understanding of the world into the strait jacket of a narrow and dogmatic view of God. Of course, both are in part right. All things must be seen in the light of what we know of God the Creator and Redeemer, if they are to be seen as meaningful and creative; but if we are to understand God as Creator aright, we must also in part see Him in the light of what we know empirically of all things.

Furthermore, philosophy and theology tend to differ with regard to their goal, or what each regards as a satisfactory answer to its questions. As we have said, though philosophy has a basis in conviction and crucial experience, it is primarily an intellectual enterprise of thinking out solutions to problems the inquiring mind has raised. Now a resolution to an intellectual problem is inevitably one that disposes of all that has been a problem to the thinking mind, and the mind alone. Philosophy seeks to resolve the problems of *thought*, not necessarily of *life*.[10]

[10] The philosopher F. H. Bradley expresses the predominantly intellectual character of philosophy in the following:

"Thinking is the attempt to satisfy a special impulse, and the attempt implies an assumption about reality. You may avoid the assumption so long as you decline to think, but, if you sit down to the game, there is only one way of playing . . . only here, that is in metaphysics, I must be allowed to reply, we are acting theoretically. We are occupied specially, and are therefore subject to special conditions; and the theoretical standard within theory

Philosophy thus drives toward the goal which the mind demands, the goal of complete intelligibility, clarity, precision, and a systematic arrangement of ideas. Where all incoherencies have been made coherent; where all paradoxes are removed in favor of rational implications and logical consistencies; where all outstanding mysteries have been clarified in one coherent system of consistent ideas; this philosophy regards as the satisfying culmination of its quest.

The theologian, however, is more apt to be wary of such demands for total coherence and final intelligibility. He feels that for our human experience existence is mysterious in its nature, and that the incoherent and paradoxical, the intellectually baffling and morally frustrating character of our experience, reflect not merely our lack of systematic thinking but also the real nature of creaturehood, especially "fallen creaturehood." And he knows from his experience of God that there is in life a principle of meaning that transcends his ordinary experience, that cannot be fitted into a neat system of coherent concepts. To the religious person the philosophical demand for total coherence and intelligibility exposes a blindness on the one hand to the real incoherencies and contradictions of life, and on the other an inadequate awareness of the deeper and more mysterious dimensions of life. He feels that we will *misunderstand* the deeper facts of our life if we seek to understand everything too clearly.

For the Christian thinker, therefore, there is in God a principle of coherence and meaning that transcends man's

---

must surely be absolute . . . If I am theoretically not satisfied, then what appears must in reality be otherwise; but if I am dissatisfied practically, the same conclusion does not hold."
Bradley, *op. cit.*, p. 135.

"For, if you ask what is truth, you are led to answer that it is that which satisfies the intellect. The contradictory and the meaningless fail to be true because in a certain way they fail to satisfy."
Bradley, *Essays on Truth and Reality*, Oxford University Press, p. 1.

ability to formulate it with clarity and precision. That is to say, he feels he can have confidence even where he cannot fully know and prove. As many theologians have pointed out, a man can have confidence in his wife that far exceeds his ability or desire to prove her "fidelity"— because she has "revealed" her character and her love to him in and through the crucial events of their life together. And if that man sought to relate himself to her only on the basis of what he could objectively prove about her fidelity, he would never know the depths of a personal relation and a personal trust which are the essence of a true marriage. Just so, the Christian community has found, in and through the crucial events of their history, that the deep meaning of existence has been revealed to them, a meaning that transcends and so can rescue the transitory and often helpless "meanings" of man's ordinary life. In response to this revelation of God's will, Christians can have a faith in the ultimate coherence and purpose of life which could never have been found in experience generally. Thus the Christian can trust God, even though he cannot completely capture God with his mind. In fact, many Christians would go further and say they can trust God only *because* they cannot completely understand Him. To reduce the divine source of meaning to the level of the ordinary created things which we can fully understand would be to lose the very essence of Christian illumination and confidence. For Christian experience is that ordinary things seem pointless and incoherent until they find a transcendent power and meaning that gives to them direction and purpose. God can only save us if He Himself is beyond the things that need salvation—and by the nature of the case, it is those things alone that we are able to study and to understand with clarity and precision. Thus theological understanding deliberately rests on faith in a God who is beyond our full comprehension, rather than on that clear delineation of ultimate principles which philosophy seeks. This position is not irrational, even though its source of meaning transcends what can

be made fully rational, because, for the theologian, the
attempt to make all things in this life completely intelligible endangers all hope of finding any ultimate meaning
and coherency therein. Thus as the methods of philosophy and theology differed sharply, so do their respective
goals. And out of this difference arises the creative tension
that is one of the concerns of this book.

We have discussed in this chapter the kinds of questions
that science, philosophy, and religion ask, and some of the
relations that these various levels of truth have to one
another. Let us draw it to a close by outlining the conclusions of these remarks as they apply specifically to the idea
of creation.

First of all, the biblical and theological use of the idea
of creation clearly shows that this idea is primarily of
religious origins and meanings. It has not in the first
instance arisen, nor has it functioned, as an answer to a
scientific question, or to a metaphysical question, about
the nature of our universe. Rather, what it has conveyed
to those who affirmed it was an answer to the religious
question about the meaning and purpose of our finite life.
And it has conveyed this meaning by pointing to the glory
and power of God who created the heavens and the earth,
and the dependence, the goodness, and the responsibility
of His creature man, set within a nature and a history that
lie under God's sovereign will. It is an idea that has been
derived not from a careful scientific or metaphysical analysis of the general experience of nature and of finite existence, but rather from the illumination that comes from
special encounters with God in revelatory experiences.
Now this means that the idea of creation should not be
thought of primarily as a scientific or philosophical idea,
to be judged prematurely on scientific or philosophical
grounds. The validity of this idea is not to be determined
merely by calling it "primitive metaphysics"—as if it were
doing poorly what modern metaphysical ideas are doing
better. It is essentially neither a scientific nor philosophi-

cal idea; it is a religious or theological idea. Its validity, therefore, is bound up with the whole debate between a religious attempt to understand our existence and a philosophical approach, a debate that has by no means been settled by the development of culture from a primitive to a sophisticated stage. And such a debate between two disciplines cannot fairly be settled according to the standards of only one of the debaters.

On the other hand, we also noted that this idea, while not primarily philosophical in origin, has significant metaphysical implications. Although it does not set out directly to answer metaphysical questions, nevertheless it cannot avoid entering the metaphysical arena. As we have noted, if God is the Creator of all, and if our finite life does depend for its existence on His power and will, then this affirmation involves an indirect answer to two metaphysical questions: what does it mean to be, and what is the ultimate reality through which things are? Thus the idea of creation inevitably challenges metaphysical conceptions of reality which are antithetical to its own primary intent, and inevitably generates a particular point of view about nature, and about historical existence, which can become systematized into a "Christian philosophy." Although the idea of creation is directly "about" God and His relation to the meaning and destiny of man's life, indirectly it is "about" the metaphysical question of reality and its nature. With this introduction, let us now see what this idea has said about God and the world He "made."

Chapter 3

WHAT THE IDEA
OF CREATION MEANS

We have suggested in our previous chapters that the doctrine of creation concerns that fundamental relation between God and the world on which depends the other significant ideas that make up the Christian Gospel. The next task, therefore, is to try to understand just what this doctrine says about God and the world. Then we can draw out the implications of this concept for Christian theology and for our own personal existence, and discuss from a common background certain problems it raises. The meaning of a doctrine can initially be found best by a review of the history of its development and use. Our question in this chapter will be, then, what has the doctrine of *creatio ex nihilo* meant for the Christian thinkers who have affirmed it?

Since the idea of creation has always been regarded as one of the fundamental concepts of Christian thought, it has appeared in every period of Christian history, and has been interpreted from the point of view of every variety of Christian theology. Sometimes it turns up as a conclusion of "Christian philosophy," as in a few early apologists, St. Thomas, and the Christian rationalists; sometimes as a revealed truth found in Holy Scripture and sacred tradition, as in Irenaeus, Tertullian, Augustine, and the Reformers; and sometimes as an implication of religious experience, as in Schleiermacher and the liberals. And, like a versatile actor, it seems able to don a limitless variety of philosophical costumes; at times it wears the idealism of Platonism (Origen, Augustine); next it appears in the more hardheaded thought of Aristotle (Thomas); then it may forsake these for the simple anthropomorphic categories of the Bible (Luther and Calvin), only to turn up later in the semipantheism of romanticism (Schleiermacher). This multiplicity of roles and costumes has led some critics to conclude that there is more variety than unity in the idea of creation. It seemed that this idea in history merely repeats in religious language the various divergent, and probably mutually contradictory, meanings of contemporary philosophical schools. Thus, it is said, there is no such thing as a "theological idea of creation" with its own intrinsic pattern of meaning; rather the theological idea is at each stage only a pious and pale reflection of the development of the history of metaphysical philosophy.

Surprisingly enough, a closer study of the development of Christian thought reveals a very different picture. What is especially striking is that despite the variety we have mentioned, there is one consistent theological idea of creation that finds expression in the theologies of every period. With regard to the fundamental relation of God to the world, almost the entire tradition of Christian thought is in substantial agreement. Apparently Christian theologians, when they wrote about creation, wished to express the same idea, and in order to do so they used concepts from the most potent and useful philosophies of their own time and place. The variety thus lies on the surface, in the differing philosophical tools each theologian employed to organize his thought. Behind this variety and expressed through it, there stands an integral and unique attitude toward God and toward existence which is derived from Christian faith and is fundamental to it. This central theological idea that runs consistently throughout Christian history is the object of our inquiry here: it is the doctrine of *creatio ex nihilo*. Let us look at two brief statements of this doctrine from two widely different periods, noting that the same fundamental ideas are expressed in each statement:

> It is proper, then, that I should begin with the first and most important head, that is, God the Creator, who made the heaven and the earth, and all the things that are therein . . . and to demonstrate that there is nothing either above Him or after Him; nor that, influenced by anyone, but of His own free will He created all things, since He is the only God, the only Lord, the only Creator, the only Father, alone containing all things, and Himself commanding all things into existence.[1] (Irenaeus)

> For this, as I have elsewhere observed, though not the principle, is yet, in the order of nature, the first lesson of faith, to remember that, whithersoever we turn our eyes, all the things which we behold are works of God . . . Thence we shall learn that God, by the power of His Word and Spirit, created out of nothing the heaven and the earth; that from them He produced all things, animate and inanimate.[2] (Calvin)

A useful summary of the main ideas in these two quotations, from Irenaeus in the second century and Calvin in the sixteenth, as in a host of others from Christian history, might be as follows: *creatio ex nihilo* means that God brought the finite world into being out of nothing through a "purposive" act of His free will. Upon analysis of this statement we find three main concepts that make up the idea of creation. They are: 1) God alone is the source of all that there is in the created universe. 2) Creatures, i.e., the finite world of created things, have a being or existence which is at one and the same time dependent upon God, and yet is real, coherent and "good." 3) The action of God, the source, in creating the world

---

[1] Irenaeus, *Against Heresies*, Book II, Chapter 1, Section 1. (About A.D. 170.)

[2] Calvin, J., *Institutes*, Book I, Chapter XIV, Section 20.

is to be understood primarily in terms of the concepts of freedom and purpose. Let us, then, follow these three affirmations as the outline for our discussion of the meaning of the idea of creation.

"God Is the Source of All That There Is"

Religious communities at the outset are seldom intellectually conscious of all they believe. Many of their most fundamental affirmations lie below the plane of clear intellectual formulation on the level of attitudes and deep convictions. These affirmations do not "come to the surface" as precise ideas until some other view threatens to take their place. Then, realizing that this new idea does not fit its own deep convictions or perhaps even contradicts them, the religious community for the first time formulates its own belief in opposition. Usually it takes the heretic to create the theologian—a fact which professional theologians should remember with more gratitude than is their wont. The result is that most theological doctrines or dogmas have a negative character; their content seems to be mainly a denial of an opposing pattern of thought. As intellectual formulations, this is their central origin and character, and all their exactness and precision resides in this negative role of denial. However, underneath every doctrine lies the deeper level of positive conviction and attitude which the dogma seeks to express and defend. To understand a doctrine, therefore, we must first of all understand what it denies, and then seek to understand the deep positive affirmation that it hopes to preserve.

This development is certainly well illustrated by the history of the idea of creation. As their Scriptures amply reveal, both Jews and Christians believed that God was the Almighty Lord of every creature, that no aspect of existence escaped His sovereign rule, or could long defy His effective power. And they realized that this total sovereignty of "the Lord" implied that He was the Creator of all things: "He Who stretcheth out the heavens as a curtain," as the Second Isaiah said, and "the Maker of heaven and earth," as the earliest Christian rule of faith stated. But the full implications of this belief in the divine creation were not completely realized by Christian minds until they found themselves confronting, both within and without the community of the Church, interpretations of creation which clearly denied many of the things that they believed on this subject. Consequently the doctrine of creation which resulted from this confrontation was a formulation that performed two rather distinct functions, that looked, so to speak, in two directions. On the one hand, its primary role was to deny the ideas that seemed to oppose Christian convictions, and, on the other, it attempted to give some intellectual expression to those convictions. The formula thus derived is the doctrine of "creation out of nothing," *creatio ex nihilo.* Its main emphasis and its main precision of meaning reside in its relation to the two opposing views of creation which it repudiates, the viewpoint of dualism and that of monism or pantheism. However, it also points to positive Christian affirmations of great religious importance about God and His creatures. To understand this doctrine, therefore, both in its development historically and in its meaning, we must first of all see what it set out to deny.

The most common conception of creation in the Hellenistic world in which Christians found themselves, can be roughly called the "dualistic" view. This view has had a long and distinguished history in religious and philosophical thought. In mythological form it appears in almost all the creation myths of the Near East, India, and the Far East, where a God of order subdues some monster or principle of chaos. It reappeared in the dramatic Orphic cosmologies, then was purified into the familiar Platonic picture of creation in the "Timaeus," and thence provided the groundwork for Aristotle's cosmology. In Christian times it formed the philosophical basis for most of the "Gnostic" systems with which Christianity carried on a life-and-death struggle until orthodox thought had successfully formulated its own, antidualistic view of creation. It has reappeared in our own time in perhaps its most impressive form in the philosophy of Whitehead.

For this view, reality is composed of two essentially different sorts of ingredients. First, there are the principles of organization in things, the formal structure of an object that makes it what it is, e.g., the structure of a chair that makes it "sittable" and therefore a chair; the structure of a man that makes him a "rational animal" and therefore a man. These structural elements of reality, without which no thing could be itself, were called by the Greeks forms or ideas. In order, however, for anything to exist, there needs to be more than structure or pattern. A contrary principle is needed; something that is to be structured, some unformed stuff that is to be organized. For example, some wood that can be made into a chair, and a body that can be ensouled—these must be there if particular things such as chairs and men are to exist. Thus opposed to forms or ideas there is in existence a passive, material principle: that which itself has no shape but which receives form and shape. Creation, then, or the "coming to be of things," is a process in which forms shape or organize matter; existing things come to be out of the union of these two mutually independent and yet complementary principles. This process of creation may have happened at a "far off event" as in Plato's "Timaeus," when a third figure, the Demiurge, unites the eternal ideas with passive "chaos" or matter to form the world: or it may be a divinely moved eternal process of the union and the separation of the two eternally subsistent principles of matter and form, as in Aristotle. In either case reality is viewed "dualistically," because there are two equal and primary principles in the universe, and existing things are made "out of matter" by the imposition on that material of pre-existent form.

It can be easily seen that this dualistic view reflects the making or creating that characterizes man's artistic and productive experience. When he makes something, or "creates" a work of art, man shapes in a new way some stuff, be it wood, stone, clay, paint or musical notes. His activity is genuinely creative; but his work presupposes a given material stuff to be reworked, and even given forms, either from nature or from his imaginative experience of nature, which are regrouped. For human beings "to create" means to impose upon a given material a form it had not possessed before. It never can mean to produce either the material itself or all relevant forms. Plato's Demiurge, who shaped the world out of chaos while gazing at the eternal ideas above him, is a cosmic projection of the Athenian artist, shaping new beauty and new order out of the "chaos" of Greek marble. Probably most people think this analogy of "making" is what Christianity means by the idea of creation; like some great carpenter or engineer, God made the universe by thus forming it out of chaos.

When they came to ponder what they believed, however, Christian thinkers were sure that they did not mean this dualistic view by their idea of creation.[3] For this view contradicted two basic affirmations about God and His world which lay at the very foundations of Christian convictions. The first of these was that God was the Almighty Sovereign of all of existence. But in a dualistic view of creation, God is only one among two or more equally fundamental and primary principles in reality. Whether the divine is considered to be the formal, structural principle, or a third craftsman or Demiurge, in either case He is not the source of the existence or being of things, but only their organizer. He fashions and shapes a principle outside Himself which already "is." That principle is, therefore, as self-sufficient and as eternal, as fundamental in reality and being, as He is; and thus it is a principle which everlastingly stands over against God, limiting His

[3] The one exception is Justin Martyr, who said that God created the world "out of unformed matter," and rather pompously proclaimed that Plato had lifted this idea from the Jewish Scriptures. Justin Martyr, *First Apology*, Sections 10, 59, 60.

sovereignty and rule over existence.[4] In a dualistic world view God is always finite, restricted by an antithetical principle or principles of equal stature and power. And as Christians almost universally agreed, such a limited God was the God neither of the Jewish Scriptures nor of the Christian community.

Secondly, a metaphysical dualism in which one principle is "divine" and the other principle not, always tends to become a moral dualism in which all good comes from the divine and all evil from the opposing principle. Thus in later Greek thought the source of goodness and fulfillment lay in the formal order of life, and the source of evil in the material, chaotic elements of reality. The world of space and time, of material changing things, of bodily desires and passions, and personal love, of death and decay, seemed therefore to the later Greek mind to be a world of evil. This evil is, moreover, necessary and unconquerable. Since existence is a unity of these two everlasting principles, one of which always brings chaos and passion in its train, existence itself is necessarily evil. The upper world of spirit is a realm of goodness; but the realm of history and communal life is a realm of everlasting meaninglessness and tragedy. By understanding reality as a union of opposing principles, one of which is divine and the other chaotic, dualism seems to make the presence of evil in life rational; but by the same token it can hardly avoid the gloomy conclusion that existence is by its nature inevitably a mixture of evil with good. And this contradicted another basic Christian conviction: namely, that all of creation was in essence and so in possibility good, and hence that evil, far from being a necessity in life, is the result of man's

[4] In his argument with Hermogenes, Tertullian points out that since an independent material principle is eternal and therefore divine, it must, in a metaphysical dualism, be equal to God Himself. Hence Christians, who recognize only one eternal God, cannot countenance a dualistic ontology, for "He would not be Lord of a substance which was coequal with himself." Tertullian, *The Treatise against Hermogenes*, Chapters 4 and 9.

freedom. As Augustine said against the Manichaean dualists, "Evil is not a substance; it is the perversion of a nature that is essentially good."

For these two reasons Christian thinkers formulated their doctrine of creation as a specific rejection of the dualism of their Greek environment, for they rightly felt that their belief affirmed something very different. As the essence of dualism was the idea that God created "out of matter," so the Christian formula stated that God created the world *ex nihilo*: not out of matter but out of nothing. By this phrase they asserted negatively that there was no complementary and equally fundamental principle of matter or chaos, out of which God created things, which could limit His sovereign rule and power. The formula *ex nihilo*, therefore, specifically denied the three implications of dualism: pre-existent matter, the finite God, and the necessary evil of dualism.

Positively, their formula was much more subtle. Certainly Christian thinkers were not by its means trying to give a positive description of the process of creation, as if God had used "nothing" instead of matter in creation. As a matter of fact, by saying "out of nothing" they were affirming that such a literal, positive description by man is impossible since the only kind of "creating" he can experience and describe is creating "out of something." But they were making two positive theological assertions of great significance.

First of all, by *creatio ex nihilo* they were affirming that God was the sole source of all existence. This was implied in something they already knew, namely, that God was the sole sovereign Lord of existence. As their experience with dualism had taught them, if any aspect of reality, e.g., its matter, is independent of God's creative power, then His sovereignty is limited. Then there are in effect two Gods, because two eternal and self-sufficient sources of existence. If, therefore, God is to be called the Lord of all, He must also be said to be the source of all;

every aspect of existence must be essentially dependent upon His power as the ground and basis of its being. In saying, "He created out of nothing," therefore, they asserted positively that, because there is no alien subsistence "out of which" He creates, everything that is, in all its aspects, comes to be solely from the power and being of God. Nothing "precedes" God on which He works; nothing is "given" to Him in creation. He is the source of *all* because He alone is Lord and God. In other words, they had discovered that in order to express the traditional monotheism of the Jewish and Christian religions, they must, in speaking of creation, insist on creation out of nothing. Monotheism inescapably required that no other principle than God, coequal or coeternal with God, is involved in the process of creation. The first positive meaning of the formula *ex nihilo*, then, implied that in creation God was the sole source of all existence, rather than merely its organizing principle. This line of argument is clearly stated by Tertullian around A.D. 210:

> The fact of God being the One and only God asserts this rule, for He is the One-only God for the only reason that He is the sole God, and the sole God for the only reason that nothing existed with Him. Thus He must also be the First, since all things are posterior to Him; all things are posterior to Him for the reason that all things are by Him; all things are by Him for the reason that they are from nothing . . . for there was no power, no material, no nature of another substance which assisted Him.[5]

The second positive implication of their idea of creation was that since all that is comes from God's will as its sole source, nothing in existence can be intrinsically evil. Every factor or principle that we find in our experience of things,

---

[5] Tertullian, *op. cit.*, Chapter 17. See also Irenaeus, *op. cit.*, Book II, Chapter 10, Sections 2 and 3; and Origen, *De Principiis*, Book II, Chapter 1, Section 4.

their material, their dynamic, and their formal elements alike, come from God as products of His will. Thus nothing is by its nature essentially separate or removed from God, or beyond His power and control. In rejecting dualism, therefore, the formula *ex nihilo* asserted at one and the same time the essential goodness of all that is, and its capacity by nature to be directed and transformed by God's recreative power. The Christian confidence in the potential goodness and the redeemability of life was implicit in this formula, and has continually been preserved by it.

When, moreover, the church had for some time pondered further its belief that God is the source of all, three other important implications about creation became clear. 1) The concept of what the act of creation "does" received a radically different meaning in its Christian form. In the dualistic view, creation meant "fashioning" as in human art, uniting form with matter to make something. Although the particular union of the two factors into the object is new, the fundamental elements of form and matter are presupposed. In dualism the most basic constituents of things are already there when the creative act takes place. Creation does not refer to the origination of the existence, being or elements of the process; it merely refers to their union into the things we know, a union which takes place out of more basic elements which are presupposed already to exist.

In the Christian doctrine of creation, however, God is the source of all, and creates out of nothing. Thus the Christian idea, far from merely representing a primitive anthropomorphic projection of human art upon the cosmos, systematically repudiates all direct analogy from human art: God creates, with no material presupposed. Two new meanings, therefore, appear in the idea of creation. (a) The first is that creation concerns *absolute origination*. *Nothing* is presupposed, no material is there, no process of nature or even of chaos is going on. "Out of nothing" refers to the absolute origination of things whereby the total process appears in existence; it does not refer to an act within an ongoing scheme of things uniting elements of existence already there. (b) Secondly, it follows that if creation concerns absolute origination, then what happened at creation is that finite *existence* or *being* is itself created. Creation does not unite given finite elements; it originates those elements. Therefore creation means primarily to bring process or finitude, in all its aspects, form and matter alike, into being out of nothingness. The movement of creation is not from unformed matter to formed object, but from the nonexistent to the existent. Things *are* because of creation. Creation refers to the origination of the being or existence of things, and so includes the bringing into being of both the matter and the form with which an object exists. That act of creation, therefore, which characterizes God's primary and essential relation to all His creatures, is an act that calls forth their existence in all its aspects out of sheer nonexistence. With this idea, we have reached perhaps the most basic and important meaning of the classical formula of *creatio ex nihilo*: creation is the divine evocation into existence, out of nothingness, of finite being in its totality. Thus God as Creator is primarily the source of this total being or existence.

While man cannot make anything out of nothing, but only out of matter already existing, yet God is at this point pre-eminently superior to men, that He Himself called into being the substance of His creation when previously it had no existence.[6] (Irenaeus)

[6] Irenaeus, *op. cit.*, Book II, Chapter 10, Section 4. Probably the clearest and strongest statements of the relation of the act of creation to the being or existence of things comes in Thomism: "Now among all effects the most universal is being itself; and hence it must be the proper effect of the first and most universal cause, God . . . Now to produce being absolutely, and not merely as this or that being, belongs to the nature of creation. Hence it is manifest that creation is the proper act of God alone." Thomas, *Summa Theologica*, Part I, Question 45, Article 5. "To create is,

For God creates, and to create is also ascribed to men; and God has being, and men are said to be, having received from God this gift also. Yet does God create as men do? . . . Perish the thought; we understand the terms in one sense of God and in another of men. For God creates in that He calls what is not into being, needing nothing thereunto; but men work some existing material . . .[7] (Athanasius)

In the next chapter we shall see how important this view of creation as the donation of *being* is to our conception of God.

2) In the second place, if in the event of creation finitude is brought into being and exists, then the divine act of creation is a totally unique act. The process of creation, however we may try to comprehend it, cannot be exactly like any natural or human process with which we are familiar. For no activity in nature or in human art brings its results into being; it may influence or rearrange what is already there, but it never produces existence itself. When natural change takes place, there must be a "state of things" of some sort from which the change sets out, else it is not understandable at all as change. When man creates, he must have material on which to work. In this sense every new beginning within the world is quite different from the creative event from which the world itself came to be. For in creation *nothing* is presupposed, except the being, the power, and the will of God; it is a totally unique event.

This means that the ways in which we talk about this event must be different from the way in which we seek to describe natural or human processes. The relation between the Creator and His creation cannot be the same as the relation of one finite event to another; hence we can-

properly speaking, to cause or produce the being of things . . . To create, therefore, belongs to God according to His being." Thomas, *op. cit.*, Question 45, Article 6.

[7] Athanasius, *De Decretis*, Chapter 3, Section 11.

not understand the former relation in exactly the terms of the latter relation. Any attempt, therefore, directly and precisely to describe creation in the terms of our experience will inevitably fail in its object. Such a description, set in the terms of finite events, will reduce the unique divine activity of the creation of finitude itself to the level of natural and human actions within finitude. Creation then becomes an event within process rather than the origination of process, and God becomes a finite being in the world, rather than its almighty Creator. The claim to be able literally to describe God's creative act does not so much reflect piety as it reveals the loss of the religious sense of the transcendent holiness and mystery of God. In thinking or speaking about this event, therefore, we can at best only use analogies. We can say that creation is "like" some process or event in our experience, only if at the same time we assert the deep way in which it is "unlike" that process. Thus because what God is and does transcends the finite experience with which we are familiar, all theological ideas must use symbols or analogies, what we shall later call "myths," to describe God and His acts.

The uniqueness and transcendence of the divine creative act also explains in further detail why this event can never be an object of scientific inquiry. The purpose of science is to trace and to understand the invariable relations between finite events within the experienced system of the world. It assumes that each event it investigates "comes to be" out of already existing finite events of the same order, and it tries to uncover their significant relations; it also assumes that every event it is concerned with is similar in basic structure to events that can be reproduced and studied here and now. Thus any scientific inquiry presupposes the existence of finite process and conducts its inquiries solely within the scope of that process. Science can therefore inform us about the character and development of the world that God has created, but it cannot and does not seek to study the event by which the whole process came into being. Because they have reference to events on two entirely different levels of being, the inquiries of science and the theological doctrine of creation cannot conflict.

3) Thirdly, this conception that everything there is issues from the being, the power, and the will of God, creates in turn a certain attitude toward the finite world in which we live, which has been enormously significant in our cultural as well as our religious life. For it is from this idea that the unique Christian understanding of "creatureliness" derives. Among the wealth of meanings that the word "creature" has for Christian faith, we shall here briefly mention three. In the first place, creaturely existence is for Christian thought intelligible and purposive in its essential nature because its source and origin lie in the will of God. The massive forces of existence, which seem so thoroughly to dwarf human meanings and so frequently to snuff out human purposes, are not the final power in reality, since they are not its ultimate origin. Man is not a tiny, rational and purposive mite, floating like flotsam on a vast irrational and blind sea. Were that so, the intelligibility and meaning of our life would depend entirely upon our own powers of wisdom and goodness. Creaturely existence would then be essentially tragic because that intelligibility and meaning, in the face of impersonal nature without and personal sin within, is a feeble light indeed. For Christians creatureliness is *essentially* intelligible and purposive, because its ultimate origin, beyond itself and beyond the nature out of which it came, is the intelligible and loving will and work of God. However mysterious they seem to our finite and sinful gaze, the depths of our existence are neither blind nor cold. And since by faith we can know the nature and purpose of the divine will in which is our ultimate origin, we can have a confidence in the underlying order, goodness, and meaning of our finite lives that could not be derived from any other assumption.

Combined with this new sense of the underlying purpose and goodness of finite life, there is also a deepened apprehension of the dependence of all creatures on something beyond themselves. Involved in the idea of creation is the clear implication that nothing in all existence, except the Lord who transcends it, is self-sufficient or everlasting. All things great and small, the mountains as well as the flowers that fade, the great nations that seem to endure as well as the most transitory life, the mighty of the earth as well as the weak, all have received their being and existence, not from themselves, but from God. None is the source of itself and its power, nor can any creature preserve itself in existence for another instant without God's power. Thus the fundamental characteristic of creatureliness is its radical dependence—dependence on all the other finite things that have helped to bring it into being, and ultimately dependence upon God, who gives being and order to the whole finite realm. All creatures are, therefore, inescapably "contingent" and transient. By contingent we mean that the existence of no finite creature is necessary, for its being cannot be derived solely from itself or its own nature; on the contrary, the existence of every creature is dependent entirely on all the external causes and factors that have helped to produce it, and ultimately on God, who brought it into being. It might not have been, because the causes of its being might not have been active. There is, therefore, no inherent logic or necessity for any creature to exist: its being is ultimately precarious and fortuitous, dependent upon many unknown factors beyond its own power to understand and to control—including the will of God. The transience of all creatures follows likewise from their radical dependence. Since its existence depends on factors beyond itself, no creature can be inherently immortal. The external causes that brought it into being can as easily hurl it out again, and they ultimately will. Creatures are "made out of nothing," and thus their being is always a precarious and temporal victory over the non-being from which they came. Only by the power of God do they receive what being they have, for non-being lurks continually at the horizon of their existence. Only He who is the source of being can transcend the threats of insecurity, of helplessness, and of nonexistence that hover about contingent and transient creaturehood. The result is that for Christian minds, however powerful and enduring one finite being may seem to be, in relation to others, all are as creatures created by God and so are utterly dependent upon Him for their existence, their structure, and their efficacy. All of creation bears inescapably this fundamental mark of "creatureliness."

It follows from this that in all of creation there is nothing worthy of man's ultimate worship, for there is nothing that is not finite, partial, and transitory. The doctrine of creation is a great bulwark against idolatry—the worship of a creature, or of one partial aspect of life, in the place of God. However beneficent and creative some power in our life may seem—for example, the power of mind—it is not divine and so cannot be made the exclusive center of life. It, too, has been created by God, and shares the partiality and the possibility for evil that all finitude shares. And however much the great powers of nature and the massive edifices of civilization may dwarf man and seem to him to be divine, to be that on which he ultimately depends and so that which he may legitimately worship, none of them is God, because all are infinitely transcended by that One on whom they in turn depend. Thus the idea of creation draws an ultimate distinction between the transcendent and self-sufficient God and His dependent creation, between the source of existence and that which derives from the source. The biblical aversion to idolatry, and the biblical understanding of sin as the claim by a creature to be God, receive their meaning and significance from this primary ontological distinction between the Creator and His creatures.

Finally, as we have noted, since God is the source of all, no aspect of creation can be intrinsically evil. In dualism, because certain aspects of life are seen to be purely evil,

they are absolutely rejected and suppressed; it was a dualistic world view that was largely responsible for Western
asceticism. And in the life of each of us, it is always the
human temptation to view our enemies as "children of
the devil," personifications of evil, combining no facets of
good with their manifest bad. Christians have committed
both these errors of asceticism and fanaticism, as have
others. But in doing so they have forsaken one basic conviction of their faith with regard to the meaning of creaturehood: namely, that each aspect of existence and each
being on earth is created by God, and so shares ultimately
in the same divine purpose and potentiality of good as do
we ourselves. Because God is the source of all there is,
while no creature is worthy of unlimited adulation, likewise no creature is deserving of unlimited scorn or hate,
because all have received their existence and power from
the same loving will.

"Creatures Are Dependent yet Real and Good"

We have seen how the Christian religious conviction
that God was sovereign Lord led to the formula *creatio ex
nihilo*, which negated a creation from matter and affirmed
in its place that God is the source of all there is. But dualism was not the only metaphysical interpretation of origins
which impinged on the Christian community. Another
powerful philosophy was monism, or, as it is called in religious thought, pantheism. This is the view which holds
that all that is, in so far as it is at all, is identical with
God.[8] The pantheist would say with regard to our present

[8] For example, this classic text from the Hindu Scriptures illustrates the pantheistic identification of our own reality with that
of the All or the Whole:
"That which is the finest essence—this whole world has that
as its soul. That is Reality. That is Atman (Soul). That art thou,
Svetaketu." Chandogya Upanishad, 6th Prapathaka, 8th Khanda.
Hume, R. E., *The Thirteen Principal Upanishads*, Oxford University Press, 1949, p. 246.

subject, "Creatures are made, not out of matter, but are out of God, for creaturely existence is a manifestation of the divine." This view is in some respects quite similar to the Christian conception we have just described. For Christian thought, too, creatures have their sole source in God and are utterly dependent upon Him for their existence. Like its dualistic counterpart, however, the pantheistic view that creatures are "made out of God" implied certain beliefs that conflicted with basic Christian attitudes, and this, then as now, made it impossible for Christian thinkers to accept monism as an explanation of our ultimate origin. In what ways, then, did the pantheistic understanding of God and of finitude conflict with that of Christian faith?

Whereas pantheism implied that finite existence was illusory and evil, Christians asserted that creaturely existence was in its basic structure real because created by God, and good if it rediscovers itself in God. Secondly, while pantheism implied that "deep down" man was divine because a part of God, Christians know that "deep down" man had rebelled against God and was no "godlet." Evil for Christians was the real act of a creature who was good and yet free to do evil, not divine and yet capable of a relation with God. For pantheism, evil existed merely in the shadowy world of diversity and matter; man's real self was God and so, like God, incapable of any sin. Because they knew both the reality and the sin of their own lives, Christians found it impossible to say that creatures were identical with God at any level of their existence. All aspects of their being were creaturely, no aspect was divine. Surprisingly, therefore, the same formula was used to separate Christian understanding from monism as had been used against dualism. Once again Christian thinkers said, "Creatures are made out of nothing." Only this time they were emphasizing not so much that creatures are not made out of matter as that they are not made out of the substance of God: *"non de deo, sed ex nihilo"*[9]—not out of God but out of nothing.

> But the things established are distinct from him who has established them, and what is made from him who has made them. For he is himself uncreated . . . and lacking nothing . . . but the things which have been made by him have received a beginning . . . [and] must necessarily in all respects have a different term [applied to them] . . .[10] (Irenaeus)

> The soul which has shown itself capable of being altered for the worse by its own will, and of being corrupted by sin, and so, of being deprived of the light of eternal truth . . . this soul, I say, is not a part of God, nor of the same nature of God, but is created by Him, and is far different from its Creator.[11] (Augustine)

[9] Augustine, *On Marriage and Concupiscence*, Chapter 48.
[10] Irenaeus, *op. cit.*, Book III, Chapter 8, Section 3.
[11] Augustine, *The City of God*, Book XI, Chapter 22.

This assumption that there is a fundamental distinction of nature or substance between God and His creatures, so that no creature can be said to be "made out of God," had been long implicit in Christian thought and life. It reached its clearest explicit form, however, in the argument with the Arians. Although the Arian controversy is not about this issue, what is significant is that the argument between the two sides assumes the absolute distinction of substance between God and creatures. The issue at stake concerned the question of the substance of the *Logos* or Son of God: Was he "of God," or was he "a creature"? For the Arians had maintained that the Son of God was a creature, "made out of nothing," and therefore not of the substance of God; while the orthodox insisted that he was "no creature," but of the true substance of God. In the course of the dispute both sides emphasized this distinction between God and creatures until it became absolutely unequivocal: "But we do not regard God the Creator of all, the Son of God, as a creature, or thing made, or as made out of nothing, for He is truly existent from Him who exists . . . He is then by nature an offspring, perfect from the Perfect, begotten before all hills . . . for it would be inconsistent with His deity for Him to be called a creature." Athanasius, *Statement of Faith*, Sections 2 and 3.

A reader unfamiliar with religious philosophy will probably be surprised that the pantheistic identification of the finite creature with God should imply, as we have suggested, that finite beings are "illusory," and that creaturely existence is a realm of evil. Is it not the greatest compliment to finitude to say that "deep down" it is God? Does it not express a confidence in human nature, to affirm that man's soul is divine? So it might seem at first. And yet, whenever the pantheistic view has appeared in a relatively undiluted form, as in classical India, in Mahayana Buddhism, in Neoplatonism, and in nineteenth-century idealism, it has represented a denial of the reality and value of individual creaturely existence. Since this is one of the strangest quirks of human thought, it may be well to spell out the logic involved.

As we have noted, pantheism may be defined as the view which affirms that all is God or a part of God; God is the underlying substance and unity of the diverse world of our experience. While pantheism does not, therefore, deny that in some sense there are finite things, and in some sense they have a relative value, the essence of this view is the idea that the reality and value of finite things consist in the degree to which they are identical to or united with God. What is not God, then, is neither real nor good. Now finite things *as finite*, that is as material, individual, partial, historical, or personal creatures, are

---

Thus because Christian thought held that there was an absolute distinction of vital religious importance between deity and creatures, the analogy of generation ("begotten"), which implied identity of substance, was henceforth applied only to the origin of the Son from the Father, and the concept of "creation out of nothing" was applied only to creatures. The analogies were kept radically separated to emphasize the absolute gulf between God and creation: "If the son, therefore not creature; if creature, not son; for great is the difference between them, and son and creature cannot be the same . . ." Athanasius, *De Decretis*, Chapter III, Section 13. Nothing could indicate more clearly the aversion of Christian faith to pantheism than this argument over the deity or the creaturehood of the Son of God.

clearly in only a very small degree identical with God. For God, as the transcendent source of all, is the negation of all these characteristics of finitude. The divine Being who is above all and in all, clearly can be neither material, individual, personal nor temporal; as the principle of the unity of all things it tends inevitably to absorb, and so to remove, these very characteristics that make things finite and diversified. If finite things *are* God, and if God transcends their finite characteristics, then inevitably the creature *as finite* becomes unreal. Only if finite things have an existence, so to speak, "of their own," separate and distinct from God, can they be said to be real as finite.

It follows that for pantheism "creation," as the origination of concrete particular individuals within space and time, is a "fall" from the unity and changelessness of the One. And since the One alone is real, this concrete world we experience is in fact merely a shadowy world of unreality, the realm of "Maya," produced only by our inability to see the real unity behind the diversity. Correspondingly, fulfillment means to move from the level of diversified and particular life as we experience it to a transcendent realm beyond everything individualized and concrete. Thus finite beings begin to find and to realize the reality and goodness of which they are capable, only in so far as they relinquish and lose their creatureliness, their material life, their uniqueness as individuals, and their ties with community and time. The gospel of pantheism is that "deep down" every finite being is the divine. But its problem is that we must go truly "deep down," beyond all diversity, if we are to find identity with God. And that descent takes us far beyond the bounds of our ordinary experience of things and of persons. For the pantheist, therefore, to remain within the realm of the finite, in its natural, its historical, and its personal forms, is to exist in the midst of diversity and therefore in the realm of illusion and meaninglessness. To study scientifically the interrelations of this realm is merely to systematize error and ignorance; and to expend one's effort to be creative in this realm is to be vulnerable to unrewarding and unmitigated sorrow. Thus pantheism always leads toward a motif of escape from space-time existence. By identifying God and the world, paradoxically it results in the denial of the reality and value of the world. It is small wonder that neither modern empirical science nor progressive modern society developed in such a cultural atmosphere.

As with dualism, Christians found this view of reality quite antithetical to their own, and so they struggled against it with a goodly vigor. Again their denial of an opposing position—not out of God but out of nothing—involved them in several positive affirmations about the meaning of creation which have had tremendous significance for Christian faith, and for our Western cultural life. First, all Christian theologians asserted that creatures were not illusory shadows whose real substance or reality was God. Rather each creature was a real existent, not identical with God but separate from Him, an existing thing with an intrinsic being, an essential structure, and certain natural powers. Within their fundamental creaturely limits all finite things were independent, real, and effective substances, able to act among other finite beings, and so able to be a secondary cause of events in space and time. Despite their dependence, contingency, and temporality, creatures possessed a given structure of self-activity which determined their reactions and actions amid other finite entities.[12] In man this inherent structure of activity is represented by freedom and intelligence, which enable

[12] "For creation means that free and individual beings are brought forth, or from the point of view of the Creator, it signifies that he has infused his own being into another thing which thereby has taken an independent existence of its own and may later on itself become productive. Thus the idea of creation, although transcending human experience, serves to explain the world as it really is in its two-fold character of individual autonomy and universal dependence." Frank, Erich, *Philosophical Understanding and Religious Truth*, Oxford University Press, 1945, p. 62.

men to be relatively independent, spontaneous centers of activity within God's world.

Two significant aspects of Christian experience underscored in Christian thought this fundamental biblical distinction between God's being and man's being. The reality of sin as a significant act against God continually reminded Christian thought that men were not divine and yet were real centers of effective action; and the reality of divine grace brought home to them that the creature was a real object of the divine concern. For Christians, therefore, man was an "image," not a shadow of God, and this meant that he existed and could be creative in a creaturely way, as God existed and was creative in a divine way. As Thomas reasoned, creation is a divine act whereby creatures are given "being." Thus while creatures do not have an essential or an eternal, a "divine," being, nevertheless they really possess being in all its aspects and with many of its powers. For all Christians, therefore, individual existing things were by no means the result of a "fall" from God. On the contrary, God had purposely established separate existents by His creative act, creatures who stood "over against" Himself, as dependent yet real centers of being and power.

Furthermore, it was fundamental to the Christian hope that in becoming related to God, man does not slough off his creaturehood. Rather he becomes, as Paul says, a "new creature"—or, in that phrase which would have horrified a pantheist, he becomes "reborn." Thus individual concrete existence is not an evil thing that is to be progressively lost in religion; it is an essentially and potentially good thing that can be recreated. Creatures are, in Christian eyes, entities capable, under God, of experiencing and embodying value, for despite their contingency and temporality, each creature has the possibility of the genuine fulfillment of its nature. For man this essential structure consists, as we noted, of personal freedom and intelligence, which make possible and even require his communion with others in responsible love. Correspondingly, man's "good" is not something that negates or transcends his creaturely humanness, but is the fulfillment, the restoration, of that very structure of freedom, intelligence, and love. Biblical faith affirms not only the reality and the creativity of the creature, but its value as well, even though it continually denies that this reality is self-caused, or that this value could be achieved in independence of God.

This Christian conception of creation as the establishment of a real world of potential, even if as yet unrealized goodness, has had a tremendous influence on our Western cultural life. Modern Western man has a down-to-earth sense that in dealing with material nature, with individual persons, and with the events and stuff of historical life—in producing food, comfort, security, in fostering the personal relations of the home, and in creating and improving his society—he is dealing with the most immediate reality he is able to experience in this life. He also has had, at least until recently, a buoyant confidence that these efforts are not illusory or vain, that man really can find satisfaction and value through achieving more security and establishing deeper human community. On the whole, however tragic his immediate situation may be, it seldom seriously occurs to modern Western man to wish to escape the world of matter and of history, as a realm of illusion or a realm of ineradicable evil, as, for example, an Indian ascetic might. If anything, he would seek to find other means to improve his lot here in space and time.

This belief that creation and therefore finite being is "good" is one of our most fundamental assumptions about life. We are apt to think that it is the natural point of view of mankind, because it is so deeply imbedded in the cultural heritage which has made us what we are. Consequently we often overlook the inheritance of ideas and convictions that form its basis, and we even assert that our Western confidence in the goodness of life can persist without its own historical foundation in the idea of creation. Now it is true that this confidence in the order and goodness of life has been furthered by the success which science has achieved in understanding and controlling the created world. However, this confidence is not so much the result of science as it is the long-term basis of science. Only because men were already convinced that they were surrounded by a world of real and orderly relations would they ever have embarked on the arduous enterprise of understanding that world. And only because they believed that a relative meaning and value could be found in natural and historical life would they have sought to control nature for human purposes, and to refashion community for the sake of human fulfillment. The optimism and buoyancy of Western culture is more an effect of the idea of the good creation than its cause.

To sum up this section; the formula *creatio ex nihilo* not only denies the dualistic "out of existing matter" when it describes creation. Just as much, it denies the pantheistic "out of God" as the origin of the reality of things. God *is* the sole source of finite existence: things are not made out of something other than and equal to God. But, equally, God is not the substance or reality of finite things; they are not made out of the divine nature but out of nothing. For the Christian, therefore, the world is neither divine nor illusory; and men are neither intrinsically evil nor are they "godlets." Their contingency and transience do not make them worthless, nor do their reality and potential value make them deity. Rather they are "creatures of God," made solely by His power and will, but made out of nothing. This concept of the "creature" who is of value and yet not divine is the firmest basis for an understanding of life that avoids both nihilism and idolatry.

"God Creates in Freedom and with Purpose"

In the two preceding sections we have seen that the Christian idea of creation assumes two corollaries: (1) God is the sole transcendent, unconditioned ground or source of all existence; and (2) creatures are dependent and yet real and good. In the one case we have apparently affirmed a strictly monistic account of origins, as opposed to any sort of dualism; and yet in the second we have seemed to assert a dualism of Creator and creature that denies any ultimate identity between the two. Perhaps now we can understand better why there are inevitable tensions between speculative philosophy and the Christian view of creation. For surely this monistic-dualistic view of reality, this description of an Absolute alongside of which, like a little chick, huddles a dependent yet real finitude, is the most paradoxical "philosophy" that can be imagined. And yet as we have gone along we have seen a wealth of meaning for human existence which only these paradoxes seem capable of generating.

We have come, therefore, to the most difficult and thorny question of all: what is the relation between this self-sufficient "Absolute" and this dependent yet real creation? How have Christians thought of the process of creation, and so of the basic relation between the transcendent Creator and His creatures? What do we *mean* when we say "God created the world"? In exploring this question, let us remember the principle we suggested earlier in this chapter: that all language about God and His relation to the world must be in terms of analogy. Since an event like creation is quite out of the ordinary, the only way we can describe it is to say it is "like" some event in our more usual experience, while keeping in mind that it is also "unlike" all the events we know. Thus, because it is inescapably analogical in character, theological language points to a meaning that transcends any clear and precise description.

As might be expected, there were in the culture that surrounded Christianity several analogies of long standing that sought to describe "how" the process of creation took place. For example, stemming from some of the oldest pagan myths and revived in Gnostic cosmologies, there

was the analogy of generation; the world had been produced by the process of mating and of birth familiar in our
experience of animal and human family life. Another analogy we have already mentioned described creation in the
terms of human art or craft; the world was made by God
out of matter, as a carpenter makes a box out of wood.
Perhaps the most sophisticated analogy, used by the later
Platonic tradition, was that of emanation or of overflow:
as rays of light emanate from the sun, and as water over-
flows from an inexhaustible fountain, so the world ema-
nates or flows from its source in God. The one thing these
various analogies had in common was that each sought to
describe the process, the "how" of creation, by likening it
to some process familiar in human experience.

Now although some Christian thinkers found themselves using these analogies to explain creation, nevertheless on the whole Christian thought felt them to be inadequate and inaccurate descriptions of what Christians
believed about God's creative relation to the world. Our
previous discussion has indicated some of these reasons.
For example, the carpenter analogy, if understood too literally, certainly implied a dualism which the fundamental
concept of *ex nihilo* denied. Likewise the analogy of generation, and its more sophisticated counterpart of emanation, implied the pantheistic conception that the world is
an aspect of the substance of God. But, most important,
Christian theologians realized that these attempts to describe the process of creation in terms of how it took place
were beyond their capacity, possibly dangerous to their
most fundamental convictions, and lastly irrelevant for
their purpose. The basic formula "out of nothing" is in
fact an explicit abandonment of any "how" explanation.
For it denies the one sort of creative process with which
we are familiar, creation out of something. By this paradoxical formula Christian thought has expressed its conviction that with regard to "how," the divine creation lies
beyond our understanding. Thus while some analogies tell-

ing us how creation occurred do appear in Christian thought,[13] they always remain outside the main theological purpose of the thinker, and, if pressed too eagerly, threaten the uniquely Christian character of his thought. Our question is, then, why is it that these analogies concerning the "how" of creation were on the whole rejected by theology?

The first reason is that it seems to be quite impossible for us to understand the "how" of a process that so completely transcends our experience as does creation. We can understand how a process occurs that is within our experience, or is really similar to other processes we have experienced. But a process quite beyond the bounds of our experience, as this one is, seems, as Kant and the empiricists have insisted, not to be a possible object of our knowledge. We cannot experience the event of absolute origination, as we might watch an artist paint, and so on what possible basis could our guess as to its nature rest? Can we even begin to conceive how God created the world "out of nothing"? To attempt, therefore, to describe the "how" of creation would be the sheerest speculation based on no conceivable experience or evidence. Clear, precise, and accurate knowledge of the processes within the world is possible to us; but such knowledge of the "how" of the ultimate origin of the world is beyond our capacity.

Secondly, it seems plain that if we seek to understand creation in terms of the common natural processes we do experience and can conceive, we shall misunderstand it. The mystery of our ultimate origins cannot be reduced to the level of our ordinary experience without distortion; the relation of God to the world cannot be understood in the terms of the world without at the same time making God a part of the world. To attempt, therefore, to understand the "how" of creation by an analogy drawn from the

[13] Augustine, Thomas, and Luther are examples: Augustine uses the Platonic analogy of participation in the Ideas, Thomas that of cause and effect, Luther the familiar analogy of speech.

processes of the world will strip the idea of creation of its own unique meaning and significance.

The most distinguished effort in Christian thought to understand the "how" of creation by an analogy from our common experience is found in Thomism. Here the analogy of cause and effect is used: God is the First Cause and the world is His dependent effect. The failure of this analogy is thus instructive of our point that a "how" explanation inevitably misunderstands creation because it reduces the relation of God with the world to the status of familiar relations within the world. On the one hand, this analogy tends to deny the necessary immanence of God by separating God from the world too radically; for in most cases we think of causes as separate entities from their effects. On the other hand, it tends to compromise the transcendence of God by drawing Him into the world system; for it inevitably makes Him a factor in the endless chain of cause and effect. If we think of God primarily as cause, the troubling yet inevitable question is always raised in our minds: "What caused Him?" In our common experience, causes are always in turn effects of something else that preceded and brought them about, and so whenever we hear about a cause, our mind naturally leaps beyond it to its own cause—as the child rightly wonders what the elephant stands on who upholds the tortoise that supports the world. Thus even the analogy of cause is not very helpful. In applying it adequately to the divine creation, that is, so as to preserve the immanence and transcendence of God and the uniqueness of the creative act, we have to make essential changes in the concept of cause from its ordinary use. In that case, however, it ceases to be a concept that can "explain" anything to us, and merely becomes a word expressive of a relation we know in other more appropriate terms. And if we do not so transform this analogy to fit this unique relation, the idea of cause destroys the conception it is seeking to clarify.

Finally, Christian thought realized that "how" explanations were antithetical to its own religious understanding of God and His relation to the world. To clarify this point, we must analyze in some detail the character of "how" explanations, and then look at an entirely different sort of explanation. Explanations in terms of "how" an event occurs are most appropriate to the study of natural processes, and for such study, as in the physical sciences, they are extremely informative. Here understanding consists of tracing the event through its various structural developments, in seeing how the action moves from one stage to another, and in finding the significant forces and principles at work in such action. In such an explanation, what we look for are the invariable and, if possible, the necessary relations between the stages of the event, relations which we can express in terms of some universal principle. The reason is that the explanation becomes more rational to our minds in precisely the degree to which we can show that the process proceeds automatically and invariably, because of the universal principles which the event illustrates. When we can say that every stage of the event is necessitated by a universal principle acting through the significant "causes" of the event, then we feel that we have explained it. For example, how do we explain an eclipse of the sun in these terms? We can explain the eclipse when we can show how all the forces at work on sun, moon, and earth necessarily determine the development of their relative positions according to the universal laws of gravity and motion. In "how" explanations we understand an occurrence when we have uncovered the necessary "causes," i.e., the invariable relations that make the event happen according to universal principles. This is the method and goal of science with regard to the natural world, and of that sort of speculative philosophy which seeks to understand the structure of the universe by means of a group of interrelated universal principles.

Now this kind of explanation in terms of "how" undoubtedly is the kind of understanding that most directly satisfies the mind seeking purely intellectual solutions to its problems. But it raises several serious issues as a way of understanding some of the mysteries of life, and especially when it seeks to provide answers to our deepest questions. Aside from the objection to speculation about ultimate processes which we have already raised, inevitably such understanding sheds no light on the question of why we are here, of what mighty purposes there are to give direction and meaning to our frail existence, or what our destiny is to be. An understanding of structure finally gives us no help in the search for meaning. For let us notice that in so far as it achieves complete success, a "how" explanation eradicates freedom and purpose from the event it seeks to comprehend. To the scientific inquirer, freedom can only represent an irrational element, because it is not totally explained by the necessary and invariable structure of relations that science seeks. Correspondingly, purpose and meaning cannot be a part of a "scientific" explanation; inevitably they involve freedom, and freedom, which is moved by intentions, is by its nature not a necessitated, impersonal, and invariable reality. Thus if our understanding of the ultimate character of our universe is completely a "how" understanding, directed by and copied on the understanding that science provides of natural events, it cannot find room for either freedom or purpose in existence. The ultimate origin of things then becomes an impersonal process with neither intention nor goal, and our own human existence becomes merely a part of that larger determined process. A "how" explanation, if made the final type of explanation, ultimately drains finitude of its meaning and promise.

There is, however, another type of explanation. In the case of human and historical events, we are not concerned solely with the structure of the development of the event, but rather we include as well an explanation in terms of the intentions or motive, the "meaning" of the action. It is true, of course, that events in human life and in history contain structural elements that make relatively invariable much of our individual and social behavior. Human actions respond to and are conditioned by developments in nature, in society, and in our own bodily and psychic mechanisms, which can be analyzed in terms of their impersonal structures. But human actions also spring from "meanings and purposes" which cannot be so analyzed; they combine with these structural elements the mystery of freedom and of decision. In this complex situation two facts stand out. First of all, we feel we have understood a human action and all its consequences only when we have understood its why, its purpose. We find the actions of others intelligible only when we know what was "in their mind" when they did what they did. Without a "why," human acts are blind and meaningless, the automatic actions of things and not of men. Secondly, we find that we must transcend and even relinquish an explanation of "how" it happened if we are to understand "why" it happened. For, as we have noted, an all-sufficient structural understanding ultimately denies reality to the freedom, and so the new meanings and purposes, of our acts. A dimension of mystery must be left beyond our structural understanding if freedom is to be a real factor in our view of human life.

As an illustration of this interweaving of kinds of explanation, let us take the example of an important decision in the career of a young medical scientist: A young doctor decides to leave a lucrative practice in the city to go to a small and poor community. Now what is the most relevant kind of explanation if we wish to understand this action? There is the development of chemical action in the young man's brain and nervous system as he makes the decision. An understanding of this structure is one sort of explanation but probably not very helpful in this case. There is also the whole complex of physical, psychical, and social forces that have played upon his character and person: here are other levels of explanation still in terms of structure. But the important point is that no one would be able to find any satisfying explanation of this surprising act in terms of these "causes." The first question every one of his friends, even his behavioristic colleagues from medical school, would ask is: "Why has he done this? Was he in trouble in the city, had his practice fallen off, or did he have some idealistic urge to be of service to a poorer community?" The odds are heavy that his friends would call him in to explain his motive in forsaking a good life, fame, advancement, and possible achievements in research, in order to practice in the country. They would regard the act as unwarranted and foolish, that is, mysterious and unexplained, until he gave them a good "reason" for it. And only if they did not regard his "motive" as a valid one, would they look for a structural explanation. If he said he was in trouble in the city, they would leave it at that; if he said he wanted to serve humanity, his more cynical friends would probably begin to talk about his neuroses. In any case, they would regard the act as reasonable, that is "explained," if his reason or motive satisfied them. All of this merely shows that every man, whatever his philosophy of man's behavior, assumes that he and his friends are free, that this freedom is directed by intentions and purposes, and so if we are to explain to ourselves what other people do, we must know their intentions. Let us note further that if anyone did think that the structural changes involved in the doctor's decision fully explained his action, then he must conclude that the act had, in fact, no effective purpose and so no humanly intelligible meaning. If the doctor did it only because of his psychic or cellular structure, he would be declared in court by other physicians to be legally irresponsible. Since such an act is not the product of freedom and intention, it has no human meaning, and so it is in effect the act of a determined object that is to be evaluated in that light alone. Like the falling of a leaf, an act without purpose is "merely caused," the determined effect of a preceding physical event, and nothing more with regard to value, meaning, or responsibility could be said of it. Only where freedom and so the power of decision are assumed, only where a purpose is evident, does an action become meaningful to itself or to others as a human action. If, then, we are to understand human behavior, we must finally explain men's acts in terms of freedom and of purposes and not simply in terms of their structural antecedents.

Explanations in terms of structure, and those in terms of free purpose and intention, do not necessarily conflict with one another, although if either tries to exclude the other completely, conflict will occur. Both are essential in understanding the mystery of human and historical action. For the complexity of human existence is such that it contains both structural and intentional elements; it is made up both of determined processes and freedom and thus it requires these very different kinds of explanation. Christian thought must accept the scientific method, which searches for the necessary interrelations between events, as a valid and important means for understanding the observable world around us. But Christianity can never accept science as a total view of finite reality, especially historical reality. For our historical experience reveals all too clearly that freedom, both human and divine, is interlaced with causal necessity in everything that happens. Since, then, the determined relations relevant to scientific inquiry give us only a partial picture of the mystery of our historical existence, there we are justified in using the categories of freedom, intention, and purpose as complementary means of explanation. For only if at some point the impersonal process and so the structural sequence is transcended in freedom, and only if our explanations go beyond the "how" and include the "why," can there be meaning in human or in divine life.

Finally, to return to our example, we have seen that if we are to understand the doctor's action we must know his purpose. Now to know the purposes and intentions of a person we must receive a personal word of explanation from him, a revelation of his will and the intent that motivated it. Purposes cannot always be seen from the outside; often they must be revealed from within, for the will and intent of a man are not always evident on the surface of his acts. Consider all the possible explanations for the doctor's leaving the city, and the impossibility of knowing the real "why" unless he himself revealed his own intentions to his friends. In dealing with persons, therefore, we can find meaning in the whole series of events their actions may initiate only when we have received this sort of revelation of intention and purpose from the depths of their personal being. Explanations of human actions and so of events in history must include, therefore, not only an analysis of the structural interrelations of the conditions and elements of the event, but even more, "revelations" of the inner and so hidden purposes and intentions that motivate the freedom of the actors in these events.[14]

Now this understanding of human behavior and of his-

[14] The philosopher of historical knowledge, Collingwood, makes this point repeatedly:

". . . because it is peculiar to history that the historian re-enacts in his own mind the thoughts and motives of the agents whose actions he is narrating, and no succession of events is an historical succession unless it consists of acts whose motives can, in principle at least, be thus reenacted."

"His work may begin by discovering the outside of an event, but it can never end there; he must always remember that the event was an action, and that his main task is to think himself into this action, to discern the thought of its agent."

"For history, the object to be discovered is not the mere event, but the thought expressed in it. To discover that thought is already to understand it. After the historian has ascertained the facts, there is no further process of inquiry into their causes. When he knows what happened, he already knows why it happened."

"The cause of the event, for him, means the thought in the mind of the person by whose agency the event came about: and this is not something other than the event, it is the inside of the event itself . . . All history is the history of thought." Collingwood, R. G., *The Idea of History*, Oxford University Press, 1946, pp. 115, 213, 214, 215. In this sense, as we shall see further in Chapter 10, the Christian understanding of creation can be said to be an understanding of the presuppositions of history, thought about in the terms with which we seek to understand historical action.

torical events is just the sort of understanding that Christians have felt that they possessed about the ultimate origins of their existence. They know that they can never comprehend the mystery from which they came by understanding *how* the world came to be. But as in the case of free human activity, they have not felt that this lack is absolutely irreparable. For the mystery of our ultimate origins has been dispelled by a revelation of the purpose for which we were brought into being. In Christian faith the claim is made to know the nature of the will of God who created the world and to know why He did so. In its communion with God in Christ, the Christian community has encountered the Almighty Power from which all of finitude has come, and it has found that the final nature of that creative will is love. Thus each Christian knows that the transcendent mystery which impinges on his life and directs it is not dark meaninglessness, but a creative purpose seeking for the fulfillment of his own small life and that of the history of which he is a part. There is for him, therefore, an answer to his question "why am I here?" The answer is that he is "here" through the free creative activity of a loving will that brought the world into being only because it was "good." The Christian understanding of creation as an act of a free and loving divine will is the sole basis for our confidence that our finite life has a meaning, a purpose, and a destiny which no immediate misfortune can eradicate.

Christian thought has seldom, therefore, claimed that it knew just *how* God had created the world, and it has never sought to understand creation in terms of that sort of explanation. The idea of creation has not been primarily a metaphysical concept, communicating to us a privileged insight into the cosmic process, far beyond experience, by which things came to be from God. On the contrary, Christian thought about creation has emphasized the other sort of explanation of our world, an explanation of the creative act in terms of freedom and of purpose. For, as we have just seen, the knowledge that Christian

faith has of God is primarily a knowledge of His loving
will, of the intention of that will to restore and redeem
His creation. In this knowledge the Christian knows that
God deals with men purposefully, and that His purpose
is love. Therefore through this revelation Christians know
that God created the world, as He has redeemed it, in
divine freedom and with a divine purpose. The idea of
creation is founded on the religious knowledge through
faith of the character of God's will; it is a certainty based
on the immediate experience of God's sovereignty and His
love in the covenant with Israel and in Christ, and the
consequent faith that existence, which is known there to
come from God, is created in the same love.

For this reason, when theologians have spoken of the
act of creation, they have used the analogy of human historical action. They have emphasized that this act was a
free and intended act on the part of God, and that the
purpose of this act was that "it was good." Realizing that
any intimation of necessity in the act of creation would
eliminate these basic religious elements from their concept, they have tended to insist that this free purpose to
create "because it was good" was the only explanation that
can be given. In effect, therefore, Christian thought has
said: "However it was accomplished, creation was an act
of divine freedom, done solely because of God's goodness
and love, that He might bring forth a good creation."

But He Himself in Himself after a fashion which we
cannot describe or conceive . . . formed them as He
pleased.[15] (Irenaeus)

And by the words, "God saw that it was good," it is
sufficiently intimated that God made what was made
not from any necessity, nor for the sake of supplying
any want, but solely from its own goodness, i.e. because
it was good.[16] (Augustine)

[15] Irenaeus, *op. cit.*, Book II, Chapter 2, Section 4.
[16] Augustine, *The City of God*, Book XI, Chapter 24.

God cannot be conceived without His eternity, power, wisdom, goodness, truth, right, and mercy . . . His goodness because there was no other cause why He should make all things, neither can He be moved by any other reason to conserve them, than for His only goodness.[17] (Calvin)

In each of these quotations, and throughout Christian thought on creation, we find this same theme: Creation is an act of divine freedom, done solely because of the divine purpose of love. This is the most fundamental knowledge that Christians have of God and of the character of His actions, and it is also the most important affirmation they could make about the ultimate origin of their own existence. To know the process by which things came to be would be only interesting; to know that it comes from a will which unites its power with a creative love is to be able to answer with confidence all our most crucial questions about the meaning and intelligibility of our existence.

In Chapter 2 we said that the idea of creation was a "religious" rather than a scientific or metaphysical idea, because it provided an answer to one of the fundamental religious questions of man's life, namely, the question of the ultimate meaning of his life as a contingent, temporal being set in the wider context of nature and of history. And we said that consequently this idea was "about" the transcendent glory and majesty of God the Creator, and the finite but potentially good character of our human existence. Now in this chapter we have explored the content of this idea more fully. We have seen that within it are three central concepts: that God is the transcendent source of all existence; that creaturely existence is dependent, contingent, and transient, and yet possesses a

[17] Calvin, J., *Commentary on the Epistle of St. Paul to the Romans*, Edinburgh, Calvin Translation Society, 1844, pp. 27–28.

reality and a value in its own fulfillment; and finally, that
the divine act of creation is to be understood not in terms
of structure but in terms of its divine purpose, as a free
act of a loving will. And we attempted to show how each
of these concepts points at one and the same time to the
sovereign power of God over all existence, and to the
meaningful character of our human life. But as our final
discussion makes very plain, this conjunction of divine
sovereign power and human meaning is possible in the
Christian faith only because through Jesus Christ the almighty divine will reveals itself as a loving will seeking
human fulfillment. And so in another sense this doctrine
turns out to be "religious" in character. For the kind of
understanding it expresses is not gained through an intellectual inquiry into the ultimate structure of things,
but is achieved through knowledge of the will and purposes of God as known in religious faith.

On the other hand, our discussion of the content of this
idea has made clear that this "religious" doctrine about
God and the world spills over into philosophy and metaphysics at every turn. We found it becoming progressively
defined through its denial of the philosophical alternatives
of dualism and pantheism, and we have found it disputing
with philosophy concerning the principles that should
direct our ultimate understanding of things. In the next
chapter we shall discuss the view of God that is implied
in this primary statement about Him that Christians affirm: Maker of heaven and earth. And there we shall be
even more concerned with this intimate relation of metaphysical and religious ideas that make up our subject.

Chapter 4

GOD THE CREATOR

Nothing is more difficult for the average Christian than thinking about God. Problems come at him from many sources and create confusion in his mind. All the half-remembered influences of his childhood religion, his vague recollections of Sunday-school phraseology and Bible stories, lead him first of all to think of God in quite literal, almost chummy terms. He remembers that God once walked in the garden; he is reminded on Sundays that God "gets angry" and "forgives." He hears in scriptural readings that God's "right hand" is mighty and is even the "place" where Jesus Christ sits—and in the somewhat blasphemous popular religion of our day, he hears God referred to as "the man upstairs" and the "someone up there who likes me." All of this leads his thoughts in the direction of the most usual picture of God in our culture: a large, powerful, kindly elder statesman who treats us much as a doting grandfather might do, with occasional moods of needed judgment but with a balance of indulgence.

Other influences, however, tend to make the Christian somewhat uneasy with this simple picture of God as an almost literal "person." Perhaps in a college philosophy course he learned that philosophers speak of ultimate reality or of substance as the eternal source of all, and he noticed that these vague abstractions sounded very much like intellectual versions of "God." In a confused sort of way he knows that his Christian idea of God should be related to what these philosophers were saying, but how to connect a vague notion of ultimate reality which is "underneath everything" to a personal, specific elder statesman who is "up there," he has not the slightest idea. Or perhaps he has heard several fairly theological sermons. In these he might be told to think of God, not as having a body, or being in any special place, but as "spirit." Or he may hear that what the scientist calls the order and wisdom of the world, and what the philosopher calls the "creative force which produces good," is what Christians call God. As a result the Christian layman finds himself trying to think about a being who is nowhere, about a vast "spirit" or "mind" that is bodiless, nerveless, and brainless, and about a "force" that can neither be measured nor felt. This muddle, in which ideas of order, evolution, and goodness are all mixed up with nothing to hitch them to, culminates in that familiar cynic's definition of God as a "vague, gray, spiritual blob." And here our churchman's mind comes to rest in serene blankness because there is no content there to think about at all. This state lasts until the next time he hears a sermon which assures him that all he need know is that God is "like Jesus." And with this the Christian layman returns with relief to that kindly bearded figure of his precollege days.

Thinking about God, then, is no easy task. We waver between literal pictures of God with too much content and vague abstractions with no content—with the result that much of the time we have no idea what we mean by God. And this is a dangerous situation for the Church. Men cannot afford to be vague about what they really believe in. They must *know* that in which they put their trust. If God is a vague amorphous nothing to us, the "nothing" will be filled by more compelling gods, the concrete idols of our cultural life, such as nation, race, and personal prestige. As the Old Testament struggle against idolatry shows, only a clear and honest concept of God can drive the fertility and tribal idols from our religious life.

Although many people may not realize it, theology may be of help to us in this problem of thinking clearly and rightly about God. Theology is "thought or speech about God"; it is the result of Church and churchmen trying seriously to think about God. The intention of theological doctrine, therefore, is not to confuse and befuddle the lay mind, but to clarify and aid it. Now theological doctrines are thoughts about God on the basis of some aspect of His activity: each doctrine describes God in terms of certain things He has done or is doing. Thus the doctrine of creation concerns itself with His creative activity in bringing the world into existence, the doctrine of providence with His rule in our historical and personal life, and the doctrine of redemption with what He has done for us in Jesus Christ and is doing for us through the means of grace in the Word and the Church.

Among the many activities of God, His creative activity is surely the one most essential for our existence. It is through this activity that we are brought into being, and it is this activity, therefore, that establishes our deepest, because our most essential, relation to God: He is our Creator and thus our Lord. Correspondingly, the doctrine of God as Creator is, perhaps, the most fundamental conception we can have of God. That is, creation is that activity of God by means of which we define what we mean by the word "God." It is quite natural, of course, that Christian devotion and Christian thought should concern themselves most with God's redeeming activity in Jesus Christ, for upon this our knowledge of God as Loving Father, and so of our hope for salvation, most directly depends. Nevertheless, the centrality of God's redeeming activity to our life and thought should not blind Christians to the divine work of creation, which, if not so close to our hearts, is just as significant for our existence and just as important if we are to think rightly about God. Through God's redeeming works we know that He is supremely righteous and supremely loving. But when we ask *who* is supremely righteous and loving, the answer

comes in terms of God's original activity, creation: the
Creator of heaven and earth, the Lord, is He who judges
and redeems us. The transcendent "Godness" of God,
what gives Him deity and so ultimate significance to our
lives, is most directly manifested to us through His creative activity as the transcendent source of all being and of
all existence. Without this transcendent aspect of "deity,"
the judgment and love of God would be ultimately unimportant to us, and the redemption promised by them impossible for God. The idea of creation, therefore, provides
the most fundamental, if not the most characteristic, definition of God in the Christian faith. Among all the activities of God, creation is that activity or attribute which
sets him apart as "God."

The idea of creation is fundamental for our conception
of God for a second reason. For it is through this idea
that we are enabled to define God in relation to all else
that is; the idea of the Creator specifies the status of God,
relative to all the other kinds of things that appear in our
experience. Among these things there are men, animals,
mountains, storms, the seas, and the earth itself; sun,
moon, and stars; and finally the great creative and destructive forces in natural existence. Inevitably we ask: "Is God
one of these, the greatest of all heroes, the brightest of all
stars, the mightiest of all natural forces? What is His relation to these things we know in our ordinary experience?
What does the word 'God' mean?" Other faiths have
given a variety of answers: in some of them God may be
a mountain or a tree; in others He may be the natural
power of life, or the underlying substance of all things, or
a mighty spiritual force within the universe, or finally, as
in humanism, the essence of humanity. But in biblical
faith He is none of these, because He is the Creator of all
that is, "Maker of heaven and earth." God's relation to all
the finite world that we directly experience, and so the
primary meaning of the word "God" as we use it in religious language, is defined by the idea of creation. Our

task in this chapter, then, is to see what this fundamental idea of creation implies concerning the nature of God.

The Transcendence of God

The first thing that has traditionally been said about God the Creator is that He is "transcendent" to His creation. What we mean by this transcendence, however, is not so obvious. When we first hear the word, its general connotations seem plain enough: God is not "part of" the ordinary world; He is "beyond," "before," and "above" the world as its supreme Ruler and Lord; what characterizes the world in weakness, death, and dissolution does not characterize Him, etc.: "The Lord hath prepared His throne in the heavens, and His kingdom ruleth over all."[1] But when we analyze the key concepts in these phrases we find their meaning fraught with problems that take us to the center of the difficulties of thought about God. For example, "not a part of," "beyond," and "above" have fairly definite spatial meanings, as does the phrase "throne in the heavens"; and "before" and "everlasting" are temporal ideas. Do we mean, then, by transcendence that God is more "up there" than are other things, and merely "older" than His creatures? If this is all we mean, then a traveler on a well-piloted space ship is more certain of finding God in "heaven" than is an earthbound churchman. Simple and literal views of the divine transcendence are not necessarily more pious than thought-out ones. A literalistic religion may not reveal so much faith as it does disrespect, for it makes God into a "great big being up there," and turns religion into a space-travel agency, with the sole task of getting people from this low place to that high place—and without space ships! Divine transcendence cannot mean merely "above" in space or "before" in time. And so while the real religious meaning of the word transcendence is clear and valid enough, it takes some careful thinking out.

[1] Psalm 103:19.

The idea of divine transcendence seems to involve three major concepts, two of which have to do with "ontology," or the problem of being and existence, and the third has to do with "epistemology," or the problem of the knowledge of God. All three of these meanings of transcendence are important, for they imply and require each other, and on them depend most of the other significant things Christians say about God. The God who is not ontologically transcendent and unconditioned is simply not a God who can save His creatures. A good ontology is a bulwark, not an enemy, of a sound Gospel theology.[2]

1. The first meaning of divine transcendence is that God "transcends" other beings in the mode of His existence. As traditional theology has put it: God "exists" in a different way than do other things; He *is* differently, He possesses a different mode or kind of being. While other things "have" existence, God "is" existence, for His essence involves His existence. Let us try to see what these rather queer, abstract and very scholastic-sounding phrases mean, because they express in ancient language an important truth.

If God is the source of the existence of all that is, then His relation to existence, to being, must be very different from the relation that other things have to their existence. Creatures are dependent; they receive their existence and being from things beyond themselves: from their parents, from environment, from a multitude of finite causes outside them, and ultimately from God, who gives being and power to all these causes. And only so long as these outside causes and influences continue to support a finite

[2] In its enthusiastic rediscovery of the "personal" and "living" God of the Bible, much contemporary theology has been apt to deny any relevance at all of ontological concepts in speaking of God. For example, "all the words used by faith to designate the attributes of God are figures taken from personal life." Aulén, G., *The Faith of the Christian Church*, Muhlenberg Press, 1954, p. 97. As we shall try to show, such a view of God, restricted entirely to "personal" categories, makes impossible certain basic affirmations about God which are essential to biblical faith.

thing, will it maintain its existence. If its food, air, or heat are shut off, it will cease to be. Finite things are contingent; they have existence at this moment in dependence upon other things, but they may lose it in a second, and must lose it in the end. They "have" existence as a gift from beyond. They "are not" existence, because it is derived from outside themselves. Existence has a sort of external rather than an internal, essential relation to all creatures. To no one creature, therefore, is existence necessary or eternal—as all of us are aware quickly enough when death comes close to us, and we realize with a shudder how precarious is our hold on "being." No creature, then, is self-sufficient, none can exist solely through himself, none is unconditioned, dependent on no factors beyond himself, for all *are* only because of influences and causes from beyond themselves. Each creature is able to be only within the systematic relations of dependence which make up the finite world order.

God as the source of all, however, is vastly different in all of this from His finite and dependent creatures. As the source of all existence, He does not receive His being from elsewhere: no other factors have united in a happy harmony to produce and maintain Him. Since He is the source of existence, and not its recipient, He is not at all dependent upon other things to bring Him into being; and correspondingly He is not at all dependent upon outside things to maintain Him in being. If, then, He is in this sense "uncreated" by anything beyond Himself because He is the Creator of all else, His existence must be derived from Himself alone. Solely dependent upon Himself, God is unconditioned by, because He is independent of, any other being. He is self-sufficient in His being, *a se* (self-derived) as theologians have said, rather than *ab alio* (derived from elsewhere), as are creatures. Or, as the scholastic theologians put it: since existence comes from Him, and therefore from His nature, His "essence involves existence," He "is" existence—whereas creatures, who are dependent upon other things, only "have" existence. While

other things exist contingently because they exist depend-
ently on things beyond their control, God exists essentially
and so necessarily since His being comes from Himself
and from nothing else at all. Thus Thomas Aquinas could
say: The fundamental name for God is "He who is,"[3] He
is "Being Itself," the unconditioned source and ground of
all existence.

It follows that God's being is in some sense eternal.
This does not mean that time is negated in God and that
He is incapable of relations to time and the passage of
years. As the Creator of time, as the Preserver and Ruler
of history, and above all as He who enters time for man's
salvation, the Christian God can never be out of touch
with time. The eternity of God, therefore, means that
God transcends the temporal passage of creaturely existence, as His self-sufficiency transcends the dependent contingency of our existence. God is the Creator and Ruler
of all temporal passage; thus He cannot Himself be subject
to it. Temporality is itself a mark of dependence and
contingency, and as such is impossible for the independent
and necessary source of all being.

Let us explore a little more fully the theological and
therefore somewhat technical reasons for this concept of
eternity. Since God receives His existence not from outside but from Himself, His being is not derived from the
moment immediately past, any more than it comes to
Him from some other contemporary being in space. God's
existence does not come to Him in the passage of moments from a disappearing past; nor can He, as the necessary source of existence, lose his existence in the passage
of moments into the future. Every creature, on the other
hand, lives each present because of a past on which it is
dependent; and each creature loses its present being when
the precarious future, which may not even include that
creature, takes the place of the present. If things are *really*

[3] Thomas Aquinas, *Summa Theologica*, Part 1, Question 13,
Article 11.

in time, then they depend upon a power beyond themselves to renew and preserve their being within the passage from moment to moment. For Christians this ground of passage is neither the "flux of Nature" (Santayana), nor "Creativity" (Whitehead), but the creating and preserving power of God. And because the ground of passage must itself transcend passage, God cannot be "in time" as creatures are "in time." If He were, then His own continued existence would be dependent upon some eternal power of being beyond Himself.

Temporality, in other words, is a mark of double dependence, and so a cause of continual anxiety to human creatures who are alienated from God. First, temporal creatures are dependent upon their own past out of which they have come; and so the loss of that past makes them feel they have lost themselves. Second, temporal creatures are dependent on the continuing creative activity of God, who is the ground of their renewed being in each moment of passage; and so the loss of God makes them feel they have lost all security for the future. If God be the ground of things in time, necessary to their continued being, He cannot Himself be temporal as they are. And if He be the source of our courage in facing the anxieties arising from our temporality, He cannot Himself be subject to that temporality. Because temporal passage reflects a creaturely dependence as much as does contingency itself, God, as the source of creatures and the basis for their courage and faith, must transcend temporal passage as He transcends all essential marks of creaturely status.[4]

4 Some biblical theologians, conscious only of the antithesis of biblical thought to Greek philosophy, have so negated the Greek concept of eternity that they have capitulated to the modern naturalistic apotheosis of temporality. Thus many of them consider that they are defending the biblical view of God by insisting that He is not "eternal" but "in time." They are right that the biblical God is not eternal in the sense of a negation of time, or of relations to time; but they are wrong in denying that He transcends passage, for He cannot be temporal as creatures are temporal. If He were merely temporal, He could not be the Creator and prov-

For these reasons, Christian thought has always maintained that God is the Eternal Creator of time, related to
temporality but transcendent to its passage. It follows
that the changes and the dissolution characteristic of creatures within time do not affect the being of God. Although He is related to time, He is not pushed, hurried,
changed, or removed by time's motion: "As for man, his
days are as grass: as a flower of the field, so he flourisheth.
For the wind passeth over it, and it is gone . . . But the
mercy of the Lord is from everlasting to everlasting . . ."[5]

---

idential Ruler; just as if He were not related to time, He could
not be the Redeemer. The Christian understanding of God paradoxically denies both the Greek concept of Eternity and the
naturalistic rejection of any transcendence of temporality. Perhaps
if these scholars understood more clearly the "mythical" character
of the temporal language of the Bible, they would not conclude
so readily from this language that God was simply "in time." For
the most potent and persuasive example of this type of thought,
see Oscar Cullmann, *Christ and Time*. Westminster Press, 1950.
Translated by F. V. Filson.

[5] Psalm 103: 15–17. Brunner well expresses this conception
of God's eternity, which transcends but does not negate time, in
the following: "His Eternity, then, is something quite different
from timelessness: it is a sovereign rule over Time and the temporal sphere, the freedom of Him who creates and gives us Time.
As for the Creator, the limitations and laws of the created world
do not limit Him, because it is He who posits them and creates
them, so also for Him the barriers of the temporal—the separation
into past, present, and future—do not exist. God includes and
comprehends Time within His Presence; He does not eliminate it,
but He fulfils it. God's being is not timeless; but it is full of time,
fulfilling time; all that is temporal is present in Him in the same
way, or, to put it more correctly: He is present in the Temporal as
a whole as He wills." Brunner, H. E., *The Christian Doctrine of
God*, Lutterworth Press, 1949, p. 270.

Surprisingly, almost the same conception is found in the quite
different theology of Tillich: "Since time is created in the ground
of the divine life, God is essentially related to it. In so far as
everything divine transcends the split between potentiality and
actuality, the same must be said of time as an element of the
divine life. Special moments of time are not separated from each
other; presence is not swallowed by past and future; yet the eternal keeps the temporal within itself. Eternity is the transcendent

In formulating this biblical idea, classical theology has insisted not only that God has "aseity," since He is self-sufficient and therefore unconditioned by anything beyond Himself, but also theology has maintained that He is eternal, since, as the continuing ground of temporal passage, He is in some sense beyond time and decay.

Lest this train of thought ring too exclusively of the dry abstractions of scholastic systems, let us listen to two Protestant writers on the subject:

> His power leads us to the consideration of his eternity; because he, from whom all things derive their origin, must necessarily be eternal and self-existent.[6] (Calvin)

> The fact that God is wholly other refers to that which distinguishes Him as Creator from the creatures. He alone is Lord, He alone is the Source of all life . . . He alone is "*a se non ab alio*" . . . Outside God there is only that which has been created, outside Him who is "*a se*," there is only that which is "*ab alio*"; thus outside the one who is entirely independent, there is only dependent being, the creature. This difference is greater than all other differences of any other kind; this is the absolute transcendence of essence of Him who alone is God.[7] (Brunner)

> Creation out of nothing is the expression of the unconditioned, sovereign Lordship of God, of His absolute transcendence, and of His absolute mystery.[8] (Brunner)

The first and most basic aspect of transcendence, therefore, points to the vast difference in being and in power

unity of the dissected moments of existential time." Tillich, P., *Systematic Theology*, University of Chicago Press, 1951, Volume I, p. 274.

[6] Calvin, J., *Institutes*, Book I, Chapter 5, Section 6.

[7] Brunner, *op. cit.*, p. 176.

[8] Brunner, H. E., *Revelation and Reason*, Westminster Press, pp. 44–45.

that there is between God, from whom all comes, and
those things which are absolutely dependent upon each
other and on Him. Thus traditional theology has said that
while both God and men can be said to exist, God's existence transcends that of His creatures so that there is at
best only an analogy between their modes of existence.
"Before," "above," and "beyond," then, refer not to time
and place, but to the significant and essential distinction
of being between Creator and creature. They imply that
while all creatures exist as conditioned and dependent,
God exists as unconditioned and self-sufficient; that while
all creatures are transitory, He is from everlasting to everlasting; that while creatures are weak and can be conquered and defeated, His power is absolute and He can
"never be moved." Countless passages could be used to
illustrate how essential to the biblical idea of God is this
ontological transcendence of the Creator over the creature.
It is expressed in the thundering commandment to liken
God to no creature, and in every hymn of praise to God
in the Psalms; it is the implication of every passage about
God's majesty and power; and it is the foundation of the
biblical confidence that although "The grass withereth, the
flower fadeth, . . . the word of our God shall stand for
ever."[9]

To recapitulate, then, God cannot be really "like" an
elder statesman with a white beard and a kindly face. For
that conception pictures Him as an ordinary being existing
as do others, and so different from them only in that He
is bigger, older, and more "up there." But since there is
no qualitative difference in mode of being, this is no real
transcendence. For however large, old, and good our elder
statesman may be, if he is really like us in the mode of
his existence, then he too is dependent, he too will pass
out of existence; and so he too needs God as the source
of his being, as the ground of his existence in time, and
as the hope of his salvation. A god who is a creature

[9] Isaiah 40:8.

among other creatures, even the biggest and highest, is no god: he has no "transcendence." He cannot be the source of finite existence, because he is merely an illustration of it. The ontological transcendence of God in the mode of His being is an absolutely basic requirement of our thought about God if He is to be understood as the Creator, and if we are to trust our life to Him and Him alone.

The Distinction between God and the World

2. Any consistent monism would understand transcendence in very much the same terms we have just used: the source of all is self-sufficient, necessary, and eternal in relation to its dependent creatures. Thus the Brahman of Hinduism transcends the "maya" of our experience; the One of Plotinus transcends the shadowy world of matter and diversity; and the Reality of Bradley transcends the appearances that make up our world. It is for this reason that many students of philosophy feel they recognize God when they study speculative metaphysics in college. Every monistic philosophy which seeks to find an ultimate substance or reality behind things deals with the transcendent source of all, and in that regard, at least, agrees with the Christian idea of God.

As we have seen, however, the biblical Creator is very different from the immanent-transcendent One of monism. And since this difference is an essential aspect of the idea of creation, it must be reflected in the concept of transcendence that stems from *creatio ex nihilo*. In talking about God, biblical language makes clear that it thinks of Him not only as "beyond" the world, but even more as "outside" the world in His real nature. Thus it is said that God "inhabits" eternity, that He "dwells in heaven," that He "has come" or "will come" into the earthly sphere in judgment and salvation. All these phrases point to an idea of transcendence which implies a *separa-*

tion between God and the world of finite things, as well as a *difference* between God and that world. What, then, do these biblical symbols from spatial relations, "outside of" and "come into," imply with regard to the transcendence of God?

The theological answer is that these symbols, which separate by spatial analogies God from the world, point to the second meaning of transcendence in Christian thought about God—a meaning that is not true for philosophical monism. This second meaning of transcendence was already implied in the basic formula of *creatio ex nihilo*— creatures are made not out of God but out of nothing. That is to say, the substantive existence of God is distinct from that of the world; God's essence and His existence are not identical with those of the world. In His essential nature, God is "outside" the world in the sense that at no level is the world God or God the world. What, then, can these theological phrases distinguishing God from the world mean, and why is this idea important?

First of all, they mean that no creature shares in divinity in any of its aspects, as if the being or substance of God had separated itself into many pieces to become the being of each creature. Nor is the whole world as a unity the divine; at its deepest level and in its most unifying principle, the world is not God. When we explore the world, and look deeply into its principles, its powers, and its nature, we do not find God as its underlying substance or unity. On every level we discover only dependent, contingent "creaturehood," whether it be at the superficial level of trees and mountains, or the deeper level of natural forces. Nothing is necessary here, and nothing is eternal; all has come to be by a power and by a will beyond the world. For Christian belief in a transcendent Creator, the whole realm of nature and of finite reality has been stripped of divinity and necessity; the gods have fled. Cleansed by the idea of creation of all arbitrary spiritual forces and all "sacred places," finite nature has been made a fit ground for empirical study and human use.

When, moreover, we look inside ourselves, we find not divine but creaturely existence. In our minds we experience intelligence, but creaturely, finite intelligence—and so equally capable of error and of truth. In our own selves we experience the possibility of responsibility, community, and love; but because we are creaturely spirits who have a finite freedom, we can also discover sin within. At no level of natural or human life do we find God, although at every level we encounter some creaturely reality that points beyond itself to God. Christians declare, therefore, that creatures are *ontologically* distinct from God, that they exist "alongside" of God, because Christians know that while nature and man are good, they are neither divine nor worthy of worship.

Furthermore, this ontological distinction between God and His creatures is the result of God's creative act, not of a "fall" or turning away from God. In fact, this ontological separation between God and the world is one of the basic meanings of creation. For, in creating, God gives His creatures distinct, concrete existence in space and time— He gives them "being." To say, then, that God transcends His creatures, and so is distinct from them, is to say that all finite entities are not only real as finite, but good— since their status as separate creatures is an intended aspect of the divine purpose.

Thirdly, to say that God transcends creation, in the sense of being distinct from it, is to make intelligible the alienation of creation from God that is so vivid a part of biblical and Christian experience. Were the natural and human worlds identical with God, a direct manifestation of His being, then no real defiance of the will of God by His human creatures would be possible. But as a real and spontaneous creature, distinct from God, man can freely turn away from God, and in his spirit lose his touch with God, although his existence as a dependent creature is still rooted in God. Men are neither essentially divine and therefore unable to be evil, nor essentially demonic and therefore unable to be good. They are, rather, creatures of God: rooted in Him as the creative power that gives them being, and yet distinct from Him, so that they can come under His judgment. God can be the judge only of a creation that is alienated from Him, and thus of a creation which is not identical with His own being.

The transcendence of God "beyond" the finite is thus a significant aspect of the biblical understanding of God and of His relation to His creatures. In that understanding, God "comes into" a real world that He has created and rules, that is not Himself but on the contrary is estranged from Himself, a world that He judges and then redeems. All of this implies, as we have seen, that creatures are essentially dependent upon God, but also essentially distinct from Him. The ontological independence of God from the world, His transcendence "over" the world in being and essence, is the inescapable condition for the kind of relatedness to the world in revelation, in judgment, and in salvation, of which the Bible teaches. Again ontology and biblical theology are complementary sides of the same religious affirmation.

Thus for good religious reasons Christians have always insisted that God transcends His creation not only in being the eternal and self-sufficient source of creatures but also in being distinct from His creatures. Although He is immanent in the world, He is not the heart, soul, or substance of the world. He is "outside" the world, which He creates and sustains by His immanent power:

> But the things established are distinct from Him who has established them, and what has been made from Him who made them. . . .[10] (Irenaeus)

> For what man of right understanding, does not perceive, that what are created and made are external to the maker . . . ?[11] (Athanasius)

[10] Irenaeus, *op. cit.*, Book III, Chapter 8, Section 3.
[11] Athanasius, *De Decretis*, Chapter 3, Section 13.

God is self-existent, enclosing all things and enclosed by none; within all according to His goodness and power, yet without all in His proper nature.[12] (Athanasius)

Because God is said to have breathed into man the breath of life, they supposed that the soul was an emanation from the substance of God . . . For if the soul of man be an emanation from the essence of God, it will follow that the Divine nature is not only mutable and subject to passions, but also to ignorance, desires and vices of every kind . . . Who would not dread such a monstrous tenet?[13] (Calvin)

The creation means something different; it means a reality distinct from God. And finally, the world must not be understood as a manifestation of God, so that God would be to some extent the Idea. God who alone is real and essential and free is one; and, heaven and earth, man and the universe are something else; and this something else is not God, though it exists through God.[14] (Barth)

Finally, we might point out that the unique biblical conception of "holiness" stems ultimately from these two aspects of the mystery of God's transcendence. Holiness is not primarily a moral attribute, as if it meant merely the perfect goodness of some superbeing with a white beard. Rather it refers to that absolute "otherness" which distinguishes the divine from all that is creaturely, and so characterizes every aspect of God. Holiness is the word that refers to the *divine* aspect of any attribute asserted of deity, the quality which makes any attribute essentially different in God than in other things, the quality that raises anything, be it power or love or anger, to the *nth* de-

[12] *Ibid.*, Chapter 3, Section 11.
[13] Calvin, J., *op. cit.*, Book I, Chapter 15, Section 5.
[14] Barth, K., *Dogmatics in Outline*, Philosophical Library, 1949, p. 55. See also Brunner, H. E., *The Christian Doctrine of Creation and Redemption*, Lutterworth Press, 1952, p. 20.

gree when it is applied to God. Thus God's goodness is
"holy," His being is "holy," His anger is "holy," His love is
"holy." Holiness, therefore, points to the unconditioned,
the transcendent element of deity which absolutely distinguishes God from all creatures; holiness is the "Godness" of God. Thus holiness and the divine transcendence
are ideas very closely associated in theology: so far as God
transcends His creation, so far is He holy.[15]

It follows, therefore, that a God who in no significant
respect is transcendent to the world or to our understanding of the world, cannot be holy. And this is what is most
wrong about calling God "the man upstairs," or thinking
of Him in literal terms as if He were a kind of grandfather.
An immanent, finite God, conditioned by the same categories and forces as we are, subject to the same perils and
mysteries and frustrations, is not holy. He is then merely
a "being among other beings"; such a being may be better
or more powerful than we, but, unless he transcends our
finitude in unconditionedness, he cannot be "holy" to us.
We can respect and even fear him, but we would never
radically surrender ourselves to him. Thus, ironically, both
the simple God of popular religion and the esoteric God of
process philosophy, by their essential lack of ontological
transcendence, are never holy enough to be objects of genuine religious concern. Biblical theology, therefore, must
take care that in seeking to avoid the impersonal abstractions of ontology, it does not lose the transcendent holiness
of God. For God's unconditioned majesty, on which all religious faith depends, is grounded ultimately in God's ontological transcendence over His creation.

The Need for Analogy and Symbol

3. A third connotation of the idea of transcendence follows from the first two. This is the transcendence of God

[15] See the excellent discussions of God's Holiness in Brunner,
The Christian Doctrine of God, pp. 157 ff., and in Aulén, *op.
cit.*, pp. 120–24.

over our limited powers to understand Him. If God is not the same as other things in His nature and being, and if He is not a part of the world which we experience and know, then obviously the knowledge of God becomes a serious problem. One aspect of this problem can be put quite simply: if we find and describe God as an entity in our ordinary experience, then clearly He is not the Creator we have been discussing—He is then a creature among creatures, and not God. On the other hand, if we cannot so locate and describe Him in terms of the names and relationships we use with other things, how can we know and understand Him at all?[16]

Conscious of this dilemma, philosophers and theologians of all persuasions have maintained that the source of all existence can only be known and described in two ways: by negation and by analogy. The first way proceeds by stating what God is *not*. For instance, we can state that He is not like an elder statesman of our ordinary experience, in so far as that image connotes creaturely dependence, contingency, and mortality. The way of negation describes the transcendent God by denying all those aspects of our experience that are representative of our limitations, our finitude, and our creatureliness. The second way, that of analogy, proceeds by giving a positive description of God through analogies from our limited experience. We state what He *is* only by comparing Him to certain significant aspects of our ordinary experience, in saying that He may be "like them." For instance, we can take certain traits of finite existence, its being, its power, its personality, its goodness, and say "God possesses these characteristics, but very differently from the way finite creatures possess them, He has them analogically." We mean by this that these words indicate a certain truth about God, but in Him their truth is different because while finite things are condi-

[16] Because our subject is not sin and its effects, but the transcendence of the Creator over His creation, we have omitted from this discussion the most serious barrier to the knowledge of God, namely the barrier to that knowledge which sin raises.

tioned, temporal, and imperfect, God is unconditioned, self-sufficient, eternal, and perfect. Thus while in many respects God is not at all "like a person," we may speak of Him as "personal." But by that word we can only mean that He is personal in a sense applicable to the kind of unconditioned being that He is. For always we must remember that our words about God are only analogies, since God's being, His goodness, and His "personness" are not just like ours. The words we use about God are symbols which only in part can describe the divine "being" that transcends our understanding and experience.

> There can be no doubt that any concrete assertion about God must be symbolic, for a concrete assertion is one that uses a segment of finite experience in order to say something about him. It transcends the content of this segment, although it also includes it. The segment of finite reality which becomes the vehicle of a concrete assertion about God is affirmed and negated at the same time.[17] (Tillich)

Because God is ontologically transcendent to His creatures, it follows, therefore, that He cannot be known as creatures are known. To try to know and describe Him in the direct terms of our finite existence is to fail to describe Him; it is to transform Him into a creature. For this reason, Christian theologians have always said that God "transcends" our understanding:

> Whatever men may think, that which is made is not like Him who made it . . . God is ineffable. We can more easily say what He is not than what He is. Thou thinkest of the earth; this is not God . . . What is He then? I could only tell Thee what He is not.[18] (Augustine)

[17] Tillich, P., *op. cit.*, p. 239.
[18] Augustine, in Psalm LXXXV, 12. Quoted in Przywara, E., *An Augustine Synthesis*, Sheed and Ward, 1945, pp. 80–81.

His essence indeed is incomprehensible, so that His majesty is not to be perceived by the human senses.[19] (Calvin)

Ultimately, it is an insult to the divine holiness to talk about God as we do of objects whose existence or non-existence can be discussed . . . The holiness of God makes it impossible to draw him into the context of ego-world and the subject-object correlation. He himself is the ground and meaning of this correlation, not an element within it.[20] (Tillich)

Thus we may conclude that a fundamental rule of theology is that all positive language about God is analogical and symbolic. We cannot speak directly or exactly about God because our ordinary experience, and our thoughts and our words that come from that experience, refer to finite things. In speaking of God, then, we must be content to talk in riddles and paradoxes: we can only say what He is by first saying what He is not; and we can only affirm something about Him if we are careful to deny at the same time its literal application. God is and remains a mystery to our thought and our language, *the* essential mystery of our existence since He is the source of that existence. And however much we may know of Him in faith, the infinity of the Divine Majesty broods over all our theological language, cautioning us that before the throne of God, "let all the earth keep silence."

Now this whole problem of the knowledge of God creates a difficult dilemma for philosophy. If philosophy is based on our ordinary experience, how can it know in any relevant sense a holy "Being" that transcends that experience? For philosophy, even the methods of negation and of analogy seem futile and meaningless. Merely to say "the absolute is not like this or not like that" is not to add creatively to our understanding and knowledge. And if in

---

[19] Calvin, *op. cit.*, Book I, Chapter 5, Section 1.
[20] Tillich, *op. cit.*, pp. 271–72.

defining God either by negation or by analogy we seem continually to negate all the finite and therefore "ungodly" traits of our experience, do we not inevitably end up with a completely abstract, bloodless, motionless, meaningless nothing?[21] We may call it Being or the Absolute, but is it not lacking in all the movement, the concreteness, and the content that must be there in any concept to make it meaningful?

Furthermore, if we affirm that we can only know God positively by analogy, what do we mean? To say on the one hand He is fundamentally different from all creatures, and yet He is like a person, is confusing. Surely our statement is meaningful only if we know Him in some sense already, at least enough to specify *how much* like a person He is. Without that prior direct knowledge, we have no idea how the word "personal" applies to this different kind of being—whether very closely or really not at all. For example, we use the phrase "like a person" to describe such disparate entities as a chimpanzee and a constellation of stars. For the phrase to be at all meaningful we must know the ways in which the chimpanzee and the stars differ from persons; we must know them in some sense already. If, then, we can know God positively *only* by analogy, are we not caught in a vicious circle? For all we know of

[21] This problem for the philosophical theologian is ably expressed by Anthony Flew in the following:

"The theologian will find himself forever saying things about God drawn from human experience. (For where else is a human being to get his vocabulary if not from this world we live in?) And then admitting that, of course, as God is transcendent, infinite, the ground of all being, and so on; this analogy breaks down in this and this respects. Again and again he is going—and I think necessarily so from the very nature of his project—to erode his promising analogy by qualifying it till there is nothing left. Till it has tacitly, or even explicitly, been admitted to break down not only in some but in all respects. His analogies are all going to suffer . . . the death by a thousand qualifications." Flew, A., *op. cit.*, p. 180.

Him, God may be so much "wholly other" that our words do not fit and so describe Him in any relevant sense at all. Unless, therefore, there is some other means of "knowing" a transcendent God, the philosopher seems endlessly frustrated: if he seeks to understand that transcendent source from which all comes, he is left amid only negations and dubious analogies when he tries to describe it.[22] No wonder many philosophers scoff at this attempt to scale the transcendent, for philosophy seems by its own empirical method to be confined to this given world and the immanent system of relations in that world.

To this problem of the knowledge of the transcendent God Christian faith has a distinctive answer. Since God in the majesty of His being transcends the world of our ordinary experience, He can be known only through His revelation of Himself within that world. Because He is transcendent, we cannot know Him by our own methods of discovery: to do so is either to reduce Him to the level of creatures whom we can understand, or else to conceive of Him negatively as an abstract, lifeless absolute. But this "unknowability" has been overcome, not by our intellectual ascent to His eminence, but by the descent of His Word into our realm. In His saving acts in history, culminating in that event in which He took on the conditions of finitude and thus became "knowable" and "visible" to us, He has revealed Himself to us. In this we do not know directly His transcendent essence and being; but we do know His inmost will, His intentions for us and for our world. Thus the gulf between the Creator and the finite creature has been bridged by revelation, and the absolute mystery of that transcendent source from which we come has been illumined to our spirits and made partially intelligible to

[22] A good example of this philosophical frustration that ends only in negation is Bradley's effort to understand the absolute which his philosophy requires as the ground of appearances, but which it is quite unable to describe meaningfully. Cf. Bradley, F. H., *Appearance and Reality*.

our minds. To Christians, therefore, the transcendence of God implies and requires the revelatory acts of God. And for this reason, Christian theology rightly feels that all that it can validly say about the transcendent God must be based upon and guided by God's revelation of Himself.[23]

This connection between God's transcendence and the need for revelation has been much emphasized in contemporary theology. Consequently to many Christians the word transcendence connotes, not so much ontological transcendence, as the unknowability of God to our ordinary scientific and philosophical knowledge, and our sole dependence upon revelation for any knowledge of God. In this emphasis it should not be forgotten that one of the most fundamental grounds for our need for God's revelation in history is the ontological transcendence of God over all of creation. A God who in His being and essence is simply "like other beings" would, if relevant at all to us, be known through our ordinary scientific and philosophical inquiries. This intimate relation between ontological transcendence and historical revelation in Christian thought about the Creator is well expressed by Brunner in the following:

[23] Calvin enunciates this rule of theology as follows:

"On this, indeed, if on any of the secret mysteries of the Scripture, we ought to philosophize with great sobriety and moderation; and also with extreme caution, lest either our ideas or our language should proceed beyond the limits of the Divine word. For how can the infinite essence of God be defined by the narrow capacity of the human mind . . . ?

. . . Wherefore let us freely leave to God the knowledge of himself . . . and we shall certainly leave it to him, if our conceptions of him correspond to the manifestations which he has given us of himself, and our inquiries concerning him are confined to His word . . . The very unhappy consequences of this temerity should warn us . . . not [to] allow ourselves to investigate God anywhere but in his sacred word, or to form any ideas of Him but such as are agreeable to his word, or to speak anything concerning him but what is derived from the same word." Calvin, *op. cit.*, Book I, Chapter 13, Section 21.

The sum total of all that in principle is accessible to man is called the "world" . . . The unconditional mystery does not belong to the world; it is Supramundane. To say that it is Supramundane, and that it can only be known through revelation, really means the same thing. *Because* it is Supramundane, it can be known only through revelation . . .[24]

As the Holy One, God is the Wholly Other, the Incomparable, the Sole Reality, who in this His incomparable uniqueness wills to be known and recognized . . . When God in His revelation steps out of His mystery, at the same time He removes the absolute barrier between Himself and all creatures . . .[25]

In this knowledge of the nature and will of God through His acts in history, the abstract and empty character of the transcendent absolute of the philosopher is overcome. God for Christians *is* transcendent and beyond all; but He is far from the bloodless abstraction of idealist philosophy. Nor does His transcendence have to be filled with the world's content in order for the conception of Him to be living and meaningful. In His saving and revelatory acts He has shown Himself to be dynamic and living, so that the Christian conception of God is filled with the most concrete content. Revelation, then, is the Christian basis for our positive knowledge of God, and for our use of every appropriate analogy to describe His nature.

We have found, then, three aspects to the important notion of the divine transcendence: 1) The transcendence of God "beyond" the world in the mode of His existence. While creatures are dependent, contingent, and temporal, as Creator He is self-sufficient and eternal. 2) The transcendence of God "outside" the world: the essence and existence of creaturely life, while continually dependent upon God, are not identical with God, so that creatures

[24] Brunner, H. E., *Revelation and Reason*, p. 23.
[25] *Ibid.*, p. 45.

are distinct beings from their Creator. 3) The consequent transcendence of God to our knowledge: as a being
or reality "other" than the world, God cannot be known in
terms of the world, and hence can only be understood
paradoxically by negation and by analogy based upon His
own revelation of Himself in the world. It is evident from
this analysis of "transcendence" that the idea of God involved here is a baffling mixture of ontology—the study of
existence, being, and the nature of reality—and of religious
faith. Religious faith springs from and worships the God
known in historical revelation in and through events and
persons within history; but the God known there is He
who transcends the world in existence and in being, and
so can be thought about correctly only if we also use this
more abstract and impersonal language of ontology. This
problem of the relation between our religious and our
metaphysical language about God will accompany us as
we proceed in our study.

The Immanence of God

Obviously the doctrine of creation has a good deal to
say about God's transcendence. Does it have anything of
equal import to declare about His immanence? Or is the
Creator only "outside" His world and not "within" it at all?
Strangely enough, the idea of creation asserts God's presence in power and in wisdom within the world as firmly as
it affirms His transcendence in "His proper nature" over
the world.

In describing the character of "creatures" we have said
that although their existence is real enough, nevertheless
it is a completely dependent existence. Their being has
come to them, not from their own nature, but from beyond themselves in God, whose creative act brought them
into being. They *are*, then, only so long as God's creative
act continues to give them being, for they do not generate
their own power to be from themselves, but as the moments of their existence pass, they receive it continually

from beyond themselves. The renewal of each creature in each succeeding moment of its existence is a victory of being over the non-being of temporal passage. In the on-rush of temporal passage, this victorious recreation in the next moment is accomplished by a power beyond ourselves, since each creature is caught within the present and cannot establish itself beyond the present. Thus, without the continuing power of God each creature would lapse back into the non-being whence it came. Were God to cease to be in things, they would simply cease to be.[26] In speaking, therefore, of creatures as continually dependent upon their Creator for their existence, the doctrine of creation implies the continuing immanence of God in all His creatures as firmly as it asserts His transcendence over them. For this reason the concept of God's continuing creation of the world in each succeeding moment of its passage is the ground for the further doctrine of God's providential rule over each aspect of creation and each moment of its duration. God is immanent in things as the creative and preserving power in which all exists; and yet as the self-sufficient and free being from which all derives its existence, God transcends infinitely all His creatures. No one has phrased this paradox of immanence and transcendence better than Athanasius: "Within all according to His good-

[26] "Whatever bodily or seminal causes, then, may be used for the production of things . . . yet the natures themselves, which are thus variously affected, are the production of none but the most high God. It is His occult power which pervades all things, and is present in all without being contaminated, which gives being to all that is, and modifies and limits its existence; so that without Him it would not be thus, or thus, nor would have any being at all." Augustine, *The City of God*, Book XII, Chapter 25. "If God should but withdraw His hand a little, all things would immediately perish and dissolve into nothing as is declared in Psalm 104:29. And indeed God is rightly acknowledged as the Creator of heaven and earth only whilst their perpetual preservation is ascribed to Him." Calvin, J., Commentary of Genesis 2:2. Quoted in Torrance, T. F., *Calvin's Doctrine of Man*, Lutterworth Press, 1949, p. 62.

ness and power, yet without all in His proper nature."[27]

Actually, immanence and transcendence are polar concepts and, like reason and faith, cannot do without each other. A completely transcendent God who has no aspect of immanence, a God who is really *wholly* other, would be out of all relation to us, and therefore quite unknowable and quite irrelevant to us. He might, it is true, enter like an invader from Mars into our world, as an interesting addition to the things that are in it. But surely if He is thus irrelevant to the essential ongoing of the world, it would be absurd to say that the world had been "lost" without Him, or "saved" by His new presence in its midst. For a transcendent God to be important and relevant to our lives, He must in some sense already be immanent in them. Correspondingly, there can be no "absolute immanence" which contains no semblance of transcendence. If God is "in things" in any significant way, then He is "in

[27] It is fashionable in the theology of our day to attempt to deny this ontological immanence of God and to emphasize only His transcendence over and separation from us. Thus one reads that biblical faith is uninterested in the presence of God in all things, for "God is present only where His love realizes itself in grace and judgment," and "all questions whether God is in the flower or in the stone, and the like, are immaterial to faith." (Aulén. *op. cit.*, pp. 150–51.) The implication of these sentences is surely that there is no relevant relation between man and God prior to the grace of judgment and of redemption. Because it wishes to emphasize the crucial importance of the gulf of sin on the one hand, and of revelation and the faith and decision that respond to it on the other, such contemporary "biblical" theology is apt to deny that there is any presence of God outside of His revealed presence and any relation to God outside of faith. If, however, the doctrine of creation is taken at all seriously, as these theologians try to do, such remarks seem somewhat out of place. If things *are* because of God's creative act, then so long as they are at all, they have an essential relation, a point of contact with God. If God is said to be Creator, then He is inescapably present in all of nature and in all of mankind. And while men can be separated from God in religion and in the spirit, neither they nor anything else can be completely separated from God's creative power so long as they are at all.

them" in a way that other beings—stones, stars, people, for instance—are not "in" other things. But if this is so, then inevitably He is different in some fundamental aspect of His being from ordinary finite entities. And thus we move inescapably back to transcendence. The Christian concept of God as Creator and Redeemer invariably connotes both transcendence and immanence, and can safely lose neither one, although the emphasis on one or the other will vary. For if God be the Creator and ground of our being and life, it follows both that He is fundamentally different from and so transcendent to all else to which we are related, and that He is involved in, and so immanent in, all else in a way that no creature can be.

Divine Freedom

In the preceding chapter we found that one essential aspect of the Christian doctrine of *creatio ex nihilo* was that creation was an act of the divine freedom, done "only because of God's goodness that He might make a good creation." And we argued briefly that this understanding of creation as an act of God's freedom provided the only basis on which a meaning and purpose to finite life as a whole, and therefore to our individual lives, could be discovered. Now let us look at the implications of divine freedom in creation for the idea of God; we shall name three.

1. The first implication in the idea of the "freedom" of God is that God is unconditioned and self-sufficient, dependent neither on the world nor on any other power for His reality. If God needs the world in order to complete or enrich His being, then His creation of the world is not "free." It is a necessitated and therefore impersonal act, to which God is compelled by His own unfulfilled nature. If He would not be fully God without the world, then producing the world is a necessary part of the process of being God. In such a case, we cannot meaningfully apply to His act of creation the categories of freedom or of purpose

which, whatever else they may mean, connote the ability to "do or not to do" and the power "to choose amid alternatives." Part of the meaning of freedom, then, requires that the only reason for creation is "that it was good." If any other reason compels it, then it is not a free act of God. God must be unconditioned to be free; a God who fundamentally depends upon the world is therefore not a God who can freely create the world. Thus the purposive relation of God to this world seems to be based upon the ontological self-sufficiency of God beyond the world.

Furthermore, if God depends upon some other principle of equal stature to create the world, if He is finite, then again He is not "free." As finite, His acts are continually conditioned by this other principle, perhaps of chaos, of matter, or of creativity. If He be finite, moreover, He is inescapably governed by the structure of being of which He is merely a part and an illustration. He is like the gods of Greece, who were under the ultimate rule of Fate, or like Whitehead's God who is "in the grip of the ultimate metaphysical ground."[28] The will of such a God is not the sovereign principle of existence but only one conditioned voice in a chorus that transcends Him. Such a restricted being is not "God," the object of our ultimate concern and trust, the free Creator, Ruler, and Redeemer of whom the Bible speaks. The unconditioned character of God, and His consequent freedom and sovereignty over all things, are essential to the biblical idea of God:

> . . . We find that there is hardly a word said about God in the Bible which does not point directly or indirectly to his freedom. In freedom he creates, in freedom he deals with the world and man, in freedom he saves and fulfils. His freedom is freedom from anything prior to him or alongside of him . . . There is no ground prior to Him which could condition His freedom; neither chaos nor non-being has power to limit or resist Him

[28] Whitehead, A. N., *Process and Reality*, Macmillan, 1929, p. 529.

. . . freedom means that that which is man's ultimate
concern is in no way dependent on man or on any finite
being or on any finite concern. Only that which is unconditional can be expressive of an unconditional concern. A conditioned God is no God.[29]

The divine freedom requires, then, that God be ontologically transcendent in the sense that He is self-sufficient
and unconditioned. A divine elder statesman, a *purely*
"personal" God, would not be free in the biblical sense.
For a conditioned person is far from the free Lord of all.
Surprisingly, then, the most important "personal" category
applied to God, His freedom, depends upon His ontological transcendence and so upon the denial that He is merely
a "person."

2. A second necessity, if we are adequately to describe
the divine freedom, is that we use "personal" and "intentional" terms, as well as ontological ones, in conceiving
of God's actions. It is not enough that God as being itself
is neither dependent upon nor limited by any power outside or beyond Him. It is also essential to His freedom that
He be spirit, and thus "intend" and "decide" to do what
He does. Without this "intentional" element, God's creation of the world becomes an impersonal process, like the
overflowing of a fountain or the emanation of light—unconditioned by other factors but still automatic, inevitable,
and therefore neither free nor meaningful. The divine freedom, therefore, connotes more than the ontological transcendence of God: it connotes also the "personal" nature
of God. For freedom is a concept invariably associated
with the whole range of powers that are used in a full
description of a human person, powers of intelligence, will,
intention, and decision:

Freedom is not absence of determination; it is spiritual
determination, as distinct from mechanical or even organic, determination. It is determination by what seems

[29] Tillich, *op. cit.,* p. 248.

good as contrasted with determination by irresistible compulsion.[30]

Thus in contrast to inorganic bodies whose behavior is adequately described . . . in terms of matter in motion, and in contrast to organisms, whose behavior is described in terms of growth and decay, human deeds are *intended* and *done*. They are not intelligible apart from the categories of *intention* and *decision*. Intention or "intentionality" was first a category of scholastic thought, indicating an objective direction, a conscious purposiveness of the human mind . . . Intention has its fulfillment in *decision* . . .[31]

A free act, therefore, implies a personal and intended act, motivated and determined by the spiritual powers of intelligence, will, and purpose. If we are to speak of God's freedom, and especially if we are to speak of a purpose or meaning in creation, we must think of God primarily, though not exclusively, in personal analogies. Thus the Christian God is neither just the underlying reality of philosophy nor the elder statesman of popular religion. Like the former, He is transcendent and unconditioned; but He is a transcendent Creator and Redeemer who can finally be understood only through the ideas and words we use to describe persons.

3. A final important element in the concept of the divine freedom in creation is what we might call the "variability" of God's action in relation to His world, or the dynamic and "living" character of God. If we say that God is "free" over His creation, then we mean that His actions are not restricted to certain universal and therefore invariable relations to the world, as if everything He did was everywhere and always the same. Rather, in agreement with His purpose, which does not change, His actions on

[30] Temple, W., *Nature, Man and God*, New York, The Macmillian Co., 1949, p. 229.
[31] Hutchinson, J. A., *Faith, Reason and Existence*, Oxford University Press, 1956, p. 102.

the world can vary as He chooses. Thus, for example, according to His consistent purpose, God in the Bible appears to and is with Israel, as He is not with the Ethiopians, although both are His children. Freedom in human life connotes this strange combination of consistency of purpose and variability of action—and so this kind of variable relation to His world is implied in the affirmation that creation was a "free act of God."

This implication has the utmost significance for the biblical conception of God. As we have emphasized, it is true that God *is* invariably and universally present in all things as the source of their existence. Were His immanent power not thus invariable and universal, these things would not be. But the essence of the biblical view of God is that He is not confined merely to that ontological relation to the world which He has as Creator. Rather He is "free" to have other sorts of relations to creatures, depending upon His "intention." Thus He can remove Himself from man's presence, as the Psalms imply; He can "come" or "appear" in judgment as in the prophetic writings; and He can be uniquely present in certain events in saving strength, as the Old Testament both recalls and prophesies, and as the whole New Testament witnesses. The biblical God is the God of history, who acts within certain unique events of history and is thus known through His "mighty deeds." In these events of history God is present as He is not present elsewhere, and reveals Himself in a manner unknown and unknowable elsewhere. This concept of "special action" at certain times and in certain places reaches its culmination in the Christian claim that the Word, "without whom was not anything made," "became flesh and dwelt among us" in a particular human individual who was born of Mary and crucified under Pontius Pilate. This paradox of the universal God who manifests Himself within a special event is classically phrased by Paul: "God was in Christ, reconciling the world unto Himself."[32] For the Bible,

[32] II Corinthians 5:19.

then, while God as Creator is omnipresent, as Judge and Redeemer He comes in specific and unique events. To take away either one of these very different types of relation to His world, either this universal ontological presence or these unique revelatory and saving appearances in historical events, is to demolish the essential structure of the Christian idea of God as both Creator and Redeemer, and to transform the Christian religion as a faith in God based on unique historical events.

Central, then, to the Christian faith is the conception that God is "free" over His creation to relate Himself to it in different ways and at specific times and places. In this faith, then, the consistency and order of the universe is not founded, as in philosophy, on the invariability and necessity of God's relation to the world. This is a far too intellectual and systematic an understanding of meaning. Rather the deep basis of Christian confidence is our knowledge of the steadfast and faithful will of Almighty God, who deals with us in various ways according to our several conditions. Thus perhaps the most significant element religiously of the freedom of God the Creator is that it establishes the possibility of God's freedom *over* His creation, so that He may "act" within the arena of historical time in revelatory and saving events. For, as the free transcendent Creator of the world, God is not a determined part of the system of the world, confined to the invariable relations of the world's structure. Rather is He free over His own creation, which thereby becomes an instrument in His hands and can be both judged and redeemed by His saving will.[33]

In this chapter we have discussed the idea of God that is implied when Christians affirm that God is the Maker

[33] It is significant that theologians like Schleiermacher, who incline toward an "impersonal" idea of God, and who assert that God "transcends" the distinction between freedom and necessity, so that in God potency and act, can and do, are identical, are precisely the theologians who are least able to conceive of God as

of heaven and earth. We have found that this is an idea
of great richness and complexity, comprising important implications of God's transcendence beyond our finitude and
our direct knowledge, His immanence within our continuing existence, and His freedom in relation to the world
that He has created. As we have tried to show, each of
these concepts is directly implied by the idea of creation,
and each of them is in turn an essential element in the
total Christian idea of God. Thus it seems apparent that
the conception of God the Creator is for Christians not
simply a primitive inheritance from an outgrown tradition,
which we can without loss to our faith transform at will.
Nor is it merely a piece of metaphysical speculation,
tacked on by theologians to the "unmetaphysical" biblical
heritage. Rather, as the foundation upon which all that is
Christianly significant about God is based, the idea of the
Creator is an indispensable and primary element in any
Christian theology.   *Summary.*

We have also discovered that this "theologian's" conception of God, not unlike that of the average churchman
with which we started, combines in a bewildering mixture
elements that at first seem incompatible. In discussing the
fundamental aspects of God's transcendence and His immanence, we could not avoid dealing with the somewhat
impersonal and abstract categories of ontology and of philosophy: here, when we spoke of God, we used such words
as "reality," "existence," "essence," "being," "power,"
"ground," "eternity"—words derived from and clarified by
philosophical analysis, and by the metaphysical quest for
ultimate reality. On the other hand, when we discussed
other aspects of God's transcendence and immanence—His
revelatory self-disclosure, His purposive freedom and in-

---

revealing himself in special and unique events. For Schleiermacher
the only intelligible divine activity is the universal causal action of
God on all things, and thus he is unable to fully comprehend
God's special activity. Cf. *The Christian Faith.* The biblical con-
cept of revelation and the idea of the Creator who is "free over
His creation" imply and require one another.

tentionality, and His dynamic, "living" relations to history
and the world—we found ourselves inevitably using terms
and symbols from human personal and historical life. It
was evident, furthermore, that no more for the theologian
than for the layman could any easy separation be made between these two aspects of God: His ontological being and
and His personal nature. Rather each aspect conditioned
and depended on the other: the ontological transcendence
and immanence of God is the necessary basis for His freedom and His redemptive activity. And this freedom and
personal activity, on the other hand, are the sole bases in
revelation for our knowledge of His transcendent being and
for any meaningful content therein. We shall discuss this
issue again. Meanwhile we can conclude that it is unwise
to try to dispense with either the ontological tradition or
the more personal tradition when we speak of the Christian God.

Chapter 5

CREATION AND THE INTELLIGIBILITY OF OUR WORLD

In our discussion of the meaning of the doctrine of creation, we have found that this concept has made significant affirmations, not only about the nature and activity of God, but also about the reality and the goodness of our finitude. Just as in the preceding chapter we explored what the idea of creation meant for our thought about God, so in this and succeeding chapters we shall seek to learn what this concept implies for our understanding of our own existence. What do Christians mean, then, when they say that creation is "good"?

As long as the simple biblical picture of the world held sway in the minds of Christians, it was fairly easy to give an answer to this question. God had created the world in six days and when His task was done creation was perfect: "And God saw everything that he had made, and, behold, it was very good."[1] For a brief period of historical existence the world was as God had planned it, for in this original creation there was no disorder and confusion, no sin and conflict, and therefore no pain, suffering, and death. Because of the Fall, these aspects of "evil" appeared in God's world, but before that tragic event all that was was good. In this view the idea of the goodness of creation possessed a definite meaning: it referred to the original perfection of God's world as it came from the Creator's hand.

With the appearance of a scientific understanding of the world's origin, this simple picture of God's creative

[1] Genesis 1:31.

activity gradually lost its hold. Almost universally it has been agreed among scientists that each form of existence has come into being as the result of a gradual development, stretching over millions of years. Consequently when modern men looked backward into the past of nature they found, not the harmonious, painless nature of Paradise, but an undeveloped and, to our eyes, a relatively chaotic universe. And when they looked back in human history they discovered, not a sinless human pair, but the neolithic and paleolithic savage. It seemed certain to all who took science seriously that no period of the past contained the "golden age" of the Genesis story, and that if we were searching for the good creation, we should not look behind us at the chaos, the mire, and the savagery out of which we have come. If creation is good at all, this cannot mean what it had always meant, namely that in the beginning the created world was perfect.

Modern liberal Protestantism accepted this scientific picture of a developing universe, and it sought to understand the goodness of creation in its light. God had created a world which, while not good at its beginning, was nevertheless becoming better, and which in some far-off day would be fully good. In evolutionary liberalism the goodness of creation was moved from the beginning of process to its culmination. The orthodox conception that Christian salvation restores for man what had been lost in the Fall was changed to the liberal theme that Christian faith completes and perfects the developing goodness of God's creative process. Again the idea of a good creation has a definite meaning: it points to the promise, inherent in God's improving world, that in the end nature and man will achieve a perfected existence.

In our own day both these meanings of the good creation have lost their power over men's minds. Like the liberals, modern Christians feel they must accept the scientific picture of the past history of nature and of mankind as authoritative: the goodness of creation does not lie behind us in an earthly Paradise at the beginning of

things. But unlike many liberals, modern Christians feel
an equal uncertainty about the future perfection of man's
earthly state. The optimistic picture of a "golden age" to
come appears to be as much an unwarranted article of
faith as was its orthodox predecessor. The fundamental
threats to the goodness of life—meaninglessness, sin, and
death—are as pervasive now as in past times, and no mere
process of biological or social development appears capable
of removing them. Modern Christians seem forced to admit that God's creation is *never* fully good, neither in the
past nor in the future. And so they are led to wonder
somewhat despairingly whether or not life can be called
good at all; and if it can, then to what aspect of our finite
existence does the "goodness of creation" refer?

Perhaps the most unfortunate answer to this question is
the one most commonly regarded as "Christian." This is
the sentimental answer. It affirms the goodness of creation
by denying the reality of any disorder or evil within our
experience. For this view, a Christian always "looks on the
bright side," always "sees nothing but good in events or
people," "remembers the silver lining," and believes that
all's well in God's world. The picture of the world fostered
here is unbelievably naïve: people are filled only with
good intentions; frustrations and fears are merely psychological since positive thought will eradicate them; and
problems are only there because we do not believe hard
enough that they are not there. This gentle world is appropriate enough for Sunday school. But when this child's
landscape, filled with ladies, bunnies, fairies, and harmless
men with clerical collars, is presented as the Christian
understanding of the world—since God's world is good—
Christianity has lost all power and relevance to the problems of life. No wonder those people who live immersed
within the tragedies of existence, amid its real frustrations
and insecurities, its deep conflicts of power, and its inescapable sufferings, are offended by the falsity of this picture of the world and suspect that those who hold it find

in this sentimentalism a helpful excuse for doing nothing about the world's various ills.

Let us note that this sentimentalism is representative neither of orthodoxy nor of liberalism at its best. Because the orthodox believer held the goodness of creation to refer to a definite period of the past, he could be and often was intensely realistic about the disorder and evil of man's present situation, without losing his faith in God's good creation. And because the liberal believed firmly in the goodness of a realizable future, he could be and was fully aware of the conflicts, the injustices, and the sufferings of man's present existence. The roots of this sentimentalism lie in the optimism of modern secular culture, and in the confusion in the mind of the church as to what it does mean by the goodness of creation. In order, then, to escape sentimentalism as well as despair, it is important that the idea of the good creation be thought out again on the most fundamental level.

Fortunately the history of Christian thought about the goodness of creation reveals that much more was meant by that concept than the simple view that creation was actually perfect "at the beginning." For most Christian thinkers the symbol of a perfect Eden pointed to an understanding of finitude which is separable from the question of the actual existence in space and time of that specific paradise. Like the affirmation that God created the world, the affirmation that creation is fundamentally good can be made as honestly and as meaningfully by modern men who accept the validity of science as it could by their grandfathers who believed in the historical existence of the Garden of Eden. Essentially the next five chapters of this book will be devoted to an exploration of the meaning and validity of this central affirmation. For, as our brief discussion of the idea of the goodness of creation has already revealed, this concept involves many complex and yet important ideas.

When thoughtful Christians have said that the world is "good," they seem to have been affirming the following things: 1) that creation, as the product of the divine wisdom, is orderly and intelligible in itself, and therefore a fit object for human inquiry, understanding, and control; 2) that the essential structure of finite, human existence is such that, despite the contingency and precariousness of our life, there can be meaning to historical existence; 3) that evil is not an essential or necessary character of our existence, but an "intruder" into a world that is by nature good; 4) that the saving activity of God, which is proclaimed by the Gospel and to which a man may relate himself in faith, can achieve the conquest of this intruding evil and realize the potential goodness which creaturehood essentially promises; 5) and, finally, that in consequence man's temporal existence is not merely a "living and a dying," but that through the temporal dimension there runs a divine purpose, to which in faith a man may relate himself so that his unique historical life can achieve meaning and purpose. The theme that dominates our whole discussion is that man's creaturely existence, his finite, contingent, and temporal life, becomes good when, in faith, man's life is centered upon his Creator. Then the many threats to the goodness of life are conquered, and life realizes its great inherent possibilities. In other words, when man's spiritual existence reflects his essential nature as a dependent creature of God, then man's life is good. This possibility that life may be reborn to its essential structure and its inherent potentiality is what Christians mean by the good creation.

The Laws of Nature

To modern Western man the most obvious evidence of the goodness of the created world is its intelligibility. Over the centuries men in our culture have increasingly believed their world to be characterized by a pervasive order of invariable relations, what have been called the "laws of nature," an order which can be understood through patient scientific inquiry. To us it seems axiomatic that the world is intelligible to our minds, and this we have found to be an important aspect of its goodness. For through scientific knowledge man has been enabled in part to control and to use nature for his own purposes. Thus he has unquestionably made his life more comfortable, more secure, more convenient. Understanding does foster the intelligent control of forces both outside and within us, and is for this reason a requisite to a full human existence.

The belief that fuller knowledge can lead directly to the good life, and that the world's intelligibility is a main element in its goodness, has led many modern people to question and even to reject the Christian faith which they had inherited. In the first place, they have been so confident that more knowledge can resolve man's most basic problems that they have felt little need for religion in order to realize the potential goodness of life. And secondly, they have felt that religious faith is somehow antithetical to a proper scientific understanding of the order of the world. Not only do they cite the historic conflict between science and theology, but they add the more profound objection that religious explanations of our world and of its order contradict scientific explanations. While a Christian says the stars are "created by the will of God," the scientist explains their existence in terms of that immanent system of natural relations discovered by empirical inquiry. While the one finds the effective cause in a supernatural will beyond all finite causes and so beyond our understanding, the other finds the effective and explanatory "causes" to lie within the world order around us. These two kinds of explanation appear to be mutually exclusive: seemingly if God created the stars, then natural causes could not have, and vice versa. Does not the religious man, therefore, have to forgo the intelligible world order which the modern scientist finds in the universe; and does not the modern intellectual, on the other hand, have to relinquish the consolations of religion if he is to affirm and to use the world order of modern knowledge?

In another chapter we have tried to show that religious and scientific explanations do not conflict, because they pose different sorts of questions in different realms of discourse. In this section our purpose is to show that the religious idea of a transcendent Creator actually made possible rather than hindered the progress of the scientific understanding of the natural order. In a real sense the modern conviction that existence is good because it is intelligible to scientific inquiry finds some of its most significant roots in the Christian belief that God created the world.

Our Greek Inheritance

Now there is little question that the tradition of knowledge which has culminated in modern science has its ultimate origin in the pre-Christian culture of Greece. Perhaps the greatest creation of the Greek spirit was the vision of reality as a "cosmos," that is, as permeated by a rational structure which the human mind could know. For the Greek thinkers, everything that is comes to be because it illustrates an intelligible or purposive form. The essence of the Greek view of nature, therefore, was that natural objects are really like human artifacts, and are to be understood by the same methods of study. A human artifact is an object, like a knife or a vase, that has been made by man for a specific and intelligible purpose. We can, therefore, understand it most helpfully if we view it as having a material substratum arranged according to the guiding principle of some intelligible, purposive form—as a knife or a vase are clearly composed of appropriate materials arranged according to the principles of "knifeness" or "vaseness." Thus when, rummaging around some old ruins, we come across a strange artifact and wish to know what it was or did, the quickest and best thing to do is to ask ourselves: "What was it for?" If we can discover, or, as we say, "intuit," that basic form or purpose according to which another man made it, then we can understand the object fully. For what artifacts are and do depends on their determining form or purpose, and not on their matter, which merely gives embodiment to the guiding form. For example, it is the essential structure of a knife as "something to cut with" that has determined the arrangements of its material parts and makes it a knife. And we can understand and use this sharp object before us when our minds have grasped this essential structural form. We need to know nothing more about an artifact once we have understood the principle according to which it was made, and so the function which makes it what it is.

Now according to the Greek view, all of reality is in this way like productions of human beings, permeated and structured with purposive forms that the mind can grasp. Thus human knowledge of the inner structure of nature is possible if the inquirer searches for and discovers these formal principles. One understands a natural object as one does an artifact, by asking the same questions: "What is it for? What is its basic principle of operation, and so of construction? What is its form?" And such questions can be answered because the natural world, like the human world of art, consists of objects whose material parts illustrate some intelligible form that the mind can grasp. Once the scientist has uncovered this form of the object, moreover, he really knows all he can or need know about it; he has penetrated to the very heart of reality. He does not need to experience or describe any further its external characteristics or patterns of behavior, since, with its form in his mind, he can predict all that is important about its activities and powers. Thus Greek science was a search for formal structures or essences: one understood a natural object or event, not through tracing its material causes or through describing its sensible characteristics, but through a rational intuition of this purposive form. This vision of a world penetrated through and through with intelligible forms is one of the greatest of the many contributions of Greece to our cultural life. It is the original basis for the

Western confidence that the world in which we live is neither arbitrary nor chaotic but exhibits an inherent order which careful thought can uncover.

The Greek vision of an orderly world was, however, an insufficient basis for the empirical sciences which the West has produced during the last few centuries. The reason lies precisely in the view of the world's order which we have just outlined, namely that for the Greeks the order of the world was an order of inherent purposive forms, rather than, as in Christian culture, an order created by a transcendent divine will. The Greek viewpoint provided no basis for the two central characteristics of modern science that have made it a fruitful form of inquiry. These two convictions are: (1) that the intelligibility and order of the natural world are to be found within its physical and material relations, rather than in its qualitative and purposive forms; and, (2) that this order is not deducible from ideas or forms in our minds, but is "contingent," and therefore discoverable only by sensory experience, and by the manipulation and study of the material aspects of natural events. As we shall show, these presuppositions of modern empirical science run directly counter to the main tendencies of Greek science. Their roots, therefore, lie in quite a different intellectual tradition from that of the Greeks, namely in the Christian belief that God created the world.[2]

For Greek science the order of the natural world came from its qualitative and purposive forms, rather than from the material aspects of its existence. This material element was merely the irrational receptacle of the form, and so was not part of the intelligible order of the object.

[2] In this discussion the author is greatly indebted to the excellent article by M. B. Foster, "The Christian Doctrine of Creation and the Rise of Modern Science," in *Mind*, Volume XLIII, 1934, and to the following studies of the same subject: Collingwood, R. G., *An Essay on Metaphysics*, Oxford University Press, 1940, Chapter 21; Chevalier, J., *La Notion du nécessaire chez Aristote et chex ses prédécèsseurs*, Lyon, A. Ray, 1914.

Consequently what the material elements of things contributed to their make-up were called "accidents" by the Greeks, and were not of concern to the Greek seeker for knowledge. For example, in understanding what a human artifact such as a knife or a vase is and does, we are not concerned with such things as its size, weight, mass, and physical relations to other things. They are interesting "accidents" of its particular material, but not essential to its "knifeness" or "vaseness." Only the qualitative arrangement of its material parts into something that "cuts" or "holds water" is important to us, and once we know that qualitative form, we can understand all we wish to know about the material elements of which it consists. Because the Greek scientist regarded nature as if it were a world of human artifacts with qualitative forms representing inherent purposes, he "looked through" all the material elements of nature in his search for its formal principles. To him the material elements were only the necessary but distorting material in which these forms resided. Consequently, the physical events, relations, and materials which make up the natural world, and which are the dominant concerns of the modern scientist, had no real interest for him.

Likewise the Greek scientist felt neither the urge nor the capacity to explore the contingent aspects of reality. The contingent is, as we have seen, what is not self-derived or logically necessary. In this context it refers to all that cannot be deduced from the inherent form, structure, or essence of an object. Now in the case of artifacts whose purpose we know, the contingent elements are few and insignificant. Knowing the purposes for which knives or vases are deliberately made, we can deduce almost all of their significant aspects from that known intelligible form. All their important arrangement of parts, their most important capabilities and ways of functioning, follow from the patterns that have determined their construction and which can be known by us. Since our minds can intuit the same form that created and structured the object,

there is to us little about the knife or the vase that is il-
logical or that seems to be the result of mere chance.
What cannot be so deduced from the form we know, is
minimal, and is really "accidental," the result of unpredictable flaws in the material and so quite beyond rational
explanation. Furthermore, these contingent features are
unknowable and unintelligible; they flow from the material, not the form, and thus cannot be made an object
of scientific study. To a science based on intelligible rational forms the contingent is both unimportant and
inexplicable.

Now the problem of a natural science based on these
assumptions is that it seems evident that in fact man cannot intuit directly the forms and purposes of natural objects. To the modern mind nature is not a realm of objects
which have been, like human artifacts, constructed according to intelligible purposes that we can intuit. We
cannot understand nature's workings as we do human
artifacts, merely by asking "for what purpose was this
thing made?"[3] The purposes for which trees, rocks, and
stars were made remain quite unknown to us, and we shall
simply not understand these objects if we seek by intuition to guess at their qualitative forms, and to make the
objects intelligible by their means. The consequence is
that in a nature whose determining principles are beyond
intuition, the area of the contingent, of that which is not
deducible from a known purpose, is almost infinitely ex-
panded. If we do not know the purpose of an object we
find, then everything about it is "contingent" to us—we
have no general principle in our minds according to which

---

[3] In fact modern science really begins with the revolt against
just this understanding of nature as a system of purposive structures. Descartes formulates this as a fundamental rule of scientific
method when he declares, as the twenty-eighth principle of knowledge, "that we must examine, not the final, but the efficient,
causes of created things."
Descartes, R., *The Principles of Philosophy*, Part I, Principle
XXVIII.

we can understand either its arrangement of parts or its behavior. In this situation a method based on intellectual intuition of the form is hopeless; our one hope of understanding the object is to develop a method that is strictly empirical. For with an empirical method the scientist does not guess at the purpose of the object; rather he studies the object as he experiences it, describing how it looks and feels, how it behaves under various conditions, and how it is physically related to other objects. Through such a study of an object whose inner purpose and organizing form remain unknown, the scientist is none the less able to find the most significant and invariable relations among its parts and with its environment. The only means by which a contingent order can be known is the empirical method of description and experiment; but, by the same token, men had to recognize that the order of the world was contingent and not intuitable, before they could come to value empirical description as the key to knowledge. So long as men assumed that an object was known through its intuited form, this sort of empirical description was both unnecessary and impossible, and so it remained quite undeveloped. Consequently the Greek view of a noncontingent order prevented rather than encouraged the development of an empirical method of inquiry.

As is already clear, the most serious lack of Greek science was its indifference to sensible experience as the avenue to knowledge. For Aristotelian science some sense experience of objects was necessary, since forms exist only in matter—after all, we must see and touch the knife to understand it as a knife. Nevertheless, just because we can tell what a human artifact is the moment we see it, study of our sensible experience of the object is unimportant in the case of artifacts. For we know the form by direct vision or intuition: we recognize what "looks like a knife" quite apart from the arduous procedures of weighing, measuring, and testing. We look at it as a whole, hoping for a flash of recognition; and if that flash of recognition does not come, no amount of weighing and measuring will help us uncover its purpose or determining form. Correspondingly, to Greek science all that was scientifically significant about an object was known directly by an intellectual act which abstracted the intelligible form from the experience of the object. Sense experience was merely the first step of a process which, if successful, transcended and then ignored sense experience. Consequently, in themselves and as an independent object of study, the data of sense experience revealed only the irrational contributions of the material; the form was known by the intellect alone. Thus a science based on empirical description and analysis was impossible for Greek thought because the data of sensation were essentially irrelevant to the aim of the inquiry, which was to know the intelligible form.

The Christian Contribution

From this analysis of Greek science, it is clear that a radical change in man's understanding of the order of nature must have occurred as the necessary presupposition for the rise of modern empirical science. For modern science makes assumptions about the order of the natural world, and about how we are to discover that order, which run directly counter to Greek thought. First of all, modern science assumes that while the world has an order of significant relations that can be studied, this is not a purposive order. In science things are not understood as if their structure and behavior were determined by human purposes. Universally it has been recognized that we cannot with our human minds "see into" nature and find our own purposes there. On the contrary, science assumes we must study nature as a contingent reality, examining her from the outside as she is perceived by our senses and as she responds to our manipulations, and from these observations gather what significant principles manifest themselves. Secondly, modern science assumes that the order of nature resides in the material aspects of natural objects and the invariable physical relations between events. Thus what modern science studies about natural objects is their mass, acceleration, physical composition, and physical relations, a clear change from the view that regarded these aspects of nature as accidents contributed by an irrational matter and therefore irrelevant to the qualitative or purposive form. Finally, putting these two ideas together, modern science assumes that only by study through our sense perceptions and through manipulation of material relations can the mysteries of nature be uncovered. Modern science is based on the empirical method, because it views the order of the world as a contingent, material, and "causative" order rather than a purposive and formal order, and such a world is intelligible to men only if it is studied empirically and experimentally. Both Greek and modern culture assume that the world is in some sense intelligible, and so both produced the enterprise of a scientific study of nature. But only a radical change from the classical presuppositions about the character of the world's order could have produced the kind of empirical science that we enjoy.

Now the conception which effected this fundamental reinterpretation of the world's order, and so provided those presuppositions of modern science, was the Christian idea of creation. It is no accident that modern science has developed in a culture formed and dominated by this conception, for when nature was thought of as possessing an order stemming from the Creator's will rather than from its own inherent intelligible forms, then modern science became possible. During the medieval period the impact of biblical concepts was confined largely to the theological understanding of the realm of grace; the understanding of the realm of nature remained almost entirely Greek. With the breakup of medievalism, however, Christian concepts began to permeate the secular spheres of ethics and of science, and both modern society and modern science were born. Let us see what these implications of the idea of creation were which enabled a Christian culture on the one hand to appropriate the significant values of the classical spirit, and yet on the other to set them in a new framework of understanding so that they became more fruitful and positive. We shall first mention two points which contributed to the Christian belief that nature contained a real order which the mind could know.

Christian tradition has always maintained that the world possesses order because of its creation through the divine wisdom. Any notion that finitude was an illusion created by ignorance, a shadowy veil of irrationality, or that process was intrinsically chaotic, was impossible for a faith that knew God as the source of meaning and wisdom and knew that He had established the world and its order. Although Christians recognized that God might forever transcend easy comprehension, nevertheless there was never any doubt that God Himself was wholly rational and wholly intelligible.[4] A world created by the divine wisdom, therefore, was inevitably a world which had an intrinsic order. Since man was created in the "image of God," it was also assumed that this order was in some way akin to the processes of human thinking, and could be known and understood, in part at least, by human intelligence. Thus, quite appropriately, early Christian thought maintained that God created through the divine Logos, the wisdom or intelligence of God. And on the same basis Christian thought adopted the classical conception of Natural Law to express the conviction that finite creatures exhibit a characteristic and immanent harmony and order which man could discover and know.

Secondly, Christians believed that the finite world was the product of the divine will as well as of the divine

---

[4] For example, the following from Irenaeus stresses the transcendence and yet the essential rationality of God: ". . . God is not as men are; and His thoughts are not like the thoughts of men . . . [but] He is wholly understanding, and wholly spirit, and wholly thought, and wholly intelligibility, and wholly reason . . ." *Op. cit.*, Book II, Chapter 13, Section 3.

wisdom. Nature was, therefore, a creature and not an appearance of God, a distinct and relatively independent reality posited into being by God's will. This emphasis of the idea of creation on the separate and real nature of the finite also made the world amenable to rational study. In pantheism all finite entities are fundamentally "appearances" of the Absolute, and so their seeming natures and their apparent relations are merely illusions which our ignorance produces. When we understand them completely we see that finite structures and relations are really not there at all, for all appearances are absorbed in a divine reality that transcends our experience completely. In the world of sensory experience, therefore, there is neither reality nor order, and so inquiry into its nature is as profitless as a "science" of the world through Alice's looking glass. According to the Christian idea of creation, however, finite entities are not identical with God, but real existents with definite structures and determinate characteristics and powers. Each can operate effectually within the realm of finitude, and can establish real relations with other finite beings. Every creature—atom, molecule, cell, plant, or animal—is a real center of structural and dynamic aspects, which make it causally effective on the one hand and structurally intelligible on the other. The world for the Christian is therefore a realm of definable structures and real relations, and so is a possible object both for scientific and for philosophical study. As a creature of the divine wisdom and the divine will, the natural universe is for Christians, as for their Greek predecessors, an orderly world. Thus Christians could appropriate in their own way what was valid in Greek culture, and provide the ultimate basis for that confidence in inquiry and the possibility of knowledge of our world which has dominated Western culture.[5]

[5] It is perhaps significant that the rise of the modern confidence in knowledge of the natural world begins with Descartes' essentially religious affirmation that "God would not deceive us,"

While in this way Christian culture could transmit the classical confidence in the order and intelligibility of the world, nevertheless two other aspects of the idea of creation effected a radical transformation in the understanding of that order and made possible the change from Greek rationalistic science to modern empirical science. First of all, a created order, while intelligible, is nevertheless contingent to our minds. Although Christians believed that God's will was wholly wise and wholly intelligent, still to them it was a deeply mysterious will: "For my thoughts are not your thoughts, neither are your ways my ways, saith the Lord. For as the heavens are higher than the earth, so are my ways higher than your ways, and my thoughts than your thoughts."[6] As both finite and sinful, our minds are quite incapable of thinking God's thoughts for Him, of concluding with confidence that what seems right, just, or even rational to us, is necessarily so in the same way to Him. No devout Jew or Christian would ever claim that he could, on the basis of his own reason, *deduce* what God could or should do. Rather he would feel that because God is transcendent, man must wait until His mysterious will reveals its intent before he can state with any confidence what that will is.[7] For knowledge of God

and as that theological basis for the confidence in the knowledge recedes, the inner assurance that we can know also recedes. Science has continued despite the increasing power of philosophical skepticism about the possibility of knowledge. But surely its modern foundations are shaky, to say the least, when all that speculative philosophers can say is, with Whitehead, "It is faith," or with Santayana, "It is animal faith," and when positivists find the question of the foundations of empirical knowledge "a nonsense question."

[6] Isaiah 55: 8–9.

[7] This is where Leibnitz' well-known "philosophy of creation" fails to express the religious spirit of Christian faith, and reflects rather a too philosophic interpretation of God. When Leibnitz says in effect: "God chose the world; therefore He must have chosen the best of all possible worlds," he is certainly implying that he can think God's thoughts for him, that what is reasonable and coercive for human minds is equally rational and coercive for

Himself, this conception of God's transcendent holiness and otherness logically requires revelation. For knowledge of the natural world which God's will has created, the same divine transcendence logically requires empirical study.

A world created by the transcendent divine will is very unlike the homely Greek world of human artifacts, in which by direct intellectual vision the guiding purpose of a natural object could be seen. For the divine purposes which have determined creation and that rule the events of nature are a mystery to our easy understanding. We know by faith that there are such purposes; but we cannot know, by merely looking at the world and thinking about it, just what they are. For God's ways are not just like ours, and therefore the products of His will are not constructed according to purposes immediately discoverable by us. A created order, therefore, is to human minds contingent. The purposive and logical structure that determine the world around us is not immediately evident to our minds, as it would be if natural objects had been made by men like ourselves. Thus a created nature must be studied from the outside, and the order of nature must be found only by means of our continuing experience of her habits and our manipulation of her relations. Knowledge of a created nature is based on sensory description rather than on intellectual intuition. The certitude that the divine will transcends our human understanding freed science from the search for final causes in nature, while the confidence that the Creator's will was intelligent kept alive the necessary assumption that nevertheless the world exhibited an intelligible order. The result was modern

---

the divine mind. There is here, then, no sense of the divine transcendence. The Christian would have confidence that the divine choice is "good," because the divine will has revealed itself as a loving will; but he would hesitate to try to determine the rules of thought which structure that divine mind, and so coerce God into choosing the "best."

empirical science, an inquiry through sense perception into the order of the natural world.[8]

Secondly, according to the idea of creation, the material and dynamic aspects of finitude share equal dignity in the divine creation with the formal aspects. Thus in the Christian world view the order of the world can exist as much within material properties of events as within spiritual or intellectual purposes. The physical composition of objects and the relations of cause and effect between events become, therefore, no longer the "accidents" of the irrational matter of which things were composed, but the actual seat of the world's order. Consequently empirical study of the physical properties of things, and of the physical relations which we call efficient causation, became the key to the understanding of nature. The idea of creation, therefore, provided the reinterpretation of order which made empirical science possible. As Greek philosophy before it had successfully done, it gave men the necessary confidence that they lived in a world that could be understood by inquiry because it possessed an intelligible order. Nevertheless, because for Christian faith the orderly world had come from the transcendent will of God, and because its order lay within the real physical relations between things, valid knowledge of the world can only be gained through careful and controlled experience of the world.

[8] Descartes, who formulated for the first time many of the basic principles of modern science, shows in Principle XXVIII the intimate relation between the understanding of nature that informed modern science, and its acceptance of the idea of creation. In fact he goes so far as almost to deduce the scientific method from the idea of the world as a created order. "We will not seek reasons of natural things from the end which God proposed to Himself in their creation and we will entirely reject from our philosophy the search of final causes, for we ought not to presume so far as to think that we are sharers in the councils of deity, but, considering Him as the efficient cause of all things, let us endeavor to discover by the natural light . . . what must be concluded regarding those effects we perceive by our senses . . ." Descartes, *Principles of Philosophy*, Principle XXVIII.

Modern culture so completely takes for granted that sensory experience and science are united notions that it is easy for us to forget that the conjunction of these two terms is an amazing cultural phenomenon. For sensory experience consists only of variable physical sensations, while the term science points to some system of invariable relations. The belief, therefore, that our wayward sensations could, in conjunction with mathematics, provide men with scientific knowledge rested upon the conviction that active, physical experience made contact with an invariable order in things. Thus behind that conviction lay the faith that whatever variability and sheer materiality the contingent world of physical experience might reveal, nevertheless it contained an order because it had been created by the divine wisdom. However much modern positivism may deny any "metaphysical foundations to science," this same faith that sensory experience reveals an objective order must lurk somewhere in the mind of each scientific experimenter—otherwise he would not spend his life searching for the "invariable relations" between experiences. The "hypothesis" of a contingent and empirically discoverable order was provided for Western culture by the idea of creation. This is an hypothesis necessary for empirical science, not in the sense that this hypothesis is used within any particular scientific experiment, but in the more general sense that it alone gives intelligibility, validity, and purpose to the whole enterprise of experimental knowledge.[9] It is evident, therefore, from the history of our most general ideas about science, that the religious concept of a transcendent Creator has

[9] This relation of the idea of creation to the enterprise of science is well expressed by Flew: The idea of creation is "yet a picture the use of which excludes certain nightmares about the nature of the universe. That the heavens were created by the word of God is not a piece of literal theory. Nevertheless the acceptance of this picture, on the one hand, excludes certain sorts of theory about what literally does go on; and, on the other hand, clears the way for other different sorts of theory also about what literally does go on." Flew, op. cit., p. 176.

not been antithetical to the scientific spirit. Intelligibility as the scientist understands it is one of the essential ingredients in the goodness of life. Christian faith affirms this to be so, and in its doctrine of creation gives the most reasonable, and historically the most effective, foundation for that intelligibility which science seeks.

The Need of Religion for Philosophy

The intelligibility of our world is not exhausted by the inquiries of the empirical scientist into its nature. Just as significant for man's fulfillment, and just as illustrative of the fundamental rationality of the created universe, is the intellectual enterprise of philosophy, rejected often by practical men and theologians alike. Their rejection, however, is never successful, for neither a sound culture nor a sound religion can long exist without the help of philosophy. The modern philosopher Whitehead is all too persuasive when he argues[10] that civilization becomes stagnant and decadent unless it is continually enlivened by the imaginative explorations of philosophy into the unknown and the unformulated. Every significant aspect of culture: science, morals, politics, law, religion, and aesthetics, depends upon certain fundamental assumptions. In every civilized society, therefore, there must be a relentless and systematic inquiry into these general ideas that form and guide our social existence to guard against the stifling effects of irrationality and arbitrariness at the most basic levels of our cultural life. The speculative philosopher raises such questions as: what is knowledge and how is it possible; what is the meaning of truth and how is it found; what do we mean by events, relations, and causality; what do men mean by the good; what is beauty; and how are we to understand the relations of

[10] Cf. Whitehead, A. N., *Science and the Modern World*, Chapters V and IX; *Adventures of Ideas*, Chapter IX; *The Function of Reason*, Chapter III.

justice, freedom, and responsibility? These questions are relevant to any thoughtful human existence. No culture can fail to answer these questions somehow, either implicitly or explicitly, either by custom or by intelligence. It is better, therefore, that these answers be explored and criticized by rational inquiry, than that they be left merely to tradition and so conceived in outdated form. If philosophy is the examination of our most general questions, the search for the final structure of each aspect of culture and of existence itself, philosophy is necessary to the vitality of civilization.

Now Christianity makes the claim to provide the ultimate basis for a meaningful human existence, and it encourages men to find that meaning within the life of culture rather than outside of it. It aims, among other things, to transform and enrich the enterprise of human civilization; it does not seek to overthrow or to flee human community. If, then, philosophy joins science, the fine arts, and the economic and political practices of men as one of the essential ingredients of civilization, it is fully as incumbent upon Christian faith to foster a creative philosophy as it is necessary for it to encourage a sound science and a vital art. Being a Christian in one's ultimate faith does not provide an automatic answer to the question "What is knowledge and how is it gained?" or to the question "What is justice, and what is beauty?" A healthy Christian culture, therefore, must be able to produce Christian philosophers as well as Christian scientists and businessmen if it is to realize, as it claims to do, the potential goodness of human life.

The desire of Christianity to transform culture is, however, not the only basis for the concern of Christian faith for the enterprise of philosophy. Rather, by their inherent nature and needs, religion and philosophy require and supplement one another, so that the health and fullness of Christianity depend in part upon its creative relation to the intelligibility which philosophy seeks. In Chapter 2 we raised this issue of dependence and yet tension between philosophy and theology, and we likened them to blood brothers who, though they fought between themselves, were stronger in union than in conflict. We pointed out that religious thought depended upon philosophy for two main reasons. First, because as religious *thought* it used words and arranged them in some sort of meaningful order, it inevitably borrowed the concepts and some of the criteria of philosophy to express this meaning. And secondly, as *religious* thought it sought to understand God as the source of all being, and therefore could not avoid relating itself to philosophy's search for ultimate reality. We are now in a better position to explore further this relation of mutual dependence. By this means we can discover how it is that the intelligibility which philosophy seeks can, like that of science, most fruitfully be realized within rather than without the framework of the Christian faith.

It is central to the Protestant understanding of religious faith that every Christian should be able himself fully to affirm his own deepest convictions, that on no important matter should he have to say: "I was told to believe this, although I myself have not the least idea what it means or whether it is true." This demand is high but necessary for real religion, for as Luther reminded Christians, "Every one of us will have to die for himself, so he must also believe for himself."[11] Now this basic Protestant principle means that the Christian faith of each man must be to him intelligible, valid, and consistent, a meaningful faith which he can fully and with integrity affirm with all his "heart, soul, and mind." He must be able to feel, when he ponders or speaks of his faith, that it makes real sense, that it answers his deepest problems and questions, and that it is, in the light of all he knows, true. If he cannot honestly say this to himself, then he cannot believe for himself; and some authority, of church, pastor, community, or custom, has done his believing for him. Protestant-

11 Pauck, W., *The Heritage of the Reformation*, Beacon Press, 1950, p. 27.

ism can consistently appeal to no external human authorities in religion; what a man cannot himself affirm to be true can have no real value or relevance to him. Protestantism does exist on the basis of the mystery of God's Word; but it cannot exist at all, if its own doctrines and ideas remain quite mysterious to its adherents.

From this basic principle it follows that in Protestantism religion is always striving to make itself meaningful and intelligible to those who affirm its truth. And this drives it continually throughout its history into the arms of cultural intelligibility and of philosophy. Just as its nature seeks no authority but that of God's Word, and so Protestantism is impelled into orthodoxy, so its spirit also seeks to make that authority intelligible, and so it is also pushed into liberalism. And the reason for this Protestant orientation to culture is plain enough. Most of the meanings and ideas which our minds comprehend come to us from our ordinary cultural experience. For example, we learn what "true" means by all sorts of varied cultural experiences: the difference between truth and lies in personal relations and politics; between fact and fiction in literature; between irresponsible claims and carefully validated statements. Correspondingly, we learn the meaning of the words "to know," "to exist," "to trust," "to love," and so on, through our experiences of communal life. Man's mind is filled with concepts and meanings drawn from his cultural experience, and these are the intellectual stuff in terms of which he makes anything intelligible to himself. Thus, when he seeks to understand and to affirm his religious faith, inevitably his mind relates this faith to these concepts from his ordinary cultural experience. When he hears that the Gospel is "true," he must immediately ask himself "How is this related to the truth I know in personal relations, or in science?" He hears that God exists and loves him; at once, if he is to understand and so affirm this, he must ask, "How is God's existence related to that of a stone, or a house, or to my own existence? How is God's love related to my mother's love, my wife's love?"

Most of this activity of relating the Gospel to ordinary experience and its concepts is done by us unconsciously; but it must be there in each of us if we are to give any meaning at all to the great Gospel phrases which we repeat about God and our salvation.

Now this means that a continual process of both amateur theologizing and amateur philosophizing is always going on in any healthy Protestantism. That is, whenever people ask the fundamental theological and religious questions: "Who and what is God; what has He said to us; how is it true; and how may we be related to Him?", at the same time, in order to make this intelligible to themselves, they must ask philosophical questions: "What is it to be; what is truth; what is it to love, to trust, to be in relation to someone?" For when we say God exists and loves, and that we must know and trust Him, we are using these concepts, drawn from our own cultural experience and so ultimately from philosophy, and are applying them to God in our relation to Him, as we know and experience that relation in His revelation to us. Thinking about religion, whether on the simplest or the most sophisticated level, is a process of uniting these two kinds of questions—questions about God and what He has done, and questions about our general experience. Every Protestant who can really affirm what he believes to be meaningful and intelligible and true, has himself gone through or borrowed from some such process of uniting theological and philosophical thought; and every preacher who seeks to proclaim the Gospel as true and meaningful for others, depends even more on such a process. Thus Protestantism, as a form of religion which stresses the free affirmation of each man of what he believes, can never separate itself from that careful and unimpeded analysis of our general ideas which is philosophy. For it is in terms of these ideas that the religious faith of even the most unintellectual person will ultimately become intelligent and so personal. The goodness of religion, as well as of life, depends upon the intelligibility which a rational understanding of general experience makes possible.

In our discussion of the idea of God the Creator, we have seen a vivid example of this dependence of theological concepts upon philosophy and its work. We found that if theology is to say of God all the significant things that the Bible affirms of Him, it must speak of His transcendence as the source of all being, and of His immanence as the dynamic creative power that upholds everything. It must be willing to describe Him as unconditioned and eternal in His being, and yet related to all finite, temporal things in His creative activity. Now any attempt to describe God in this way will use metaphysical language, since metaphysics is that inquiry which deals with the being or existence of things, and which develops and defines such concepts as reality, existence, temporality, transcendence, dependence, and so on. Revelation no more delivers a heaven-sent metaphysical language than it gives us a divine natural science. It is from philosophical inquiry, which seeks to analyze in experience what finite being is and what relations are, that these concepts must be drawn. It is true, of course, that because of revelation and the knowledge of God that we gain thereby, we think differently in our metaphysics about what existence is, about what relations are, and about what time is, than we had done before. But if we are to formulate that difference, and so make coherent and intelligible what Christians believe about God and His world, we must express that new understanding of God's ultimate being, of change, of relation, and of time, in the terms which only metaphysics and philosophy can provide. A philosophical inquiry within the life of Christian faith itself is, therefore, a necessity in order that our faith be intelligible and meaningful to those who hold it—independently of argument with those who do not share that faith. The problem of relating Christian theology to philosophy is not resolved by an attempt to rid theology of all philosophical traces. Rather it can only be resolved by conducting a philosophical inquiry capable of expressing that attitude toward existence characteristic of Christian men.

The Limits of Philosophy

Although it is true that philosophy is an important ingredient in a mature Christian life, it is also true that philosophy finds its own fulfillment only in religious faith, and in the theology that formulates that faith. For in its own essential structure philosophy reveals certain recurrent problems that tend to destroy it unless they are resolved from beyond philosophy. Philosophy as traditionally understood is the search for the universal structures of experience, for the general principles that underlie every aspect of our life. As an activity carried on by the inquiring intellect of man, it seeks to satisfy the mind's intellectual demands for clarity, precision, and wholeness. Hence it searches for a coherent system of general principles that will include within its scope every aspect of experience. It tries to express in one unifying set of ideas the final principles of reality, to bring into the clear light of human knowledge the ultimate mystery of all existence. Inevitably, however, its success is thwarted by certain insoluble problems that continually arise.

First of all, philosophy is frustrated by the problem of its own foundation. Included within the experience which philosophy seeks to understand in terms of a rational system is the experience of knowing. Thus an essential element in any philosophy is an understanding of how knowledge is ultimately possible, a vindication in terms of rational understanding of how man can have valid knowledge of the world he supposes he experiences. Clearly such validation is possible only if some ground can be given for a dependable relation between the object of knowledge and the subject who knows. But how can philosophy, as a part of knowledge, establish and describe a relation to something beyond knowledge? The philosophic quest for a complete and orderly system breaks down at this point,

for the foundation of knowledge itself, namely, the relation of experience to an objective world, cannot be made a
part of any system of experience. The extreme reactions of
philosophy to this problem seek to avoid the dilemma by
denying that knowledge is a relation to any objective reality. Idealism tends to absorb all of objective reality into
a system made up solely of experience, while positivism
tends to deny the possibility of any understanding beyond
the mere data of sensory experience. But neither alternative will really work. Sooner or later the idealist has to admit that his experience touches something beyond its own
content, and he is forced back into the problem of the
relation of experience to its object. And at some point the
positivist, whether in the role of scientist or citizen, must
admit that both his philosophy and his active life are based
on certain assumptions about the order and structure of
the reality with which he deals; and so he too faces the
problem of the relation between his own sensory experience and its object. Most moderate philosophers solve this
problem in terms of a "faith" that cannot be included
within philosophy because it is its basis: perhaps an "animal faith" that our experience is in dependable relation
to an external world, or a more sophisticated "intuition"
that objective existence is harmonious with our intellects.
Every philosophical system, therefore, must transcend itself on the issue of its own foundation. Its very basis lies
beyond the system itself, and so beyond rational inquiry
and rational validation. Philosophy requires for its own fulfillment, therefore, both an inquiry which can examine and
test the "faith" of man, and a secure and intelligible faith
on which it may be grounded.

Secondly, if philosophy succeeds in formulating a systematic understanding of all experienced reality, it then
faces another dilemma. By its very success in establishing
its system, it brings inevitably into the light of clear rational expression the ultimate principles of existence. It
reduces to the sequences and relations we can easily understand, the ultimate relationships that pertain to the depths

of reality. Thus in its search for a rational order of ultimate principles, philosophy tends to banish all mystery. But existence, while revealing an ultimate coherence and meaning, will not be completely reduced to any clear and precise sequence of relationships. There are depths of freedom, of creativity, and even of incoherence, within the mystery of being, which defy the attempt to organize life into simple rational patterns. Thus ironically the very goal of philosophy is fatal to full understanding.

For example, those philosophers who see in the physical sciences the most helpful kind of ordered system try to reduce all the relations within existence to the determinate, invariable relations that used to be called efficient causation in the sciences. On the other hand, those philosophers who are more fascinated with the ordered relations between abstract ideas, tend to understand all experience in terms of a system of rational implication drawn from their experience of mathematics or of logic. Both efforts result in a universe which is philosophically satisfying because it is structured entirely by an intelligible rational order: the one of determinate causation, the other of logical implication. But both succeed as philosophies only because they banish from their systems certain elements of experience which are recurrent and undeniable. The "feel" of existence as we know and experience it in ourselves, with its omnipresent sense of freedom, its spontaneity, its infinite contingency and creativity, is lacking in these ordered pictures. Likewise the insistent intuitions that our purposes are effective and our individuality is of value, belie systems in which all is determined from beyond ourselves, and in which the individual is merely a part of a coherent whole. The evidence of personal and historical life, where personal relations are willed and intentional if they are personal at all, and where decisions seem validly momentous because all is not determined from outside, points to a mystery of freedom in existence which no rational system can capture and control. Above all, the very experience of philosophical inquiry, in which we assert something for no other reason than its inherent validity, denies a total system of causation or determination. Unless the philosopher will admit that he holds his own system merely because of causes affecting his mind, rather than because it seems to him to be true, he must agree that in the experience of truth the universal system of causation is broken by the mind's freedom.

These experiences of spontaneous action, of creativity and affection, of personal responsibility and purpose, and of intellectual truth, point to a dimension of existence which can be confined within no simple rational order.[12] There *is* order in our world, and hence science and philosophy are possible. But when we try to reduce the world of our experience to the kinds of order we can clearly formulate, we falsify and misunderstand our experience. Thus our understanding of existence must transcend the ordering capacity of philosophy by some other way of grasping meaning. The ultimate principle of reality and coherence in existence cannot be formulated in the same terms we use to deal with the ordinary sequences of our experience; the ground of finite relations cannot be finally understood

[12] Reinhold Niebuhr has emphasized this point, namely that the vivid experience of our own freedom, and therefore of the self-transcending dimension of human existence, points to a depth and freedom in ultimate reality which no system of rational coherence can delineate:

"Genuine freedom, with the implied possibility of violating the natural and rational structures of the world, cannot be conceived in any natural or rational scheme of coherence." "Coherence, Incoherence and the Christian Faith," in Niebuhr, R., *Christian Realism and Political Problems*, p. 178.

"The most important characteristic of a religion of revelation is this two-fold emphasis upon the transcendence of God and upon His intimate relation with the world. In this divine transcendence the spirit of man finds a home in which it can understand its stature of freedom. But there also it finds the limits of its freedom, the judgment which is spoken against it and, ultimately, the mercy which makes such a judgment sufferable." Niebuhr, R., *The Nature and Destiny of Man*, New York, Charles Scribner's Sons, 1941, Volume I, p. 126.

in the terms of finite relations. Christians can readily understand this problem for philosophy. Knowing that the order of created life stems from the transcendent God and is continually upheld by His mysterious power, they recognize that beyond the order they can see and understand there is a mystery of freedom, of being, and of meaning, which cannot be grasped clearly by our minds but which is the ground of all order.

As we have remarked before, when philosophy seeks to express this mystery which transcends our clear understanding, it flounders. For seemingly philosophy can only understand the transcendent in terms of the absolute; and with an absolute, philosophy comes to the end of real comprehension. As a wag remarked of a famous idealist: "His absolute is only the dark night in which all cows are black." Philosophical absolutes are omnivorous mysteries, which on the one hand devour all of finite reality into themselves, and on the other can be described only in terms of negation. For it is impossible to devise a rational understanding of the relation between an absolute and the finite without denying the reality and value of the finite. And it seems just as difficult in philosophy to describe, in any helpful sense at all, an absolute which unconditionally transcends every aspect of finite experience. In another context we have pointed out the theological solution to this problem in terms of the personal nature of God and of the revelation of His nature and will within the realm of the finite. At this moment, however, our concern is with the effect of this dilemma upon philosophy.

Philosophy seeks for rational understanding and therefore for a total view of all reality. But each time it tries to formulate this total view, it fails. It cannot complete a total system inclusive of its own foundation and of those elements of freedom, purpose, and individuality which appear in our experience. Inevitably a depth or dimension of experience reveals itself which is fundamental to philosophy, and to the order it seeks, but which is not to be included within that order. Thus philosophy points beyond all the levels of order which it can usefully describe, to a mystery from which all order derives. If it forgets this mystery it ceases to give an intelligible account of existence; and yet it cannot in its own terms be intelligible about the mystery itself. Philosophy, therefore, can fulfill itself only through some mode of inquiry, some aspect of meaning, that transcends philosophy. The whole philosophical enterprise, though necessary to cultural and Christian life alike, is incapable of satisfying its own goal of unity and wholeness. Ultimately it depends upon the completion which faith alone can provide. Far better than philosophy can, theology based on faith points to that transcendent principle which is known as the source of order, yet cannot be reduced to any finite order; which transcends human definition, yet undergirds the orderly sequences of our experience.[13]

Religious Truth and Scientific Truth

So far we have discussed the intimate relation between science and philosophy on the one hand and Christian faith on the other. We have suggested that the great task of science and philosophy to make the natural and social worlds around us intelligible to our minds and malleable to our purposes is ultimately dependent upon the assumptions implied by the Christian doctrine of creation. On the other hand, an intelligible Christian life within society requires full Christian participation in these two intellectual enterprises. No sincere Christian can drive his Hydromatic automobile to the doctor's office at one mo-

[13] "This faith in the sovereignty of a divine creator, judge and redeemer is not subject to rational proof, because it stands beyond and above the rational coherences of the world and can therefore not be proved by an analysis of these coherences. But a scientific and philosophical analysis of these coherences is not incapable of revealing where they point beyond themselves to a freedom which is not in them, to contradictions between each other which suggest a profounder mystery and meaning beyond them." Niebuhr, R., *Christian Realism and Political Problems*, p. 203.

ment and deny the validity and relevance of science the next. Nor can he appeal in a court of law to the "principles of justice" and then berate philosophy and reason in the name of faith. If Christians are to live within modern culture, they must not only accept the principles of science and philosophy but foster their pursuits. And this raises the fundamental problem of this chapter: is it possible to reconcile the different levels of truth in science and philosophy, and in revelation? Can a man be a scientist or a philosopher, and still be a convinced Christian?

In our study of the idea of creation we have found that faith draws a sharp line of distinction between the created world and the Creator. On the one side there is the universe which we experience through our senses. This is the created world which exists in space and time, and which is for our experience most helpfully understood as a structured system of invariable relationships commonly called "causal." The ultimate principles of "causality" in nature, and especially in history, will almost certainly always remain a mystery to our knowledge, and surely the determined causal systems that our minds create in response to events, are no direct picture of the mysterious forces at work in the world and in ourselves. Nevertheless, it remains true that for the purposes of understanding this material and sensible world, the method of empirical science is our most accurate and dependable tool. All our "factual" questions about the created world of nature are scientific questions and with regard to these questions, scientific inquiry represents the ultimate court of appeal. If we ask how old the earth is, what physical factors produced it, how big it is, what is "up there" in the sky, etc., we should go to the scientist, not the preacher, for our answer. And the same rule applies to "observable" facts of any sort. If we ask what happened in history, meaning what observable events took place, we should go to the science of history for our answer. The whole realm of spatiotemporal facts, what can or could be observed about the created world through the senses of man, is a fit arena for scientific investigation, and in this area, for the Christian as for the secularist, scientific method is the most dependable avenue to truth. Truth about the observable character, structure, processes, and facts of the created world, and truth about its development in history, is scientific truth—it is not "religious truth"—for its concern is God's creation, not God and His activities. And let us always remember that no *truth* about God's creation can be antithetical to Christian truth. The same God who created the world has revealed Himself in Jesus Christ; thus whatever is true about the world can be no threat to Christian faith. To be sure, the Christian does not believe that the scientific method exhausts the whole realm of truth; but what is known according to scientific criteria is a valid part of the whole area of God's truth.

On the other side, Christians believe that this created world, with its system of complex interrelations and its spatiotemporal facts, is dependent upon a deeper dimension of reality and being. The world is not self-sufficient, but dependent on God as its Creator and its continual preserver. Every fact and event, and every system of facts and events, comes to be and is upheld by the active, creative power of God, which continually gives to every creature its power to be in each new moment, and its power to act and relate itself to other creatures. Thus for the Christian every aspect of finitude exists, so to speak, in two dimensions: it is related on the spatiotemporal level to the whole orderly system of finite causes and influences; but it is also related, beyond that whole system, to its source and ground, which is the continuing creative activity of God. For example, to the inquiring mind of the scientist a tree points beyond its own existence to the seed, the air, the soil, the sun, and the water from which it came. On each one of these finite "causes" the tree is dependent, and its dependence on other things reaches back to the near infinity of influences that form that tree, and that make up the system of invariable or "causal" relations which the scientist can and should study. But also the tree reveals to faith a dimension of ultimate dependence upon its Creator God. For God gave being and order to the whole sequence out of which the tree appeared, and in each continuing instant of the tree's life He is the immediate source of its renewed existence, for it is by His continuing power alone that all things are and continue to be.

This "religious" dimension of the tree's life is not observable by the scientific method. God's creative activity is not a part of a finite sequence among finite entities, a sequence that is available to sense experience and testing because it can be manipulated by the scientist. A scientist comes to understand the causes of an event by rearranging the factors he thinks might have brought the event about, and by basing his conclusions on their presence or absence when the event occurs. If one factor is not active when the event occurs, he knows it is *not* a cause; if a second factor is present as predicted when the event occurs, he knows that factor *may* be a cause. Scientific method, therefore, can deal only with variable factors which may or may not be present in an event. It has no way of testing factors which are universally present, for it can set up no experiment that reveals the absence of such a universal factor. But God's presence, if there at all, is not such a variable and manipulatable factor: over it the scientist has no control, and if it were absent, then no event at all of any sort would take place. Consequently there can be no form of scientific experiment which could test the hypothesis of the creative activity of God, since no sensory experiment could conceivably reveal the presence or absence of God.[14] The scientist as a Christian

14 The inability of scientific experiments to disprove religious doctrines has led to some unnecessary misunderstanding concerning the validity and status of religious ideas. Philosophers of science rightly insist that a meaningful scientific hypothesis must be capable of disproof. That is, experiments must be conceivable in which the hypothesis may not hold if it is false. If every conceivable situation equally fails to "disprove" the hypothesis, then the

believer may see this deeper dimension in the creatures
he studies, and in the whole creative process of the earth's
development; but as a scientist he is confined by his
method to the sequence of finite spatiotemporal events
and relations and can only report on them. Thus God's
creative activity is no part of any valid astronomical, biological, or geological textbook, although to the mind of the
Christian it is the implication and inference of every study
of natural processes.

Now this deeper dimension of existence, where we are
concerned with the relation of God to His creatures, rather
than the relations of creatures to one another, is the area
of "religious truth." Here the word "religious" has two
important meanings which distinguish it from other kinds
of truth. First, its object is always God and His activity.
Religious truth concerns God first of all, and His creatures
only insofar as they are related to God. It is not about
their relations to one another. It is a religious truth about
the tree and about the world to say that they are created

---

hypothesis as no scientific meaning and status. Religious doctrines are often mistakenly cited as examples of such "meaningless" scientific hypotheses because, as it is correctly seen, no particular event can disprove them. For example, no particular
situation in history shows that the providential activity of God is
a false concept. This argument, however, merely illustrates our
present point, namely that theological doctrines are not of the
same order as scientific hypotheses. For if true, theological doctrines, such as creation and providence, necessarily hold of all
events alike. If it be valid to say that God creates all creatures,
then *ipso facto* no creature could "reveal" the absence of God.
This sort of theological doctrine, therefore, is not an hypothesis
with a limited scope or a probable status. Rather they are like
metaphysical propositions which, if valid, hold of all events
equally, since they concern the necessary and essential structure
of things. Thus, as Whitehead says, "existence never takes a
holiday from their sway." (*Process and Reality*, p. 7.) For the
positivistic scientist the comparable "untestable" hypothesis is
that of an invariable order of relations which he assumes in every
experiment, but of which he could by experiment find no negative
instances.

and upheld by God; it is a scientific truth about them to say that they are produced by such and such finite causes and relations. Religious truth always concerns the relation of God to the finite, never merely the relation of finite events to each other.

Secondly, since religious truth deals with God alone, it is always of "ultimate concern" to man. It has an "unconditional" meaning for his life and his existence. Truth on the finite level, truth about one's relations to other beings and other persons, may be about things that are very important to happiness, health, even life—but it is never of *ultimate* importance to us. In the end a mature man can get along without the help of any other one creature, for on no creature does he depend essentially, even on a parent or a loved one. There is always an inward autonomy in any developed creature that balances and makes relative his dependence on others. Consequently no man can surrender his soul in utter dependence on another finite being without destroying his selfhood. Absolute dependence of one creature on another is religious idolatry and psychological neurosis. But absolute dependence upon God is the sole condition for a free and fulfilled life. On God, as the source of my existence and my redemption, I do depend ultimately, for no creature can even exist, much less be itself, without Him. Thus this relation is one of ultimate significance, and thus truth concerning it is of ultimate concern to me.

Religious truth, then, is different from scientific truth because its object, God, is not one of the many creatures of the world with which science is concerned. He is the transcendent source of all existence, and thus He is radically different from all that depends upon Him for being. As my Creator, He stands in a different relation to me as creature than do other things, a relation which is much more essential to my life than is any other relation. Religious truth, then, does not tell us any new "facts" about other finite things in the created world, nor add at all to our descriptions of its observable character, structure,

or development. The Bible is not an almanac of cosmological, geological and historical facts. It is, as revelation,
the Word of God, speaking of the divine activity in and
through the facts of space and time. What the Bible does
say to us about the world is that whatever the character
and history of the nature around us, it is the creation of
God, who upholds it by His almighty power and redeems
it by His gracious will.

The source of religious truth is also understandably
different from the source of scientific truth. The scientist
searches, within sensory experience of all sorts, for the
significant facts and interrelations that inform him of the
structure of the world. But such inquiry will not disclose
the God who transcends the world's structure. The deeper
dimension of existence, with which religious truth is concerned, has been "revealed" to man in and through special
historical events. Admittedly these events could be
observed just like other events, because they occurred
within material nature and within history. Jesus of Nazareth was a real man of flesh and blood, who was observed
by any person who encountered him, be he an indifferent
scoffer, a hating persecutor, or a believing disciple. Since
all the revelatory events to which the Bible witnesses are
in this sense truly "historical," they can be studied and
understood from the point of view of historical science.
But though these events are from one viewpoint like all
other happenings, nevertheless for Christians they bear a
unique relation to God's activity in history. Through these
events, which the Bible calls "the mighty acts of God in
history," God is present and active in a manner not to be
found elsewhere; and so for Christians they are especially
and uniquely revelatory of God's nature, purposes, and
will toward man. While they remain facts which can be
studied by historical science, they are also for faith events
which have revelatory power. For example, the Christian
affirms that in Jesus of Nazareth God was uniquely present, so that in this man's life and death God's nature
and will can be seen and known. Now this deeper mean-

ing in the historical facts about the man Jesus is not simply derived from biographical data. "Flesh and blood" could reveal the living Jesus of history to any man of his place and time; but that He was the Christ, that in Him God "became flesh and dwelt among us," only the Holy Spirit could reveal. The divine dimension and significance of these events, their special relation to God's activity of revelation and salvation, is known only to faith. The historian, as a scientific inquirer, sees in these facts only a prophetic carpenter who died; the believing Christian has found the atoning and risen Savior of the World.

For the Christian, then, certain events in history, which at first glance seem much like other happenings, contain a special and unique significance and meaning. Through them he is for the first time aware of the God in whose presence he and all creation have been living all the time —for through them the light of the divine countenance shines as nowhere else. This "knowledge" in no way contradicts what he knows of nature and history through science; it supplements it by revealing the deeper dimensions of God's creative, providential, and redeeming activity in the life of His creation. Thus it does illumine the meaning of both nature and history for those who have eyes to see. For by revelation the Christian knows the Creator to whom all dependent finitude had pointed; by revelation he knows the sovereign will that gives meaning to all the apparently meaningless events of history. He can thus be both a scientist and a Christian, with a sense neither of fear nor of conflict.

The Possibility of a Christian Philosopher

Now let us turn to the more difficult question: can the Christian be a philosopher as well as a scientist? We have emphasized repeatedly the importance of philosophical inquiry to Christian life, both in its relations to culture and in its own internal completion. We have, however, also noted the difficulties of a philosophical attempt to

understand and to comprehend God. Autonomous philosophy, or as it is called in a religious context, "natural
theology," if it seeks to transcend the finite at all, seems
fated either to reduce God to a part of the structure of
the world, or to lose Him in abstraction and negation. In
any case, the impersonal concepts of philosophy tend, as
we have seen, to deny to God any freedom, intentionality,
or personal character. Thus for many Christians our
religious thought cannot be subservient to philosophy, for
a strictly philosophical conception of God seems to be an
impossible vehicle for the Gospel.

On the other hand, apparently philosophy cannot be
subservient to theology. For if philosophy is ruled by goals
and standards that are not its own, it ceases to be itself.
Philosophy is a search for the general structure of things
within all of experience, and unless its conclusions are
derived from an empirical and universal study, they are
not valid philosophically. A Christian thinker cannot deduce from revelation any conclusions about the character
of the created world in any of its aspects, and claim them
to be a part of genuine philosophy. How, then, can a
Christian be a philosopher if his knowledge of God and
the relation of creatures to God is derived from revelation, and yet his philosophical understanding of the world
is gained from an empirical study of its nature? This is
an important question for Christian faith if Christianity
is to claim the intelligibility which philosophy represents
as a part of the Christian goodness of life.

Inescapably all philosophy, secular or Christian, has an
"existential" source. Every philosophical inquiry must
make certain assumptions before it can begin at all. First
of all, the inquirer must assume at the onset that certain
kinds of experiences are valid clues to the reality, whatever it may be, which he seeks to understand; otherwise
his mind has no significant material upon which it can
work. Thus naturalistic and empirical philosophies presuppose that sensory experience is the only dependable
avenue to valid knowledge, while idealistic philosophies
tend to regard sensory experience as mere appearance,

compared with the less precise internal experience of the creative self. Rationalistic philosophy regards the experience of clear and abstract deductive thinking as the key to the nature of reality, while existentialist philosophies feel that the deep, uneasy experiences of "subjectivity," of the self in its creativity, its decisions, its anxieties, and its conditionedness, bring the closest touch with reality that we have. None of these can "prove," within their system, the validity of their choice of significant experience. Rather this choice is one of the determining presuppositions of their thinking, from which the character of their philosophy flows. One of the basic "prephilosophical" foundations of philosophy, therefore, is the determination by the philosopher of what within experience he shall take to be real and significant, or the most valid sign of what is real and significant. And this starting point is validated only by its self-evidence to the philosopher and his followers, not by any sort of coercive proof.

The second initial assumption that determines the character of a philosophy concerns a decision about the *kind* of order or intelligibility which reality is felt to exhibit, and so the most appropriate way of conceiving the intelligibility of things. Every philosopher assumes that the world is in some way intelligible, else he would not seek to understand his experience. But their philosophies vary almost infinitely with regard to the kind of coherence they hold the universe to contain. To some, the world is to be understood in terms of determinative causal sequences; to others it becomes coherent only as a logical order; to still others, the ultimately intelligibility of the world lies beyond our patterns of thought, so that neither our ideas of causality nor our modes of logic are ultimately relevant. Again, none of these can "prove" either that experience is thus intelligible, or that it contains the kind of order they claim it to have. Basic assumptions about the nature of things are never proved to us, for all proof depends upon them: without an assumption that some facts are relevant to reality, and some order holds true there, how could we prove anything at all? Thus the assumptions of philosophers about the intelligibility of things, just like their assumptions about reality, rest on "prephilosophical intuitions," or decisions which are the foundations rather than the conclusions of their philosophy. In this sense philosophy might be called the experiment of seeing if one's assumptions as to what is real in experience, and as to how that reality may be made coherent, can be applied to all experience. A philosophy is convincing to the onlooker, not because these assumptions are ever proved, but because for him the whole of experience, looked at from this point of view, seems to become more coherent and intelligible than ever before. In this sense, the ultimate presuppositions of any philosophy are based on "self-evidence" rather than on proof.[15]

When we ask where these assumptions came from, we must answer that their origin lies buried in the mysterious depths of the philosopher's own personal experience, or that of his culture and tradition. They have come to him as basic insights or intuitions that illuminated his life and made him able to understand it. In some significant experience, when what had been unintelligible and chaotic

[15] One of the most precise "rationalists" of the modern period, A. N. Whitehead, agrees on this point:

"The thesis that I am developing conceives 'proof,' in the strict sense of that term, as a feeble second-rate procedure . . . Unless proof has produced self-evidence and thereby rendered itself unnecessary, it has issued in a second-rate state of mind . . . Self-evidence is the basic fact on which all greatness supports itself. But 'proof' is one of the roots by which self-evidence is often obtained.

"As an example of this doctrine, in philosophical writings proof should be at a minimum. The whole effort should be to display the self-evidence of basic truths, concerning the nature of things and their connection. It should be noticed that logical proof starts from premises, and that premises are based upon evidence. Thus evidence is presupposed by logic; at least, it is presupposed by the assumption that logic has any importance.

"Philosophy is the attempt to make manifest the fundamental evidence as to the nature of things."

Whitehead, A. N., Modes of Thought, The Macmillan Co., 1938, pp. 66 and 67.

suddenly became coherent, he felt that he had made contact with what is real and intelligible in existence. And on the basis of that personally significant and transforming experience, he has henceforth philosophized. Many men in our age have found the experiences of science illuminating and releasing, and have transferred its assumptions to philosophy—thus naturalism and positivism have arisen. Others have found the mathematical experience of order particularly revealing of the nature of things, and have become "rationalistic" in philosophical character. An experience, then, that has been transforming in their personal life as the point where their life most clearly encountered reality and coherence has become for each of them the basis on which he tries to understand all else. Philosophy is thus the process in which a man dares the risk of thinking out his basic faith in the face of all the facts; it involves the great courage to measure one's "stance" against every conceivable fact and every conceivable rejection.[16]

Philosophy, then, searches through all of experience as objectively as it can for the basic structures that underlie that experience. But it is no unguided or haphazard search. Rather it is informed and directed by prior principles

[16] Two excellent statements of this understanding of philosophy are the following:

"Thus philosophical reflection is not the cause of that ultimate, comprehensive decision which determines the manner of a man's life and purpose, but rather its effect and expression. So understood, my philosophy represents the result of my effort to give a carefully articulated, objective and all-inclusive account of life and reality as they appear to me from my point of view, an effort sustained by my desire to commend my point of view by demonstrating that it is one from which it is possible to see life steadily and to see it whole." Casserley, J. V. L., *The Christian in Philosophy*, Faber & Faber, Ltd., 1949, p. 193.

"And at the creative point of experience there comes an inevitable power of positive response; the thinker finds himself saying 'yes' freely with his whole being. I do not believe that any of the great metaphysicians have cast around looking for some interesting idea on which they might be able to construct a theory. They have been charged with a sense of the importance and sig-

about what is real and what is intelligible. And its final
character will be determined both by the experiences with
which it deals, and by the basic principles with which it
starts. That is why it is always difficult to disprove and
often difficult even to understand another philosophical
viewpoint. For the facts that another point of view regards
as significant and real we may feel to be superficial or
illusory; and the order and coherence that seem convincing
and relevant to them seem mere sophistry to us. Ultimate
viewpoints, whether in philosophy or religion, have diffi-
culty in finding a common ground.

If this is the characteristic nature of all philosophies,
then we can see how there can be a Christian philosophy
that is both truly philosophical and yet Christian. For the
Christian has found his life illumined and restored
through a series of significant and transforming experiences. An existence which had been unintelligible and
chaotic before, suddenly has become illumined and coherent. In that experience his life has taken on a new meaning, and things have begun at last "to make sense." The
reason was that here he seemed to be in touch for the
first time with what was ultimately real and ultimately
meaningful, and he understood for the first the true nature
of the purpose of his own life. The Christian, it is true,
hesitates to call this significant experience an "insight,"
because its characteristic quality was that he was grasped
by a power not his own, which therein revealed itself to
him. His own new understanding of himself and his
world is more of a response to what happened to him
there than it is a "discovery" on his part. Thus he con-
fesses that he is the recipient of revelation, rather than
an originator of insight. Like the secular philosopher,
however, his new thinking springs from an experience that

---

nificance of some spiritual or intellectual experience, and the ex-
citement of this has driven them on to attempt to give intelligible
form to other vague reaches of experience with reference to this
basic thought." Emmett, D. M., *The Nature of Metaphysical
Thinking*, The Macmillan Co., 1945, p. 198.

has ultimate significance for his life. Of course, in this encounter with God in revelation he finds much more than a new understanding: grace is power and love as well as truth. But it *is* truth for the Christian, and it is at this point that the processes of his *thought* show their continuity with the thought of the secular philosopher.

Now among the many things that the thoughtful Christian understands in a new way in this experience, is the character and status of his own finitude, and that of the world around him. He knows himself now to be a creature of God amid other creatures, and this knowledge affects his whole basic attitude toward his experience of himself and of other things. First of all, he knows that both his own total being and the being of the finite things he encounters are real and yet dependent beyond themselves on a transcendent power. Thus he takes both sensory and internal experience, both his physical contacts with material things and his inward experiences of personal relationships, of anxiety and of guilt, as significant clues to the meaning and structure of finitude and of human life. And secondly, he knows now that while there is an inherent order to his life, it is an order that points beyond itself to a deeper meaning. His own life's coherence had proved not to be self-sufficient; it needed a grace from beyond itself to be made coherent. Thus when he looks at the world he knows that while he can find order there, nevertheless the final source of meaning transcends both his science and his philosophy.

Within the significant experience that has illumined his life, therefore, the Christian has found the creaturely world to be a dependent reality and a transcended order, and he has a sense of what experiences are significant clues to what is real and what sort of order he may expect to find. He has the same kind of basic presuppositions as any other philosopher, derived from a similar crucial and transforming experience. And so, with these two basic principles, he is as fully able as any other thinker to examine experience as it comes, in order to find its underlying

structures. In seeking to make the finite world intelligible
to his mind, he is completely free to go only to experience,
and derive therefrom the concepts and conclusions that
will characterize his philosophy. Like any other philosophy
that is sound, his thought is a combination of basic principles and of empirical inquiry. Since, then, his principles
are expressive of the Christian understanding of existence,
his inquiry is both truly philosophical and truly Christian.
Christian faith, therefore, is in no way more alien to true
philosophy than it is to true science. Rather, if rightly
understood, it can become the foundation for the most
intelligible and coherent understanding of ourselves and
the world around us.[17]

[17] According to our argument, the bases of a Christian philosophy are the "intuitions" of a dependent, contingent, and yet real
finitude, and a transcended order (respectively, the principles of
reality and of coherence which are present in any philosophy).
With regard, therefore, to the ultimate possibility and the content
of a Christian philosophy, we are in some agreement with the
newer movements of Thomism (e.g., E. L. Mascall, D'Arcy, Mar-
itain, and Farrar). But we disagree with their understanding of
the sources in experience of this philosophy. To us it is very dubious that these specifically "Christian" intuitions, expressive as
they are of the direct implications of the idea of creation, come
to us from philosophical insights drawn from our general experience of "finite being." Too many able philosophers have had
radically different intuitions of the character and implications of
the finite being open to the experience of all of us; some of these
have found that finitude "unreal" and "appearance," while others
have found it the sole relevant and intelligible reality. We seem to
have different intuitions of the nature of finitude, dependent upon
our own most fundamental approach to life, dependent, that is,
on our deepest experiences, and so on our "faith." Thus it seems
to us that these specifically Christian intuitions of the character,
reality, and order of finite being are the implications of the Christian experience of or encounter with revelation. Arising out of
this deep source in his "existence," those intuitions become determinative of the Christian philosopher's whole approach to finite
being, and so formative of his philosophy. This alone can explain
why these basic intuitions appear only to the minds of Christian
thinkers, and are notably absent (to the surprise of the Thomists)
from either monists or pluralistic naturalists.

Chapter 6

CREATION AND THE MEANING
OF LIFE

Although intelligibility is surely an important facet of the "goodness" of existence, our age has learned that it is not its sole guarantee, or even its most important component. A generation ago men did consider reason and intelligible order to be the main foundations to whatever goodness life might possess. They felt that the growing scientific knowledge of nature and of society could so extend human control over the structure of life as to make it good for all. Ironically our period has no less faith in the power of science to uncover the intrinsic intelligibility of the cosmos; and yet through our philosophy, literature, drama, and, more important, our individual consciousness, runs a current of uneasiness and futility. A generation which has witnessed the triumph of human knowledge and control is also experiencing the deepest doubts about the goodness and meaning of life. We have learned, therefore, that knowledge about the character and structure of existence does not necessarily involve a joyous and confident participation in existence. This vivid contemporary experience of a "knowing" culture that is also a "despairing" culture, leads us to state that for men existence must be "meaningful" as well as "intelligible" if it is to be called good. What, then, do we mean when we speak of "meaning in life" or of "meaninglessness"?

As a provisional, descriptive definition we may say that to most people life possesses "meaning" when they have confidence that their life is moving steadily toward the realization of their goals. These goals will, in all probability, represent what to them are "values" in life: possessions, achievements, and relationships that will satisfy their deepest needs and give opportunity for the use of their most creative powers. Such satisfaction we might, I presume, call "happiness." If, then, happiness is the aim of most human lives, the experience of meaning in life is the experience of the *potential* realization of happiness. Thus while a happy life is surely meaningful, a meaningful life is not necessarily happy. Our work is often meaningful under conditions which preclude the immediate satisfaction of our deepest needs. What is essential for the sense of meaning is that what we do seems to be leading to this satisfaction, to be building toward the realization of the goals of our life. Without this sense of the potentiality of satisfaction, of moving toward fulfillment, life becomes devoid of meaning, it becomes "meaningless." Meaning implies, then, that our life exists within an environment of events coherent enough so that what we do can be regarded as an effective means for what we want; unless there is this coherent relation of means and ends, our life seems to us pointless.

The Happiness Man Seeks

Now the content of these goals or ends, the character of the happiness man seeks, varies greatly from culture to culture and from age to age. The basic needs of man remain, of course, constant; but the sense of their relative value, and so the emphasis on this or the other goal, varies. To some cultures (for example, the classical Indian), man is fulfilled only if his spiritual life is developed to a very high degree; to others man is fulfilled when his mind has attained wisdom and understanding; and to a third variety, human happiness comes when the body is made comfortable and secure. In each culture most individuals absorb quite unconsciously these fundamental goals and purposes that direct them. What their parents and community regard as good, useful, and conducive to happiness they accept as such, and mold their lives accordingly. Thus, although their life embodies a definite concept of meaning, based on a definite view of what fulfills man and makes him happy, most people are quite unaware of the fact that they have adopted these meanings and goals that determine their existence—like the men of Athens, they worship at the shrine of an unknown god. They do, however, become aware of the problem of "meaning in life" when some event occurs or some problem arises which seems to thwart the realization of these accepted goals in life. Then, having peered briefly into the gulf of "meaninglessness," they begin to look for the meaning which they feel they have lost, but which up to that time they had unconsciously assumed. We live in such a time today, when the assumed meanings of life have been gravely threatened, and when, consequently, there is an almost universal uneasiness and anxiety at this loss. The deep restlessness and desperate searching, whenever man's small edifices of meaning crumble around him, indicate more clearly than anything else that man is so created that a secure meaning in life is a requirement of his nature: "Thou hast formed us for Thyself, and our hearts are restless till they can find rest in Thee."[1] Our question is, then, what are the significant experiences that bring about this feeling that life has lost its meaning? If we can answer this question, then perhaps we can begin to show the way in which meaning is found in human life, and so how the Christian faith creates its own sense of confidence in the meaningfulness of existence.

Most young Americans begin life with unexplored and uncomplicated assumptions of meaning. From their culture they have absorbed a few rather simple goals in life, things which they take for granted are essential for fulfillment and happiness. They hope to find a job that will be

[1] Augustine, *Confessions*, Book I, Chapter 1.

creative, and that will bring them increasing economic
security, physical comfort, and social prestige. They expect
to have a home and friends that will provide love and
warm associations; and they anticipate leisure time for
pleasant diversions such as fishing, boating, or golf. This
is, in effect, the predominant American scheme of "meaning," symbolized by the two-car garage, the barbecue pit
in the back yard, the comfortable chair before the TV set,
the country club, and the retirement plan—all suffused
with the love and affection of a happy home. The meaning of life for most people is quite simply dependent
upon the achievement of these goals of economic, material, social, and emotional security. So long as they believe they are on the road to the possession of these good
things that are taken to ensure happiness, most people
would feel that their lives were meaningful, and would
therefore leave the question of the "deeper" meanings of
life quite unexamined. It is not surprising, therefore, that
such folk are inclined to wonder what Europeans mean
when they call our culture "superficial" or "shallow."
Quite reasonably they ask, "What's wrong with this view
of life's purposes and goals? Why should we see life more
profoundly?"

The answer, of course, is not that they *should* have a
deeper view of life's meaning, but that sooner or later they
will *have* to. For the old saw is true which says that life is
no bed of roses. Something always seems to get in the way,
to frustrate this dream, and to raise into our consciousness
the pressing question of the deeper meanings of life. For a
life supported only by the flimsy meanings of the American dream is endlessly vulnerable. The "slings and arrows
of outrageous fortune" can play havoc with such a view of
life; or, as a Hellenistic man might have put it, "the god-
desses of Fortune and Blind Chance," or the demon of
Inner Disorder, will inevitably frustrate the hope of this
sort of happiness. Against the pressure of these forces, the
simple material and emotional securities of life disinte-

grate and vanish, and the ordinary man finds life devoid of purpose. Without a deeper view of meaning, there can be in the long run no meaning to life at all. The modern sense of meaninglessness is largely due to our sudden awareness that something seems always to thwart the "bourgeois" dream, and thus, having found no other view of life's meaning, many of us experience futility and pointlessness.

Let us look at some examples of this disintegration of the simpler meanings of life. Such disintegration of meaning may come first of all from an external event, natural or historical (or, as our pagan friend would have said, from the goddess Fortuna), which makes the fulfillment of these simple and normal human goals impossible. Sickness, accident, or death may claim a man, or one of his loved ones; an economic reverse may make his lifework insecure or even bankrupt; a war may call him away from work and home, and send him back maimed—if it sends him back at all. The same war may, as for countless young men in Europe, sweep across his community, and make it impossible for anyone therein to find economic or social security or comfort. A totalitarian revolution may, as for the young men of courage and conviction in Germany, Poland, and Hungary, make his whole life a nightmare of fear, a life in which he may be hunted, imprisoned, and even destroyed.

In any of these circumstances a man has forced upon him the question of meaning, and, what is more, although he may find another, deeper answer, at least it is certain that he cannot answer this question in terms of the "simple" goals of material and social security in which his culture had found meaning. Every aspect of normal fulfillment which he had been encouraged to value—pleasure, comfort, security and affection—has been snatched from him by these misfortunes. Consequently, his existence seems separated by insurmountable barriers from all that he had thought necessary to make him happy.

Unless he finds some other basis for meaning, therefore, life will seem hostile and ruthless, devoid of promise of fulfillment. Above all, whatever he does will seem to him pointless. Standing beside a loved one's grave, lying in a hospital bed, unable to find a promising job, a victim of war and its ravages, a lost inmate of a refugee camp—in any one of these only too familiar roles, the average human being cannot help but ask himself, "What point is there to my life?" And the meaning of this poignant question is then crystal clear: if the point of living is the fulfillment of these goals of security, comfort, and love, then when fortune makes this fulfillment impossible, there is literally no point to a man's life and work. What he does day by day is no longer a coherent means to the ends he values; it is a treadmill leading nowhere. A man's experience of meaninglessness comes in the first instance because bad fortune, or, as it is often called, fate, prevents his achievement of the accepted goals and values of normal life.

Moreover, even if we have not faced the tragedy of bad fortune ourselves, we are still not free of this fear of meaninglessness. We can lose confidence in the ability of our culture to escape these external threats to life's fulfillment; we can fear their immanent possibility and become convinced that they will overcome us in the future. Thus much of our Western world has lost confidence in the capacity of its culture to ward off bad fortune and so to satisfy our needs. Especially in devastated Europe, many people no longer "believe in" the fundamental structures of our culture: individual freedom, democracy, and individual enterprise, as the most effective means of making life full and happy. Some of these people may then turn to other "ideologies," fascistic or communistic, as better able to prevent bad fortune. Others, fearing these alternatives more, merely lose the certainty of the victory of this weakened culture over totalitarianism, and move within it in an atmosphere of pointlessness, indifference, and foreboding concerning tragedy yet to come.[2] In all periods of cultural crisis, such as in the breakup of the Roman Empire, or at the end of the Middle Ages, or in our own day, a similar mood of meaninglessness and of futility arises because the obvious meanings of life—physical comfort, economic security, and loving relations—are threatened by the massive forces of fortune, and so the possibility of realizing the goals of life seems to have lost its grounding in reality.

We have said elsewhere that to be a finite creature is to be dependent and contingent. To say this is not merely to utter a philosophic abstraction. It is to describe our human existence as it is actually experienced. Existence and its meanings *are* dependent and insecure. They are dependent upon and conditioned by great forces beyond our control—the forces of life and death, of nature, society, and history. As Tillich remarks, creaturehood "from the inside" is experienced as anxiety,[3] the anxiety which comes from an awareness of this basic dependence. Whenever, therefore, we become conscious of the essential contingency of our life and its fulfillment, and when the forces that we cannot control seem to thwart our every hope, then in desperation we ask, "what possible meaning can this dependent existence of mine have?" The problem of meaning springs initially from the contingency and so insecurity of man as a finite creature, crucially subject to external forces beyond his power that determine his weal or woe. At some time or another, man inevitably encounters what he has in the past called fortune or fate, and unless he knows the Providence of God, this mystery will overwhelm all the small securities with which he shores up the meaning of his life. In the last chapter on science, we were concerned with the problem of making intelligible

2 The novels of Arthur Koestler portray this mood of indifference, listlessness, pointlessness, and despair in a West that has lost its confidence in itself as a viable and effective cultural form, and so has lost its will to defend and support itself.

3 Tillich, P., *Systematic Theology*, Volume I, pp. 191–92.

the contingency of the natural world around us; the question before us now is the more important problem of making meaningful the contingency of our own finite being.

Our problems of meaning, however, are not confined to the influence of the external forces of "fate" on our lives. Cultures that are economically, socially, and politically secure, as is our present American culture, nevertheless contain many subtle inward forces which seem bound to destroy the simple dream of the serene, comfortable home in the suburbs. Even in a prosperous and peaceful environment it is not so easy to achieve satisfaction and happiness as we had thought. Our job may seem to us uncreative and pointless, so that we feel bored and restless; because of rivalry at the office we feel bitter that others are advanced while our own worth goes unrecognized; because of emotional difficulties at home we discover that even our family relationships are breaking apart. Even if we are financially secure, therefore, we may find ourselves inwardly unhappy, living a pointless life among people who are competitors rather than friends, in a home filled with tensions rather than love. Thus the most efficient culture, motivated by too simple goals, may nevertheless be filled with frustrated people. In America today many people are as far from happiness as in war-torn Europe, as the appalling number of broken homes, the frequency of mental disorder, and the problems of drug addiction, alcoholism, and delinquency clearly reveal. And since the meaning of our American life has been bound up with the achievement of a loving as well as a comfortable home, those who are outwardly secure but who still suffer from an inner lack of fulfillment cannot avoid the question of meaning. In this instance, meaninglessness is caused not so much by bad fortune as by inner alienation from our true selves and from one another; and the search for meaning thus entails the search for inner reconciliation and healing.

If an answer to this inner question of meaning is not found, people are driven to cynicism or escape. The

cynicism manifests itself in that ruthless and lonely competition for prestige and power reflected in almost every
"realistic" novel about our business and social life. When
loving relations seem denied to us, apparently one alternative form of meaning for which we grasp is personal
"success." The escape manifests itself in a flight from all
personal responsibilities and commitments, whether to
one's vocation, one's family, or one's character. Many of
the most prosperous segments of American life are permeated by an endless search for new thrills, a continual
"playing around" with other men's wives, and the com-
forting unreality of the bottle. Whenever there is such
cynicism or escape, we may be sure that the question of
the meaning of life has been raised, at least implicitly,
and has been answered in the negative. For these secure
people, life is full of magnificent means to do anything
they might wish. But because inwardly they have no commitment either to worth-while ends or to people, these
means become boring and flat—and life seems meaningless
until either the struggle for power or the bottle gives it
back its glow. And suffused throughout this whole atmosphere of competition, of restlessness, and of futility is a
sharper, but often deeply repressed, twinge of guilt—a
feeling of being unclean, of having been untrue to ourselves, our friends, our wives, our children. Guilt before
whom, we do not know, whether before others, before our
consciences, or before God—but there it is! And we just
wish that we could get back to the old innocence, the old
meaning, of that secure and happy home with the creative
job and the loving family, which seems as far from the
sordid reality of our life as Eden itself—as perhaps it is.

Human existence has no such simple and direct meaning or goodness as the humanistic American dream, published weekly in our home magazines and monthly in the
Digest, has envisioned. A comfortable chair, a hi-fi set, a
powerful car, the protection of a deodorant, a college
romance, and a paying job, cannot even in combination

provide meaning for our life. Existence is far too subject
to threat from without and perversion from within to be
defended by these feeble weapons against fate and the
devil. We have tended in America to look upon the radical
contingency and the inner perversion of our life as exceptional, and to use a screen of technological gadgets to
hide from our gaze the inevitable sorrows, frustrations,
and turmoil of life. At our simplest level we feel that
these ultimate problems of frailty and sin can be dealt
with by science and machines. But science can at best
only ward off the threats of fate, through engineering and
medicine; and at worst, only increase the deadliness of the
threats to our life through nuclear weapons. And when we
try to construct a positive "philosophy of life" to handle
these threats to life's meaning, about all we can manage is
to invent a new gadget in the spiritual realm. We give
people simple formulas and recipes for thinking positively, for having faith in themselves, with the tacit
assumption that positive thought and brimming self-con-
fidence will drive the sorrow and despair away. The
problem of meaning, however, is not to be resolved merely
by the recipes of do-it-yourself pamphlets. It springs too
directly from the very nature of our finitude and dependence, and it involves too clearly the deepest problems of
our selfhood, to be eliminated by "techniques," either
material or spiritual.

The Conditions for a Meaningful Life

How then is the problem of meaning to be resolved?
For the Christian this resolution can be found only in
the Christian Gospel, and in the relation to God which
faith in that Gospel brings. Since, however, we are not yet
in a position to make the full, positive answer of this
Gospel clear, let us try to see in a general way what conditions would make possible the discovery of meaning in
life. Our examples have shown that the sense of positive

meaning is threatened both by external events and by inner disorder, by things that happen to us and things that happen in us. And we have indicated that there seems to be no immediate "know-how" in prospect by which these external and internal threats to our happiness can be eradicated. Are meaning and happiness, then, not possible for contingent, alienated man?

The answer is, of course, that the threats to meaning which we have cited destroy only meanings that are superficially grounded. If we regard, as do most humanists, physical security and loving relations as easily realizable goals in life, then the discovery of man's contingency and of his inner alienation will quickly dissolve any sense of meaning. If, however, our sense of meaning is more firmly based, then even these experiences will become less threatening and can be faced with courage and vitality.

Let us take, for example, the experience of bad fortune. Clearly in certain circumstances men can lose all hope for immediate physical comfort, loving relations, and even security of life, and still retain a magnificent sense of meaning in their work. In a war situation people can endure a great deal of immediate privation and pain without a sense of despair. In fact, many men have felt more "meaning" in their uncomfortable and hazardous life as soldiers than they do in their comfortable but often pointless life in suburbia. Why is this? The answer is that the misfortunes of war, with all its privation, pain, and suffering, were enclosed within a larger intelligible purpose which those who suffered from them could affirm. These misfortunes were seen as necessary steps toward a goal which their victims could understand and value. Almost any amount of privation and suffering becomes bearable, that is, it brings no threats to the fundamental meaning of life, whenever we can see that they take their place within an intelligible order of events leading to a goal. Whenever man can discern such an intelligible order within the historical events in which they participate, there the meaning of their life lies beyond the reach of immediate tragedy.

On the other hand, whenever no such intelligible order is apparent, then any amount of misfortune is almost unbearable. Such events as the arbitrary loss of one's job or of one's health or the sudden death of a young person, because they are arbitrary and irrational, threaten our basic sense of meaning. The actual pain and suffering may be less; what makes them almost unsupportable is their pointlessness, the fact that they come to us, not as signs of a future culmination for which we hope and wait, but as deadly symbols of a fundamental irrationality in existence itself. They come at us from meaninglessness, and they point toward an equal meaninglessness. Suddenly we seem, through them, to have made contact with an abyss of chaos; they seem to reveal to us that things, at their most fundamental level, are out of joint, blind, arbitrary—and this is a very frightening feeling. Tyche, the blind goddess of chance and fate, was feared and worshiped, not because Hellenistic man was afraid merely of the discomforts of cold and hunger. Rather it was because he was terrified of the blindness of the fate that seemed to rule his life. It was the unconditional abyss of meaninglessness, not the restricted misfortunes of life, that threatened him. For this reason it has not been the technical development of deep freezes and central heating that has dissipated in our culture the fear of fate and provided a sense of meaning. Rather it has been the sense, derived from the Christian faith in Providence, of an intelligible order to historical life within which privations can be meaningfully accepted. The contingency of finite man in the face of fortune calls for the Providence of God if life is to have meaning. Behind the small meanings of our individual lives there must stand a more ultimate coherence that gives to them stability, and to us a basis for courage when they are threatened.

An intelligible and purposive order in which our life

can participate is, however, required not only by the external buffetings of fortune; it is also required by the danger of inner emptiness. As we have seen, our contemporary experience of meaninglessness in the West is in many cases not caused by the malevolence and blindness of events. Rather it seems to stem largely from an emptiness and indifference in our own reaction to them. Possessions and achievements that were supposed to evoke our enthusiasm fail to do so; when they are ours we find ourselves still bored, unable to respond deeply to them or to be moved by them. In this mood, life is like a cup of weak coffee, unworthy of our effort because there is no real flavor there. The immensely popular novels of the French authoress, Françoise Sagan, reflect this aspect of meaninglessness. She portrays life threatened by no loss of essential necessities, nor buffeted by any cruel external fate; all the characters live comfortable, secure lives. Nevertheless, existence is joyless and therefore pointless. The reason is that these people are unable to respond deeply to anything, to value anything, to be ultimately concerned about anything. What this sort of person lacks is not the means to ends he values, as with the victim of bad fortune; he suffers from the more serious loss of significant ends in life which give direction, purpose and value to his activities. Hence every experience is reduced to the level of tasting: momentary, distracting, but unmoving and unexhilarating. These people touch life only on the level of sensation; lacking significant ends that call forth their commitment, their whole being is unable to participate in what they do. Thus while the senses are "fulfilled," the deeper levels of the self are left untouched. Consequently the self itself can feel only boredom. Meaninglessness here is due to an incapacity of the self to find anything in life significant, be it pleasant or unpleasant, successful or unsuccessful. What is lacking here is a purpose beyond the self that can grasp the whole self, a purpose that would give to the whole self the power of enthusiasm, of enjoyment, and therefore a basis for creative effort. Meaning in life, therefore, involves committed and personal participation in deeper purposes which can capture the concern and loyalty of the self, and give value to its experience.[4]

This is perhaps the most profound and devastating criticism of both the simple American values of material security and comfort and of secular cultures generally. Even when "fate" allows us to possess security and comfort, these goals cannot give sufficient meaning to life, because they have no capacity to stir and move man's total self. The self must be rooted in a dimension of significance beyond its own comfort and pleasure if it is to value anything, including itself. And if it can find no ultimate significance in what it does, nothing that it does will long retain any significance at all. Consequently ultimate restlessness, boredom, and pointlessness may be the end result of even the most secure of secular cultures. One further requirement, therefore, of a meaningful life is that a per-

[4] An exceedingly perceptive modern drama, Beckett's *Waiting for Godot*, illustrates many of these elements of contemporary meaninglessness. Our basic yearning for fulfillment and our utter dependence on factors beyond our control for its realization are powerfully symbolized by "Godot," who "will surely come tomorrow," and who, when he comes, "will save us." The only meaningful thing we can do, therefore, is to wait for Godot. In the meantime, nothing we do has any real significance; it merely "passes the time," as what we do in a waiting room is at best merely distracting, not significant. Since nothing before Godot's advent has importance or concern, there is no event important enough to remember, nor is there a basis or capacity for decision: the characters repeatedly decide to go, and remain still. But Godot's promise to come is never fulfilled. Thus the only thing that could give meaning and significance to life remains perpetually postponed. Consequently distinctions of value utterly vanish; even the tragic becomes comic and futile. When Estragon and Vladimir attempt to commit suicide, Estragon's pants fall down. Life is not a participation in meaning but essentially a waiting for meaning, and thus every aspect of existence is drained of real significance, although, happily for the audience, by no means drained of its humor.

son find a "vocation" for his life, a task to accomplish that has significance because it is a part of the ultimate purpose that runs through the moments of history.[5] The need of man's spirit for commitment to something of ultimate significance also calls for the providential purpose of God if his life is to have meaning. And that purpose, or ultimate coherence, within historical destiny, requires that all of being have its origin in God. As the contingent being of man's life points beyond his existence to God as the ground of being, so the contingent meanings of his life point beyond themselves to God as the fount of all meaning.

Our analysis of the components of meaning in life reveals, therefore, three factors necessary to a sense of meaning: the hope of the ultimate fulfillment of our deepest needs, a vision of an intelligible and purposive order of significance in which our life can participate, and some promise of inner health and unity. Wherever any of these elements of meaning are lacking, there the sense of the goodness of life is threatened; and where all three are absent, there despair, cynicism, or flight from life may result.

It is interesting to note that in these three elements of meaning we can detect the bases for modern man's three dominant secular faiths. Our age has produced three forms

[5] One of the most important reasons for the power of both Fascist and Communist ideology in recent times is that each of them provides an ultimate meaning and an ultimate commitment, however false, to man's life. To men whose activities are rooted in no deep significance, and so seem pointless and boring, the appeal of such ideology is almost irresistible. Thus what each Nazi follower did helped to "found the ten-thousand-year Reich," and what each Communist accomplishes participates in the inevitable march of the Dialectic of History. In each case there is something of ultimate significance to which a man can commit his life, and so in which he can again find the basis for valuing, for activity, for courage—for meaning. If one adds to this appeal the fact that such ideologies also promise to deal effectively with the menace of bad fortune, one can see their compelling power.

of "religion," in its most general sense, each of which answers one or more of these three facets of meaning. The modern faith in technical science has its origin in our belief that through science the external threats to the meaning of our life, such as sickness, natural disaster, poverty, and inadequacy of comfort, could be eradicated from life. Secondly, the recent liberal faith in historical progress, and its opposite number, the Marxist faith in a dialectic of history, in turn answer the need to see threatening or seemingly meaningless events in some sort of intelligible and purposive order leading to fulfillment. The liberal champion for truth and justice can bear the pains of his present battle if he believes he is building a better world. The Marxist has been able to stand the suffering, persecution, and poverty that have been the lot of the worker, because he is sure that in the intelligible order of history there is a reason for that suffering and a coming end to its duration. Finally, the quite contemporary "faith" in psychoanalysis has its origin in the perennial yearning for healing within, in the desire to eradicate our inner disorders, and the confidence that psychological skill can do this for us all. Each of these three "religions" of modern man, that of science, of history, and of psychological healing, receives power in our cultural life from the anxious search for meaning which is an inescapable part of man's finite life. Each one of these has a hopeful answer for one aspect of the meaning which life seeks. But no one of them can cover all the facets of meaning which undergird life, and so no one is sufficiently strong to bear all of life's tensions. Is there no religious faith, then, that can include what is valid in our science, in our hope for progress, and in our psychological skill, and also contain within its own scope a genuine promise of ultimate fulfillment, intelligibility, purpose, and healing? This is the basic question which our cultural life must answer if it is to have the confidence and the courage sufficient to conquer the real threats to its existence.

The Inscrutability of Finite Existence

The meaning of human life is, as we have found, threatened by disaster from without, and by emptiness and dissension from within. This has always been the case, and probably always will be. The basic precariousness and contingency of finite existence, and its sense of inner alienation, have been constant elements in history, and hence the factors which in our contemporary life seem to destroy meaning are factors which can be reduplicated in every human situation. Religion is no passing phase of human experience, because religion seeks to provide a framework of meaning for a life that inevitably searches for meaning.

Because these threats to meaning have been a perennial aspect of human existence, it has never been the case that mankind could take the "goodness" of life on earth for granted. A confidence in the possibility of fulfillment, a lively sense of the intelligible and purposive order of historical existence, and a deep experience of inner healing have been rare in life, never its normal expectancy. Indeed most cultures other than our own have felt that the life of the human creature, immersed in the unpredictability of nature and of history, is not good. Conscious of the continual buffetings of an irrational fortune, of the sorrow that befalls every man who loves, and above all of the uncontrollability of our inner spirits, thoughtful pre-Christian men found creaturely life not a gift to be prized but a burden to be borne or a cage to be evacuated. The "natural" man is not the carefree, life-affirming pagan that secularism has painted him. He is, in fact, a frightened creature, conscious of his own weakness and terrified of the massive powers and fates that determine his life. Confidence in the meaning of life is, therefore, a religious and cultural achievement, not a natural possession.

In the great Indian and Hellenic cultures, with the exception of certain optimistic periods when culture flourished grandly, the predominant evaluation of the meaning of life was negative. Let us look at a few examples from these civilizations so as to illustrate the contrast with the biblical understanding of existence. In each of them the meaning and goodness of life is essentially threatened in such a way that no fulfillment, intelligible purpose, or healing is possible within the terms of finite, historical existence. Let us also note how remarkably similar to our own are the ills which drive these thinkers to despair about human life on earth.

In the earliest Greek poetry we find these thoughts about the finitude, the precariousness, and the dark inscrutability of man's life:

Wisdom is not within man's scope; for our brief day we live like beasts, knowing nothing of how heaven will bring each thing to its accomplishment.[6]

Like the leaves, for a span of time we rejoice in the flowers of youth . . . On either hand are the black Fates, the one holding the fullness of miserable age, the other of death.[7]

A man never attains the whole of his desire; his helplessness sets bounds that hold him back. We men know nothing, and our thoughts are vain; it is only the gods that accomplish all things to their mind.[8]

Best of all things is it, never to be born upon this earth, never to see the rays of the burning sun. And, when man is born, it is best that he should journey with all speed to the gates of Death, and, wrapping himself in a close covering of earth, should lie at rest.[9]

[6] Semonides of Amorgos, Fragment I, Cornford, S. M., *Greek Religious Thought*, Beacon Press, 1950, p. 37.
[7] Mimnermus of Colophon (c. 650–600 B.C.), *ibid.*, p. 37.
[8] Theognis, Elegies 133 (c. 450 B.C.), *ibid.*, p. 38.
[9] Theognis, Elegies 425, *ibid.*, p. 39.

Alas, ye wretched, ye unblessed race of mortal beings,
Of what strifes and of what groans were ye born.[10]

This deep pessimism about finite existence, this feeling
that our dependent, precarious life, buffeted from without
and within, was fundamentally meaningless, did not last
throughout Hellenic culture. In time it was broken by the
rise of the secure and prosperous Greek city state, and
by the power of the Greek vision of existence as a rational
order which the mind of man could understand. But soon,
as these two facets of Greek culture disintegrated, the
sense of brooding tragedy, of inevitable worthlessness, and
of recurrent misery in life—and the desire to retire spiritually from it—grew apace. Let us see these powerful expressions from three later Hellenic thinkers:

Soon, very soon, thou wilt be ashes, or a skeleton, and
either a name or not even a name; but name is sound
and echo. And the things which are much valued in life
are empty and rotten and trifling, and like little dogs
biting one another, and little children quarreling, laugh-
ing and then straightway weeping. But fidelity and mod-
esty and justice and truth are fled "Up to Olympus
from the widespread earth."[11]

There neither were formerly, nor are there now, nor will
there be again, more or fewer evils in the world (than
have always been). For the nature of all things is one
in the same, and the generation of evils is always the
same.[12]

It is not easy, indeed, for one who is not a philosopher
to ascertain the origin of evils, though it is sufficient for
the multitude to say that they do not proceed from God

[10] Empedocles, Fragment 400 (c. 450 B.C.) Nahm, M. C.,
Selections from Early Greek Philosophy, F. S. Crofts & Co., 1947,
p. 140.
[11] Marcus Aurelius, *Meditations*, Book 5, Section 33.
[12] Celsus, quoted in Origen, *Against Celsus*, Book 4, Chapter
62.

but cleave to matter, and have their abode among mortal things; while the course of mortal things being the same from beginning to end, the same things must always, agreeably to the appointed cycles, recur in the past, present, and future.[13]

It is the soul that accepts unmeasure, excess and shortcoming which brings forth licentiousness, cowardice, and all other flaws of the soul . . . Such a soul is not purely itself . . . and this is because it is merged in a body made of matter.[14]

The sphere of sense is of the Soul in its slumber, for all of Soul that is in body is asleep and the true getting-up is not bodily but from the body; in any movement that takes the body with it there is no more than a passage from sleep to sleep . . . the veritable waking is from corporal things.[15]

The memory of friends, children, wife, country, the lower man retains with emotion, the authentic man passively. The loftier soul must desire to come to a happy forgetfulness of all that had reached it through the lower . . . In this world itself, all is best when human interests and the memory of them have been put out of the way.[16]

Then, moving into another culture, we find an even gloomier assessment of the prospects of creaturely existence, as the following from the literature of early Buddhism manifest:

And what, oh priests, is the noble truth of misery? Birth is misery; old age is misery; disease is misery; death is

[13] Celsus, quoted in Origen, *Against Celsus*, Book 4, Chapter 65.
[14] Plotinus, Ennead 1, Section 8, quoted from Turnbull, G., *The Essence of Plotinus*, translated by Stephen Mackenna, Oxford University Press, 1948, p. 55.
[15] Plotinus, Ennead 3, Section 6, *ibid.*, p. 102.
[16] Plotinus, Ennead 4, Section 3–4, *ibid.*, p. 126–27.

misery; sorrow, lamentation, misery, grief and despair are misery.[17]

In him who has intercourse (with others) affections arise, (and then) the pain which follows affection; considering the misery that originates in affection let one wander alone like a rhinoceros.[18]

All things, oh priests, are on fire . . . With the fire of passion, say I, with the fire of hatred, with the fire of infatuation; with birth, old age, death, sorrow, lamentation, misery, grief and despair are they on fire . . . Perceiving this, oh priests, the learned and noble disciple conceives an aversion for the eye . . . conceives an aversion for the mind . . . for ideas . . . for mind-consciousness . . . and whatever sensation, pleasant, unpleasant or indifferent . . . for that also he conceives an aversion . . . and in conceiving this aversion he becomes free . . . and he knows that rebirth is exhausted . . . and that he is no more for this world.[19]

In these quotations we may be startled to find that men of other times and places were faced with much the same agonizing problems of meaning as we are. They, too, felt overwhelmed by the sorrow of sickness and death, and by the arbitrary destruction of their hopes by fortune. But they drew more devastating conclusions from these experiences than we do. For to them to be mortal, to love and be loved, to strive for the goods of the world, was to be vulnerable to an outrageous and ruthless fate, and to lay misery on misery. And the more sophisticated of these ancients were conscious of an inner turmoil, a dislocation in themselves, which drove them to defeat their own security

[17] The Four Intent Contemplations, Sutta 22, Dīgha Nikāya, Warren, H. C., *Buddhism in Translation*, Harvard University Press, 1900, p. 368.
[18] Khaggavisânasutta, #2, The Sutta-Nipâta, Translated by V. Fausböll, *Sacred Books of the East*, Volume X, Part II, Oxford University Press, 1924, p. 6.
[19] "The Fire Sermon," Warren, *op. cit.*, pp. 352–53.

and enjoyment. They knew nothing of "neuroses," but surely they knew the need for inner healing.

The philosophical explanations for this human situation of meaninglessness, of outer and inner frustration, varied: to some it was because human souls had been incarnated in matter; to others because man had descended from his true home with the divine; to still others, it was because the eternal and necessary nature of things was a purposeless flux, which destroyed as blindly as it created. To the Buddha, the meaninglessness of life was caused by the inevitable passion and attachment one feels so long as he thinks of himself as an existing, individual being. The significant constant amid the philosophical variety, however, was that to all of them finite existence essentially involves frustration and misery. It means need, sickness, and death; it means inner turmoil, restlessness, and despair. Thus for all alike meaninglessness is inevitable for individual life in the body and in history, because individuality, matter, and time are essentially realms of evil. If we were to speak in theological categories, we would say that in each of these views creation and the Fall are identified: to *be* an individual in space and time is to be immersed in a tragic existence. As a consequence, the only answer to life's essential meaninglessness is resignation, renunciation, or flight. Cleave not to finite things, leave people and the world behind, move within, or upward to the One, or cease to care. These are the repeated pleas of the writers we have quoted. It appears that one dominant answer to the question of the meaningfulness or goodness of human existence—a question raised by experiences common to all men of all places, times, and cultures—is that there is and can be no meaning in historical life. And it also appears that this answer arises in every situation where men cannot distinguish between the essential goodness of life and the intrusion of evil into it. Wherever finitude and evil, creation and the Fall, are identified, there meaning becomes an impossibility.

The Biblical Affirmation of Life

Now this answer to the question of meaning has not been characteristic of the Christian West, although it has appeared whenever Christian culture has absorbed these other cultural strains. On the whole, while Christian faith has been realistic about the threats with which life confronts us, it has consistently and increasingly affirmed the essential goodness and so the potential meaning of finite life, and the possibility of victory over all that threatens that meaning. This faith entered a cultural environment which was diffused with the pessimistic mood we have just described: to the late Hellenic world, material and historical life was dominated by brooding fates, and enveloped by omnipresent and inevitable evil. In real measure classical and medieval Christianity absorbed this mood, especially as the collapse of classical civilization proceeded to completion. But implicit in Christianity was the biblical conviction that creation was essentially good and so potentially meaningful, a conviction so strong and so central that in time it conquered the alien Hellenistic and oriental elements which led to consistent pessimism. Out of the developed Christian culture has come, therefore, the Western appreciation of and interest in the concrete individual entity, corporeal, contingent, and historical though he or it may be. And from that appreciation of the actual has developed the concern for the natural world from which science has resulted, and the concern for individual and communal life from which our humanitarian, democratic culture has proceeded. Thus the biblical consciousness of the goodness and meaning of our finitude has been perhaps the most creative single element in our cultural life, contributing alike to our intellectual and social progress.[20]

[20] To anyone familiar with Christian theology it will be clear that Christianity is as critical of modern Western optimism as it is of Old World or contemporary pessimism. Since, however, the main criticism of an overly optimistic view of life stems more

In the biblical view God is the purposive creator of the whole of existence so that the created world is regarded as fundamentally good rather than as essentially evil. Thus for the Christian mind existence as such, the mere fact of being at all, is good, because creaturely being has been brought forth out of nothing by a good God. We shall show in the following paragraphs three elements of the content of this essential goodness of finite being. First, however, let us note that immediately in this view the creation of finitude and the appearance of evil are distinguished from one another, a distinction symbolized and expressed by the myth of the historical fall of Adam following in time upon God's creation of the world. Now this distinction between creation and evil radically changes the whole understanding of life's meaning. Whereas in Hellenistic and Indian cultures life was essentially meaningless because finitude and evil were identified, in Christian faith life is potentially meaningful because finite existence is essentially good rather than evil. In other words, because of the belief in creation, the undeniable evil in life does not lead to the conclusion that there is and can be no meaning in finite existence; it merely implies that an essentially good life has become perverted. It is true that in such a view the problem of the origin of evil is made more puzzling, and the problem of the healing of life's perversion becomes more crucial—as we shall see in the next two chapters. Nevertheless the distinction between creation and evil is the foundation on which any view of life's meaning is to be based. Without this distinction the mere fact of existence means the denial of meaning; with this distinction the essential structure of finite existence is seen to be good, and there is opened

---

from the Christian understanding of man's sin than from the idea of creation, we shall concentrate our attention on the antipessimistic aspect of Christian convictions. For the Christian criticism of modern secular optimism the reader is referred to another book in this series, namely, E. E. Cherbonnier, *Hardness of Heart*, Doubleday & Company, Inc., 1955.

up the possibility of a meaningful life in finitude and in history.

In our analysis of the pessimistic strains in the Hellenic and Indian cultures, we found that these denials of life's essential goodness rang the changes on certain fundamental structural aspects of existence which were felt to preclude the possibility of meaning. One of these was the sense of the vulnerability of dependent man to blind fate, the feeling that man's existence was determined by ultimately incoherent and irrational forces that crushed all his efforts to fulfill himself. Another was the conviction that man's existence in an evil material body, and within the emotional relations of human community, so distorted his true life that no meaning could be found here on earth. And all concluded that the historical environment of man's life, with its unpredictable natural setting and its demonic historical fates, was a realm within which no fulfillment could be found. These essential elements of the structure of finitude: its contingent vulnerability, its material and emotional bases, and its historical setting, were, therefore, regarded in all of them as essentially evil. Our question is, then, in what ways did the Christian faith in the "good" creation establish the essential goodness of each of these fundamental structures of creaturely life, so that life as we find it was felt to be at least potentially meaningful?

Faith in Historical Destiny

1. The first implication of the idea of creation for the potential meaning of finite life deals with the problem of man's vulnerable being within a seemingly irrational existence. Christian faith in God the Creator answers this problem by denying this ultimate irrationality, and replacing it by faith in the meaningful but still mysterious providence of God. For the belief in the creation of all being by a transcendent God lays the foundation for that ultimate coherence and purpose within existence which we call providence. Earlier in this chapter we found that the

problems of the meaning of man's life continually raised this question of providence. As we noted, the threats to life's normal, surface meanings, threats both of bad fortune and of inner boredom, drive men to search for an intelligible order of events in history, and an ultimate significance to their daily activities, which could give meaning to life even within the experiences of insecurity and mortality. Now in a world created by a transcendent and purposive God, such an ultimate coherence and significance is possible. For all of being has an inherent coherence because it stems from the same ultimate source, and each facet of being shares in this coherence since none could be at all without God's will. A secure faith in an ultimate order and coherence that includes the entire context of man's existence, both natural and historical, is implied by the belief in creation; the first consequence of the knowledge of God the Creator is the affirmation that there is a providence that surrounds our life.

As a result, the contingency of creaturely life, the fact that it is dependent upon massive forces beyond itself both for existence and for significance, is no compromise to its essential goodness and its potential meaning. All the forces of nature and of history that impinge upon each creature stem as well from the same creative will, and so themselves ultimately participate in the same coherence of created existence. There is, then, no essential characteristic of existence that is antithetical to the meaning and fulfillment of each creaturely life—for all of being has its origin in God. Hence the sole condition for meaning and goodness is that each creature fulfill its own nature, become itself, live out its created purpose. All else, both within it and outside it, is directed by the same sovereign will that brought it into being. And because there is a deeper coherence to life, each creature can participate in an ultimately significant purpose if it will, and in that participation find fulfillment and meaning. The belief that existence finds its ultimate origin in God sets each creaturely life in a context of coherence and significance impossible on any other terms. For such an ultimate context is not discoverable by observation in a life suffused, as is ours, by unpredictable tragedy; it can be known only by faith. And the sole basis for such a faith is the knowledge of the Creator. Without such knowledge, there is no basis for this context of coherence and significance, and without that context the meaning of life quickly evaporates.

It is in this affirmation of life's fundamental coherence and meaning because it has an ultimate origin in a transcendent God that we see perhaps the most striking contrast between the Christian view of existence and that of secularism or naturalism. For the latter there is no such thing as a meaningful ultimate origin to existence, and the questions of such an origin and meaning are nonsensical, futile, and irrelevant. The argument of the naturalist goes something like this. Since we can only ask questions within the scope of our given daily experience, any affirmations beyond this limit of our experience are pathetically naïve. This experience of ours begins *within* existence; existence is the assumed context and condition of experience; we are its children, and we were not there when the existence that produces us was itself originated. How, then, can we know anything about the origin of that from which we, and all our experience, derive? How can we get behind the very conditions of our life to find out about the "whence" of those conditions? Thus the transcendent origins of our life are forever dark to us; the deeper dimensions of the existence in which we participate are to us total mystery, and so are irrational to our minds. Consequently, we can say nothing of a fundamental coherence, goodness, or purpose in being as such. As far as we are concerned, the factors that produce us are subject to no ultimately coherent origin, and so we can only say that they rush blindly whither they will. The only coherence that our lives can know or affirm is the small garden which our human powers can create out of the wasteland of the totality of being.

However, the argument continues, our inability to an-

swer the questions of ultimate origins and of ultimate coherence does not matter, since the goodness of our life in
no way depends upon an ultimate meaning within existence itself. Our life is involved in "small meanings," local
fulfillments and achievements, partial victories over those
things that resist our human purposes. Surely these are
enough for us, since their success calls forth all our creative powers. Why search for an ultimate meaning or coherence to being, when it only draws one away from his
real business, the establishment of partial meanings in the
here and now? Thus the naturalistic portion of American
culture points to the growth of health and education, to
the spread of tolerance and science, of democracy and
peace, of physical security and bodily comfort, and says
with confidence: "Here are small but real meanings in life.
Having these, we know and care nothing of an ultimate
meaning and origin. We are content with these partial
achievements, and do not need God in an existence in
which such human and tentative values are possible." This
is the strongest defense of the skeptical humanist against
religion: he feels no need of a creator in a life full of partial meanings and partial goods.

One crucial question in this debate between Christian
and naturalist is certainly whether such an affirmation of
"small meanings" is possible to one skeptical of and indifferent to the questions of ultimate origins and ultimate
coherence. To the Christian this is not possible, for the
day-to-day meanings of life are dependent upon a fundamental structure of coherence and meaning within existence itself which can come only from its transcendent
source in God. Thus without that transcendent origin there
is no basis for thinking, as the secularist strangely seems
to do, that life contains any dependable potentiality for
local meanings. Where a transcendent Creator is not
known, the human meanings of life are defenseless against
the onslaughts of destiny. Let us look briefly at this Christian argument.

No one doubts that life is often replete with "small meanings," with partial victories of what we call good over the resistant forces of things. Life can become more secure, happy, and full, and these concerns are worthy of our utmost efforts. Nevertheless, we must ask something about the larger conditions for these small meanings, for in some historical situations they are simply not possible, and then to say we can base the meaning of our life on them is futile. Can a man gain a sense of life's potential meaningfulness from the growth of education, tolerance, and security in a police state? Can these partial meanings be a source of courage for life in a history that seems to be turning from democracy to communism, from order and peace to disorder and conflict? The fact is that the small meanings of life are, like all creaturely things, dependent, contingent, and transient. They are made possible in human experience because of vast forces—natural, social, and historical—far beyond human control or prediction. A harmony among these great forces is necessary to provide the conditions essential for the existence of the small meanings of our immediate life. These larger factors, upon which we depend more than we like to admit, include not only the regularity and benevolence of the forces of nature, but, even more relevantly, the peace and order of international politics, and the rationality and stability of world economics. And these factors are in turn dependent on the unpredictable and uncontrollable relations between various human ideologies, and on the state of human fears and passions. A basic fluctuation or change in any of these larger factors can send our small meanings toppling.

Thus the local meanings of life float on the surface of the vast river of historical destiny whose course largely determines their possibility. The question, therefore, of the nature and direction of that river is scarcely an irrelevant one. If there is in the fundamental structure of things a coherence and a purpose that includes within its scope all the forces that determine our life, then there is some security for our small meanings, and we can safely base our life upon them—as the secularist seeks to do. If, however, these local values rest on a blind nature and an undirected history, then this necessary sense of fundamental coherence has no footing—nor does the secularist faith that these small meanings will always "be there" to make life good have any ground. In such a universe, why assume that order is more basic than conflict, that intelligence will prevail over instinct, that love and goodness are more fundamental and permanent than hate and fear? How, then, can we count on there being "small meanings" at all, when that conflict, that instinct, and that hate can so quickly disintegrate them? The pre-Christian naturalists never dreamed of making the assumption that blind fortune will always so smile on man's little values. Thus, without some presupposition of fundamental coherence and meaning, there is no legitimate basis for a confidence in the permanent possibility of life's small meanings—and without some such confidence a sense of the meaningfulness of life itself quickly disappears. The secularist's affirmation that the observable achievements of life can make it meaningful is thus either a description of the obvious fact that at that particular moment all is going well—in which case there is in that description no basis for courage if tragedy should strike, and these empirical meanings evaporate—or it is an unexamined and ungrounded affirmation of the same ultimate coherence which the naturalist had scorned. Furthermore, without an ultimate significance in which our life can participate, the small meanings of life cease to be meaningful. Our small purposes must be related to a total purpose if they are to retain our commitment. If life loses its ultimate significance, it can scarcely hold anything significant—as our analysis of people who lost their hold on important ends has shown.

Confidence in an ultimate coherence and meaning within existence itself is, however, just the sort of affirmation that the naturalist cannot legitimately make. For his view is confined to an analysis of immediate experience, and thus he can speak neither of the ultimate origin nor of the essential structure of existence. The naturalistic man can only note the way the various aspects of existence happen to relate to each other in his momentary experience of them. Able to analyze only the "given," he can gain confidence only if within that "given" the apparently benevolent factors are predominant. But if at that moment of history, the irrational forces in history seem dominant, then he can appeal to no more fundamental coherence behind that experienced irrationality; and he can look to no more ultimate scheme of meaning which might include the great forces beyond human control—forces which nonetheless set the conditions for human success or failure. His sense of meaning is thus totally dependent upon the ups and downs of human success, for he can be confident about life only so far as nature and history are formed and conquered by man's creative powers and purposes. But, as we have seen, our small purposes are too often frustrated and defeated in history to be the sole support of our confidence and courage. To depend for our sense of meaning upon the observable victory of our human goals is to be easily vulnerable to pessimism and despair. There are times in history when our confidence in the meaning of life must be grounded in faith, and not in observation alone. But here the naturalist is caught, for in his world there is nothing but observable progress on which he can found his courage.

This is the reason that secular cultures, and the people within them, tend to fluctuate between optimism and pessimism. On the one hand they can be exceedingly optimistic when observation seems to show that nature and history are amenable to human intelligence and will, as in the nineteenth and early twentieth centuries. On the other hand, they become intensely pessimistic, as in our day, when the unmanageable forces of life seem to dwarf and defeat all human powers. A life based on immediate, empirical meanings does not often generate the vitality and courage to face tragedy, for in the nature of the case, the experience of tragedy strips a secular view of life of its only

possible ground of meaning. Nor can such a life relate its
small values to a permanent significance, and so escape the
sense of boredom and worthlessness. Unless men can answer the question "why am I here?" on an ultimate level,
there is no possibility of a continuing confidence in, and
an affirmation of, any meanings in life, be they small or
large.[21]

If, however, the meaning of life is founded upon a transcendent principle, and so is known by faith, then courage
and significance are possible even within apparent meaninglessness. If all that is is created and upheld by the
sovereign will of God, then existence has a coherence and a
meaning far beyond the balance of its momentary interrelationships. For its being as a whole is related, beyond
itself and beyond all its finite relations, to the very fount
of order and meaning through its creation by God. Despite any present incoherence in life, therefore, there is
"built in" to all the factors of life—nature, history, and
individual life alike—a meaning, a fundamental coherence,

[21] The paralysis of spirit when no ultimate purpose for existence is known is powerfully expressed by Thomas Mann in the
following description of the plight of Hans Kastorp: "A man lives
not only his personal life as an individual, but also, consciously
or unconsciously, the life of his epoch and of his contemporaries
. . . All sort of personal aims, ends, hopes, prospects hover before the eyes of the individual, and out of these he derives the
inspiration to ambition and achievement. Now, if the life about
him, if his own time seem, however outwardly stimulating, to be
at bottom empty of such food for his aspirations; if he privately
recognizes it to be hopeless, viewless, helpless, opposing only a
hollow silence to all the questions man puts, consciously or unconsciously, yet somehow puts, as to the final, absolute, and abstract meaning in all his efforts and activities; then, in such a
case, a certain laming of the personality is bound to occur, the
more inevitably the more upright the character in question; a sort
of palsy, as it were, which may even extend from his spiritual
and moral over into his physical and organic part. In an age that
affords no satisfying answer to the eternal question of 'Why?'
'To what end . . . ?' [only the exceptional man escapes medi-
ocrity]." Thomas Mann, *The Magic Mountain*, Alfred A. Knopf,
1947, p. 32.

and a purpose which they receive from their source. A man or a culture that knows this by faith can have confidence, whatever his situation amid the finite factors of life, however conclusive the evidence at the moment may seem that "truth is forever on the scaffold, wrong forever on the throne." His courage is not dependent upon the ups and downs of history, or the variability of his own small aims, hopes, and prospects. He knows the Creator of all and thus he knows that, whatever life may look like to his immediate observation, life is good, for God has made it. And he knows that his own life and works, if related to this deeper purpose of God, can participate in an ultimate significance which can give continuing value to his own small ends. Through his certainty that at the origin of his existence there is not an unknown abyss, but God, he can escape the meaninglessness of a life subject to external fortune and inner futility. In any situation he can find courage and meaning.

Our contemporary Western naturalism has inherited from its Christian background this deep confidence in life or process *per se*. Hence the devastating effects on meaning which its denial of an ultimate origin and an ultimate coherence in God logically bring have not yet been felt by our secular culture. Because, however, it scorns the idea of a transcendent creator, naturalism has divested itself of the sole intelligible basis for its own faith that process can involve fulfillment and significance. Only if existence as a whole comes under the purposive will of God is there the slightest ground for confidence in its ultimate meaning. And only if we can grasp some assurance of life's ultimate coherence and purpose can we affirm the immediate meanings of our day-to-day life. For as the Greeks and Hindus knew well, if historical meanings are based solely on the finite powers of human reason and freedom, there is then no basis in history or experience to believe that other nonrational forces, either within or without man, will not be continually victorious over creative human purposes. Thus it would not be at all surprising if to modern secular man also, the aspect of the ongoing process, which now appears to him as "benevolent," should change and become, as it did for the Greeks, the inscrutable and soulless visage of Blind Fate.

The New Value of Material Existence

2. The idea of creation not only set man's life within an ultimate context of coherence and significance; it also gave to the essential structure of concrete creaturely life a reality and value that it had never had before. Finite existence, as we actually experience it, is immersed in space and time, enmeshed in a body, and related to each event and person in its environment by strong emotional bonds. These fundamental conditions of creaturely life were in biblical faith seen to be good because God created the totality of all these factors. On this issue, too, the classical attempt to understand the meaning and goodness of life solely in terms of the observable elements in our experience ultimately defeated itself. Developed classical culture understood the meaning of human life to be based on what seemed to their observation to be the most creative power within existence: rational order. In their experience this order has revealed itself in two general forms: the harmonizing power of reason in nature and in the human self, and the law and order of the city state in the community. Because they thought that nature and human nature were a rational "cosmos" governed by rational laws, and the community a political "cosmos" governed by its divine laws, they believed that existence as a whole and human society in particular had the possibility of fulfillment. The meaning of life for the Greeks was founded on the power of reason to impose its order on the unformed stuff of man's individual and communal life.

This view of life's meaning, however, denied a creative role to the material and dynamic aspects of existence. If rational order is the source of meaning, then clearly all that negates or resists that order, and all that in no way participates in it, will be viewed as antithetical to meaning. But then the dynamic, emotional, and material elements of life become negative, because they represent the powers in man's existence that seem to upset the cool, ordering self-control of the mind. Thus in philosophy, in political theory, and in religion alike, the value and creativity of the emotions and of bodily vitality were progressively negated in Greek thought. The result was that as the culture developed, the body came to be shunned and abhorred as a meaningless "tomb," and all emotional attachments rejected if life was to be fulfilled.[22] The goal of individual human life was a rigid rational self-control, involving on the one hand a state of total indifference to bodily needs and feelings, and on the other an emotional passionlessness and withdrawal. Correspondingly, the goal of society was an unchanging order of life in which no spontaneous variety or emotional ties were allowed.[23] In neither case could this culture find value or reality in vital and emotional forces. Existence is seen as a mixture of two antithetical principles, form and matter. The problem of life revolves around their inevitable antithesis, and the fulfillment of life was achieved by the conquest and the repression of the one by the other. In its optimistic phase, classical culture felt that mind could successfully order and control vitality and matter. In its pessimistic period, this control was believed to be only a rare preliminary to flight from the whole material realm, where the soul—or as Plotinus called it, "the real man"—was quite free from the burden of emotional and material existence.

[22] For example, let us look at the following from the Stoic Epictetus: "Let him then who wishes to be free not wish for anything or avoid anything that depends on others; or else he is bound to be a slave. . . . If it ever happens to you to be directed to things outside, so that you desire to please another, know that you have lost your life's plan." *The Manual of Epictetus*, Sections 14, 23, from *The Stoic and Epicurean Philosophers*, pp. 471, 473.

[23] See Plato's Republic, Books 4–6, and *The Laws*, as well as the Stoic writings of Marcus Aurelius.

With the introduction of the Christian faith into the classical world, a new attitude to the material, dynamic, and emotional forces of life appears. Consequently, as the culture developed, there resulted an appreciation of concrete historical life unknown in the ancient world. Here existence was not seen as split down the middle between a meaningful ordering principle and a meaningless dynamic and material factor. Rather, according to the Christian idea of creation, each finite being in all its aspects was called into existence by God's purposive will. Thus every facet of an entity and every significant factor in man's life is potentially creative, and involved essentially in any real human fulfillment. The divine is no longer *one* of the elements of existence, thus reducing the others in value. Rather the divine is the source of *all* aspects of being so that all share in value.[24] God had created matter as well as form, the early church asserted; hence material being is

[24] The change in the status of the dynamic and emotional forces of life is nowhere seen more clearly than in Augustine's view of God and of man. In Greek thought the divine was purely formal order, and was separated from emotions which for the Greeks spelled only dependence and need. Correspondingly man's perfection lay within his intellectual, and not his emotional, existence, and so his salvation was to suppress and escape the emotional in passionlessness. In Augustine, however, God is not only Eternal Being and Truth but Love as well; and all three are fully and equally divine: "For the essence of God, whereby He is, has altogether nothing changeable, neither in eternity, nor in truth, nor in will; since there truth is eternal, love eternal; and there love is true, eternity true; and there eternity is loved, and truth is loved." Augustine, *De Trinitate*, Book IV, Preface.

Correspondingly man, as made in God's image, not only exists and knows; equally he loves, and "delights in his being." In each case the emotional category is as real and as important as the categories of being and of order. The result is a certainty within self-awareness of the existence and value of concrete life unknown before: "For we both are, and know that we are, and delight in our being and our knowledge of it . . . But, without any delusive representation of images or phantasms, I am most certain that I am, and that I know and delight in this." Augustine, *The City of God*, Book XI, Chapter 26.

not in itself meaningless, since its existence is a result of the divine will. God, who is Himself love as well as rationality, had given to man feelings and affections; these were, therefore, good and not to be denied but purified. Thus, as opposed to the contemporary pagan writers, Christians insisted that the whole man included body as well as soul, and would be "saved" only within the body and not by its loss. And they also declared that human fulfillment included a reorientation of the emotions and the mind alike, rather than the denial of the one and the supremacy of the other. The basic problem of life, therefore, was no longer the achievement of the victory of one factor of man's nature over another. Rather the central issue of life hinged on the relation of every aspect of man's being, "heart, soul, and mind," to his Creator. In a positive relation of creature and Creator, all the aspects of life, including even the physical and emotional, became essential parts of human fulfillment and human meaning. Having come from God, they could, if used in the service of God, become contributing factors in a meaningful life. Western man was thus pointed toward the discovery of a meaningful historical existence: for under God he could now learn to accept, to appreciate, and to improve his own bodily life in material nature, and his emotional life in human community.

Finally, as a result of this same reinterpretation of existence, the unity, the reality, and the meaning of each individual existent is for the first time fully and powerfully affirmed. In classical culture the formal structure of an entity, be it of a man, a state, or of an object, was its principle of reality and of value. Now this formal structure is what every individual within a species has in common with every other individual. All men, said Plato, participate in the same Idea of Manness, and all men, said Aristotle, have the same form. What distinguished one man from another was the material element in which the common form was embodied. Individual uniqueness, what makes a person distinctively "himself," was seen to be grounded not at the highest point of man's nature, in his unique spirit or personness, but in the less real and less valuable strata of his existence, in his bodily life. Because man was "cut in two" between a universal and general spiritual part and an individuating and lesser material part, the individual person in his concrete uniqueness was viewed as an unfortunate deviation from the generic type, rather than as the goal and crown of creation.

According to the idea of creation, however, the creative act of God was the source of more than the form, which was shared by the other members of the species. God's act was understood to be the direct source of the total being of the unique individual. This total being was shared with no other individual, for it included, along with the common formal structure, those very elements of material, vital, and spiritual existence which differentiated the individual as an unique entity from others of his kind. The whole man, and therefore the unique man, had been created by God in all his wholeness and uniqueness. Because it was directly the result of God's creative act, individual being, rather than universal form, became the locus of meaning and value. Thus again a transcendent principle of creation became the source of a new meaning where one would least expect to find it, in the status of persons as unique, individual existents.

Man's New Role in History

3. Perhaps the most fundamental reorientation which the idea of God's creation effected, however, was in giving a new status to man's existence within history. Since man's life is lived in history as well as in material nature, a positive evaluation of the meaningfulness of historical life is necessary if life is to be considered good. We shall return to this topic when we discuss the problem of time; let us introduce it in this context.

First of all, the new appreciation of the material, dynamic, and individual aspects of existence which Christianity brought gave historical existence a new meaning. History takes place within material nature, and its meaningfulness can never be affirmed if the goodness of the natural setting of life is denied. Moreover, the actors in history are whole men, bodies and spirits, creatures in the full sense of that term, not eternal ideas or subsistent souls. Hence a fundamental shift from the classical concentration on eternal and necessary forms to the Christian concern for contingent, material, and particular existences was necessary to create a real concern for history, either in individual beings or in mankind as a whole. No longer did material and natural life stand for an essential separation from the soul's true home in eternity. Rather, in the Christian view, history has a direct link with ultimate meaning, since it was for life in nature and in history that we had been purposely created by God, and in which we are called to serve God with all our physical powers and all our unique individual gifts. In the idea of creation, then, neither the bodily basis for man's historical life nor the natural setting for his actions in history are negated. Because both nature and time are seen as a part of the essential and important purpose of God, Christianity, in contrast to the emphasis of late Hellenic thought on the sole value of the spiritual and eternal world, regarded nature and history as arenas within which important and significant events could take place.[25]

[25] On this point of the relation of creation to ultimately significant historical events, it is interesting to note that those Gnostic groups who denied that a real incarnation of the divine into "flesh" and temporality was possible also denied that God had created the world. To many of them material and temporal existence was the product of an inferior, evil demiurge and so was in itself antithetical to all meaning and goodness. Hence to them it was inconceivable that in that realm a divine and ultimately significant event could occur. Christian thinkers, such as Irenaeus and Tertullian, saw clearly, therefore, that the doctrine of creation was a necessary basis for the possibility of crucial historical events, and so of the incarnation, and thus that the church's Gospel of Jesus Christ depended on the prior assertion that God was the "Maker of heaven and earth."

It was not, however, only its positive evaluation of physical and temporal existence which made the idea of creation fruitful of a sense of history. Many primitive naturalistic religions have revered the natural setting of man's
life, and the material and physical powers important to
him, and yet such cultures had no concern for or understanding of history. History is enacted in nature, and therefore is never valued if nature is viewed as essentially evil.
But history also transcends nature, and therefore a dimension of life deeper than the natural must be seen if
history is to be regarded as meaningful.

The life of nature always impressed the thoughtful in
early civilizations as cyclical and impersonal in character.
They noted that the fundamental rhythm of nature was
the recurrence of the coming to be and the passing away of
vegetative and animal life, and that individual entities
were really only instruments for this repetitive renewal
of the species. In the natural cycle, therefore, no essentially
new elements or unrepeatable events that are of more than
momentary significance appear. For while particular and
unique events may affect the individuals of a species, such
happenings rarely influence the species as a whole. Consequently views of life drawn from a reverence for nature
invariably emphasized repetition, and were never able to
affirm the unique, the personal, and the historical.[26] Furthermore, because there is neither freedom nor mind in
nature, no new creative kinds of events happen, and no

[26] Anyone who has seen the beautiful natural wildlife films
of the Disney Studios, for example *Perri*, will quickly absorb this
cyclical mood. In attempting to portray nature's fundamental
workings, these photographers inevitably adopt the full cycle of
the year's seasons as their fundamental structure of meaning; and
they find significance in this cycle of growth and decay, of birth
and death, in the fact that the individual animals within the
cycle are, by their life and death, maintaining the ever-recurrent
processes of natural life. If this same cyclical understanding of
the life of nature's animals were to be applied to the totality of
existence, natural and historical, one would come very close to
the mood of ancient naturalism.

departures from the past are remembered and conserved. To the eyes of the ordinary observer, therefore, there is and can be no dynamic and cumulative, no historical character to natural life.[27] Apparently what has always been will always be again, and so the life of the individual entity or of the social organism is submerged in the impersonal, recurrent cycles of nature. If, then, man's life is understood solely in the terms of his natural environment, as occurs in nonidealistic Greek thought and in much modern philosophy, history disappears within the cycles of nature, and the unique freedom of historical existence, with its significant and unrepeatable events, never appears in permanent strength.

History takes on meaning, then, when man not only sees himself as a creature in a "good" nature, but, more importantly, has distinguished himself from nature. He must realize that he alone among God's creatures is not completely dominated by nature; he must become conscious of his own unique capacity for self-direction and meaning, and therefore of being in some sense transcendent to the repetitive natural order in which he participates. Only then does an awareness of those elements of purpose, freedom, uniqueness, and individuality, which are the stuff of history, arise. Essential, therefore, to a sense of the real character of history and its development is a comprehension of man which sees both the contrast between man and nature and the embeddedness of man

[27] In this sense, the modern idea of evolutionary development is a triumph of historical categories of thought in the natural sciences. For, according to this view, there is an irreversible, cumulative development that lies behind the repetitive cycles of the life of the species. Consequently what has been, will not always be, since the new, the creative, and the unique do appear in nature. It is no accident that this triumph of the categories of history over those of nature occurred in the nineteenth century, when the conception of a dynamic history had become assumed throughout the West, and that this entire concept of an irreversible, dynamic, and meaningful history developed in a culture long saturated with biblical concepts of time.

within nature. If man is understood as totally out of relation to nature because he is regarded as purely soul or
mind, or if man is understood as totally immersed in nature and so as purely creature, then no understanding of
history arises. Greek idealism lost a sense of history because it could not understand the value of the natural
world and of time; Greek naturalism never achieved historical consciousness because it understood existence only
in terms of the cycles of natural life. In either case, man
understands the meaning of his life in such a way that his
existence as a unique, creative and historical being is
buried underneath either his concern for a return to eternity or his concern for his relations to natural and tribal
forces.

The Christian doctrine of creation provided just the
framework needed for a positive appreciation of man's
historical existence. It is no surprise, therefore, that the
doctrine of creation and a developed philosophy of history
entered Western culture together. As we have noted, in
Christian faith man is seen as a creaturely part of God's
total creation, all of whose aspects are the result of a divinely purposed act. Hence man's goal is not to escape a
meaningless natural and temporal environment and to flee
from the world. Rather he has been placed by God here
in this concrete moment for a particular historical "calling"
as a part of the divine plan. Obedient service, not flight,
is thus the mark of piety, and such service is an historical
enterprise involving material, emotional, purposive, and
communal action. The Christian understanding of man
as a material creature made the spatiotemporal locus of
history a meaningful object of man's concern under God.

In biblical faith, however, man was also understood as
more than nature, as a creature made in "the image of
God." The fundamental orientation of man's life was
thus to God his Creator and to God's will, rather than to
the creaturely world around him. The real tension in the
existence of biblical man was that which he felt before
God's judgment, not what he experienced in the face of

natural powers. And the real hope of his life was in God's grace and salvation, not in the return of the vegetative powers of fertility. Thus while he saw himself as a creature with inescapable natural needs ("give us this day our daily bread"), nevertheless biblical man understood himself as a being related more fundamentally to God than to the nature that surrounded him. As a creature of God, related in faith and obedience beyond nature to the transcendent Lord of nature, he distinguished himself from all other natural creatures ("he shall have dominion over all creatures"), he had no ultimate fear of natural powers ("the fear of the *Lord* is the beginning of wisdom"), and he regarded the aim of his life to be his fidelity in historical action to the covenant of his nation with the Lord. Under God he had been freed from ultimate subservience to natural forces, and had become a conscious, creative participant in history.

In the Old Testament this struggle between man as a purely natural creature and man as a historical being is reflected in the conflict over the worship of the fertility Baalim or of Yahweh, the Lord of history. In the victory over the Baalim as the ultimate powers of man's life, we witness, therefore, a crucial break with man's subservience to nature, similar in power and scope to the transcendence over nature which Greek philosophical idealism represented. The difference between these two departures from primitive natural life, however, is significant for the consciousness of history. While Greek philosophy transcended nature into eternity, biblical thought transcended nature into the realm of history. Biblical man is historical man; a creature of the Lord of history, man is both a part of a good nature and also transcendent in spirit, in freedom, and so in creativity to the order of the natural world. When man has this sense of a meaningful participation in the natural world, plus a sense of transcendence over it, then there is possible a complete understanding of the full dimensions of human existence. Only when man sees his life as coming from a source beyond nature, and yet creative of it, does man live as man, embedded in nature and yet at the same time a creative participant in history.

In these various ways the idea of creation provided the basis for a confidence that finite life in all its concreteness, its materiality, its individuality, and its temporality, was potentially meaningful and good. For the belief in God the Creator established the certain hope for human fulfillment, rather than frustration, and for creative, meaningful historic activity, rather than resignation and renunciation. To the Christian, nothing in all of existence was essentially or by necessity alien to the true purposes of each human creature, since all that is came from the same will, which gave its purpose to each finite being. And further, no aspect of man's life, either his bodily or his emotional nature, was necessarily opposed to his fulfillment, since each of these aspects had been given him by God as a creative part of his full being. Finally, since he now saw himself as a finite creature whose central relation is to God his Lord and Maker, man discovered a new meaning and dignity to his historical existence. Tempted neither to submerge his existence in nature nor to flee to eternity, he found himself called by God to discover the meaning of his life in historical service in the here and now. Thus through the Christian faith, and especially through its belief in creation, Western man was led to affirm the potential goodness of finite historical life. Despite its essential contingency, life is good because it holds the possibility of fulfillment within its experienced conditions of materiality, concreteness, and temporality—for all that is has its ultimate source in the purposive will of God.

In this chapter we have by no means exhausted the question of the goodness of life. Every facet of meaning which we have mentioned is daily threatened by what we men call evil. We have merely sought to show that for Christians there is nothing essentially and structurally wrong with life, as if by being born we entered meaninglessness. We have therefore established one of the most significant of Christian affirmations about evil: that it is an "intruder" into an existence which is structurally and potentially good. How Christianity understands this unwanted intrusion and the relation of evil to the Gospel are problems for our two succeeding chapters.

Chapter 7

CREATION AND EVIL

Our attention in the last two chapters has been focused on the Christian affirmation that creation is good. We have discovered that the world as we experience it is a contingent world, in which each fact and entity is dependent on forces beyond it, and so a world whose order and meaning are not easily evident. We have also discovered that for the Christian this contingent creation can be a realm of intelligible order and of potential meaning, because it is created by God's wisdom and for his purposes. In Christian belief, we are not born into an arbitrary, chaotic world, nor are we thrust into an existence that necessarily involves suffering and meaninglessness. These two aspects of contingent finitude, its potential intelligibility and its potential meaningfulness, are the foundations of its goodness. Without them, created existence would be essentially evil and could never become good at all—and resignation and flight from life would be the only valid answers to our own ultimate questions.

While these foundations are necessary if life is to be called meaningful, nevertheless our experience indicates that by themselves alone they are by no means sufficient to establish the goodness of life. For "evil" bestrides our existence like a conqueror. God's creation may be as theoretically intelligible and as potentially good as we have said, but the practical fact is that it is suffused with evil of all kinds. By evil we mean that which thwarts continuously and seriously the potential goodness of creation, destroy-

ing alike its intelligibility and meaning and making life as
we experience it so threatening, so full of sorrow, suffering,
and apparent pointlessness. Historically the presence of
this undeniable evil in the world has been the most powerful argument against a religious interpretation of the
world. And there can be little question that for many sincere Christians, both the intellectual question of evil and
vivid personal experiences of evil, in war and disease, in
sin and death, have done more to shake their faith in
God than anything else. If, then, Christians are to affirm
with conviction their faith in God as the source of a good
creation, they must do so on the basis of a faith that is
able both to comprehend and to overcome the evil that is
so evident an aspect of their existence. In this chapter
we shall discuss the Christian comprehension of this
strange fact of evil; in the next we shall be concerned
with the Christian conquest of evil.

First of all, the theologian must admit to the thoughtful
inquirer that the existence of evil poses no such intellectual problems for other points of view as it does for the
Christian faith. In fact, in secular philosophies of life the
presence of evil seems to be a continual confirmation of
their basic principles. The task of philosophy is to describe existence as the philosopher finds it. Thus when he
finds evil pervasive throughout existence, he assumes it
to be the natural result of the structure of things. In each
philosophy, therefore, what we call evil is explained as
the product of some basic factor or aspect of existence.
In dualism it is said to arise from matter, in monism from
the universal facts of ignorance and of individuality, and
in naturalism from the blind workings of natural forces. In
each case, evil is made intelligible because its cause is
found in some essential structure of experience and reality.
Consequently whenever evil appears, it is no surprise; the
philosopher is not taken off guard; evil does not upset the
careful rationality of his system, because its presence illustrates one of the basic principles of the system. Only
if existence is *supposed* to be better than it is, is the pres-

ence of evil puzzling to the philosopher and embarrassing to his philosophy, and this assumption no descriptive philosophy can make. Thus in dualism, monism, or naturalism, we find points of view that are quite free of the intellectual problem of evil which disturbs the Christian thinker. They should be reminded, however, that they have not by explaining it, banished the *reality* of evil from existence, and that it may be a more difficult matter to deal creatively with the evil we experience in life than it is to outline its causes in one's philosophy.

The Intellectual Dilemma for Christianity

For the Christian, on the other hand, the presence of evil seems to disprove rather than to strengthen every one of his leading convictions. Especially is this true of the idea of creation, which poses the question of evil in its most baffling form. Indeed, each implication of *creatio ex nihilo* seems to make evil more and more unintelligible and inexplicable. The first affirmation of *creatio ex nihilo,* that God is the source of all that is, means that He is ultimately responsible for the totality of all that exists: no aspect of the universe exists apart from Him, and no nook or cranny of the universe is closed to His overwhelming power. Since all that is comes from Him and is upheld solely by Him, there is apparently no "place" from which evil could come except from God or from what He directly creates. How then can the Christian ever make sense of evil if he insists that an omnipotent and yet loving God created the world? It seems plain that in the face of evil the skeptic must be right: either a good God did not create all that there is, or else He who created all is not good.

Furthermore, the idea of creation affirms that finite creatures are real and good. The reality of the finite means that the relations between them, and so their experiences of these relations, are not illusory or imaginary but real. Whenever there is conflict or suffering in the finite we are dealing with a real aspect of the world. The goodness of finitude means, moreover, that the innate goal of finitude is its own fulfillment, that the purpose of creaturely existence is that each of God's creatures achieve the fullest excellence of which its nature is capable. Any thwarting of fulfillment, therefore, is really a wrong against the basic purpose of creation itself. Thus for the Christian there can be no question of denying or minimizing the reality or terribleness of evil by saying "It only seems bad to us." Our feeling that things are not as they should be cannot be blamed on our lack of perspective, as if from God's point of view all was well. Whenever a creature confronts or experiences fundamental frustration or suffering, whenever its fulfillment is basically thwarted by death, or by perversion, there real evil occurs.

Finally, this point is driven even further home by the last important affirmation of the doctrine of creation, that God is in some sense "personal," and that therefore we can speak to Him as intentionally and purposefully creating and upholding His creatures. Christian piety has always assumed that this means God knows and cares so completely for each one of His creatures, great or small, that if "five sparrows are sold for two farthings, not one is forgotten before God."[1] The teachings of Jesus make crystal clear that what happens to each person in space and time "counts" for God, and is continually the object of His loving concern. An impersonal absolute or an underlying substance might be blissfully unconscious of the individual sufferings of finitude, because the discordance of these sufferings was resolved, like the minor chords of a symphony, in the total harmony of the whole. But a "personal" God, who knows and cares for each individual creature in and for itself, has no such easy escape from finite suffering. To such a God the total harmony of the universe cannot compensate for the suffering of an individual creature. Thus for Christian faith evil, as the suffering and frustra-

[1] Luke 12: 6–7.

tion of God's creatures, is not only a real fact in itself; even more, it is significant for God Himself.

In fact, the whole message of the Christian Gospel is ultimately based on the assertion that the evils and sufferings that oppress men's lives are so real and so significant to God that He wills to share them and bear them for men. Therefore it is fatal to the structure of Christian belief if evil is either minimized in its intensity or understood so that it becomes unreal to God.[2] In this sense it could be argued that Christian faith takes evil more seriously than any other viewpoint. For idealism, eternity remains untouched by the sufferings of the finite, and evil becomes finally an illusion of our ignorance. For naturalism, where there is no eternity, suffering has no ultimate significance, since it dies with each creature that dies: where nothing is of more than passing significance, evil can have no real status and meaning. For Christian faith, however, evil is intensely real and not only to those creatures who suffer from it. Indeed, it "cries out to heaven itself," and there, according to the Christian Gospel, it leaves its mark on God's love, so that He becomes "mighty to save."

Evil, then, is real and terrible to God and to His creatures alike; and yet if it comes from anywhere, it must have come from some intended part of God's creation. This is the intellectual dilemma with which a Christian believer is faced when he surveys the world. As we shall

[2] This is why most philosophical and many theological solutions to the problem of evil in terms of a "transcendent harmony" are not helpful to the Christian. It is a denial of God's care for each creature to say, whether with Plotinus, Augustine, Thomas, Bradley, or Whitehead, that since the disharmonies on the finite level become harmonious from the divine perspective, evil is a resolvable problem. What these philosophers are in fact saying is that for God, or at least from His perspective, evil as experienced by finite creatures is not real, but only an error due to a finite point of view. But this is to deny two basic Christian affirmations: (1) that no real aspect of finite experience is an "illusion," and (2) that God is concerned with precisely the finite creature as it exists here and now.

see, there are various ways in which he can make the presence of evil partially intelligible in Christian terms. Especially is this true of the human evil we call sin. For sin
comes from the misuse of man's freedom, which is a part
of God's good creation. But those other aspects of evil
which seem the direct result of the given character of creation are not so easily understood: the conflict in nature of
life with life, with all the suffering that it entails; the
natural evils that plague man's existence, such as floods,
famines, plagues, sickness, and insanity; and finally the
universal and often tragic scourge of death—these are traits
of existence which can never be fitted intelligibly by our
minds into the pattern of God's creation. For them there
is and can be no completely rational explanation in terms
of a Christian understanding of life. Christians can understand why such an explanation is impossible to them, and
thus be content with a faith that gives them the courage
to face all forms of evil. But it is well to admit at the outset that Christian faith, in contrast to many another philosophy, has no complete intellectual solution to the problem of natural evil.

The question of evil, then, is no subsidiary issue for
Christian faith. The reality of evil in our world is at
once the greatest intellectual threat to the convincing
power of Christian theology, and the single characteristic
of our human existence which gives to Christian faith its
continual meaning and creative power in men's lives. On
the one hand, as we have shown, everything that Christians say about God and about their life seems contradicted by this pervasive fact of evil. And yet on the other
hand, it is true that everything Christians believe about
God and about human life, provides the only force strong
enough to conquer the radical power of evil over men's
minds and hearts. Surprisingly enough, when we explore
the Christian interpretation of evil more deeply, we find
that those very Christian affirmations that raise the intellectual problem of evil with such intensity become the
conditions for its ultimate defeat in obedience and faith.

Let us, therefore, look more closely at these Christian affirmations that both raise and conquer the problem of evil.

The Christian Understanding of Evil

Certainly that affirmation which seems most clearly to be contradicted by the presence of evil is the claim that the essential structure of finitude is good. Nevertheless it is this claim which gives to the Christian interpretation of evil its unique power to understand human sin, and to the Christian believer his unique confidence and hope in the conquest of evil in life. For the real significance of the idea of the good creation is that finitude is not essentially and so inescapably characterized by its experienced evil. On the contrary, if finitude was created good, then the evil of existence is a perversion of the essential nature of our life, not an inevitable characteristic of it. Consequently if human life could be returned to its essential nature, if it could find itself again, evil would no longer be its dominant trait. "Rebirth" and "New Life" for man are only possible in a world whose basic structure is good, and the gloomy alternatives of resignation or flight cease to be the only answers to life's problems. The idea of the good creation, therefore, is in no sense a denial of evil. Rather this conviction has been the sole condition for understanding evil as a *perversion* rather than a *necessity* of our existence, and so for understanding human life as redeemable. The belief that creation was essentially good was one of the deepest reasons that Christianity came into the old world as a message of joy and hope.

We can perhaps appreciate the significance of this Christian understanding of evil as perversion if we look again at the other explanations of evil. As we have noted, philosophical explanations of the appearance of evil provide a rational answer to our question: "Where did it come from?" But involved in this ability to satisfy our minds on the intellectual level is an incapacity on the "existential" level. For these philosophies are quite unable to provide any grounds for hope or confidence that actual evil can ever be removed from personal, social, or historical existence. The very rationality of their explanation, namely that evil is an essential aspect of existence, accounts for the depth and permanence of their pessimism, namely that, as an essential aspect of existence, evil will continue to be as it always was. Philosophy has been able to provide serenity in the face of an evil that was intelligible because it was necessary; but it concurrently has prompted resignation and despair because of that same necessity.

As we noted earlier, in dualistic philosophy the presence of evil is rational because it is caused by one of the constituent elements of being, namely matter. But, by the same token, evil is a necessary aspect of finitude as such. Since finite existence arises out of the very mixture of matter and form which causes evil, the career of finitude and the presence of evil exactly coincide. The only way to eradicate evil in dualism is thus to "unmix the mixture" which comprises creaturely existence, and to let the soul rise out of its bodily prison into eternity again. So long as one remains finite, and therefore a mixture of form with matter, one is immersed in evil.

If we consider the second great philosophical alternative, monism, again we find that finitude and evil cannot be separated. In monism "sin," suffering, ignorance, and error are explained because each finite center of consciousness mistakenly regards itself as a real locus or point of experience and value. It says "I" to this experience and this thought, and "mine" to this or that object. It is therefore immersed in the fortunes and the passions of a finite ego, sinning through selfishness, and suffering through its concern with things, objects, and people. Evil is experienced because each finite center is ignorant of its true identity with the Whole, where selfishness is lost in the loss of the self, and where the suffering of each individual is transmuted into mere shadows within the tapestry of the Whole. Thus for monism evil progressively disappears as finitude disappears; the individual's burdens of sin and suffering vanish to the exact extent that his concern for and concentration on his own individual finite experience vanishes. The presence of evil in finite experience is rationally explained because finite experience in itself is evil, a "fall" from the unity and harmony of the One. But for the same reason, no redemption of the creature is possible, for creaturehood and suffering are understood to appear and to disappear together.

Finally, the most pervasive of contemporary viewpoints, naturalism, reflects the same inherent pessimism in the face of the question of evil. For it, evil is a fully intelligible aspect of human experience, because creaturely life is the product of natural causes without purpose or direction. Manifestly these causes at times are to us creative and good, since they combine to produce man and his values; but equally clearly they are destructive and evil, since the same forces conspire to remove him again. What we call "evil" is, therefore, to be expected for finite creatures because they are subject to powerful but blind forces beyond their control, all-determining powers which buffet them from without and propel them helplessly from within. The basis of our existence and our values is a purposeless, material flux—what is more natural then that we and our values alike, created by the flux, should also be endlessly destroyed by it? Consequently, only where the naturalist appeals to the modern faith in cosmic progress, or where he asserts that man's reason and will can benevolently dominate these forces of destiny, is naturalism able to escape a mood of utter pessimism about life. But such appeals to cosmic purpose, and to a benevolent and free human wisdom, contravene the naturalist's own principle of blind causation and the cumulative evidence of our experience. Whenever it remains true to its own methods and insights, therefore, naturalism culminates in the same "dread of finitude" which characterizes dualism and monism, and which certainly pervaded the mood of all ancient naturalistic philosophy.[3] In each case, the attempt to make evil completely intelligible results only in an overpowering sense of evil's necessity.

In contrast to these philosophical accounts of evil, traditional Christian faith has understood evil not as the realization of finite nature but as its distortion. Since God was believed to have created everything that is, nothing in existence could be "by nature" evil. The essential structure of finite beings: their individuality, their existence in space and time, their contingency, their materiality, the animal characteristics of vitality and motion, and the human equipment of emotions, intelligence, memory, and foresight, were all regarded as good because they were creatures of God's purpose. None of them, therefore, could be the cause of evil, for then God would be its cause. On the contrary, in a good creation evil could arise only when these good things were misused, distorted, and perverted. For Christian thought, therefore, evil arose only from freedom. For freedom was just the kind of finite structure which, although good in itself as a creation of God, nevertheless had the capacity to pervert and distort itself, and so to misuse both its own powers and its own goods. Freedom was the capability of man to turn from God to himself, to make his own pleasure and security rather than obedience to God his ultimate end, and so to come to hate his neighbor rather than to love him. Freedom is the mystery of the self as the spontaneous center of its own reactions and activities, the self-transcendence of man which makes him able to *use* his own powers. It is what transforms man from a thing to a person,

[3] George Santayana is an excellent example of a modern naturalist who refuses either to minimize the reality of evil and suffering, or to introduce an illicit principle of progressive development into his system. The result is the same "dread of finite existence," and the same resignation and retirement from life, that characterized ancient naturalistic philosophy. Cf. especially his book *The Realm of Spirit*, Charles Scribner's Sons, 1942.

from an object to a subject.[4] At one and the same time, freedom is the essential structure of man that gives human life its uniqueness and value, and also its potentiality for evil. For by the same capacity freely to will to cleave to God and thereby to fulfill himself, man is able also to will his separation from God and the consequent distortion of his nature. Because of freedom, the essential goodness of creaturely life has a possibility of becoming evil.

The biblical conviction that all of creation is good led, therefore, to the insight that human evil has its seat solely in man's freedom. So long as men did not know God the Creator of all, they could blame evil on matter, individuality, or process, on the "fate" of being finite rather than on themselves. Thus the ancient world had strong concepts neither of man's freedom nor of his responsibility: man was the victim of creation rather than its distorter. And thus the ancient world knew no possibility of redemption within finitude and history. Since evil arose from the essential nature of finitude, man could escape from evil only by a flight from finitude into eternity. In a good creation, however, it was seen that evil could arise only from the capacity to misuse what is good, namely from human freedom. And consequently Christian man became suddenly conscious of his own great potentialities for spontaneous creativity, of his unlimited responsibility for evil, and

[4] Scientists who say they discover no such freedom in their investigations of man would do well to direct their attention, not upon man as an object of scientific inquiry—and so inevitably stripped of his freedom as "subject"—but on man as the inquirer, upon themselves as scientists. There they would, by introspection, find a curiosity to know, a commitment to the truth, and a conviction that tested hypotheses are to be asserted because they are true—all of which presuppose freedom. For if all of these—the curiosity, the commitment, and the assertion of the truth—are present in the scientist himself merely as determined effects of natural causes, then his scientific hypotheses have no status preferable to those resulting from indolence, prejudice, and superstition, which, on the hypothesis of determinism, are equally determined by natural causes and therefore equally "valid" or "invalid."

finally of the possibility of real rebirth. In his *Confessions*, Augustine vividly illustrates this Christian discovery of the mystery of the free self, and its relation to the good creation and to evil:

> . . . Although I . . . was firmly persuaded that Thou our Lord, the true God, who madest not only our souls but our bodies, and not our souls and bodies alone, but all creatures and all things, wast uncontaminable and inconvertible and in no part mutable, yet understood I not readily and clearly what was the cause of evil . . . for I perceived that through seeking after the origin of evil, they [the Manichean philosophers] were filled with malice, in that they liked better to think that Thy Substance did suffer evil than that their own did commit it.
>
> And I directed my attention to discern what I now heard, that free will was the cause of our doing evil, and Thy righteous judgment of our suffering it . . . But this raised me towards Thy light, that I knew as well that I had a will as that I had life: when, therefore, I was willing or unwilling to do anything, I was most certain that it was none but myself that was willing and unwilling; and immediately I perceived that there was the cause of my sin.[5]

For classical Christian thought, therefore, evil arose within a good creation solely from the freedom involved in that creation. Since its seat is in freedom rather than essential structure, evil is historical rather than ontological in character. As a part of the structure of man, freedom is ontological, and its presence in human life is necessary if man is to be man. But as the voluntary use of that structure, evil is historical, and its presence is never necessary if man is to be man. Evil "happens" because of freedom, but it does not need to happen; it is voluntary and

---

[5] Augustine, *The Confessions*, Book 7, Chapter 3. See also *The City of God*, Book 12, Chapter 8, for the same point.

so not a part of God's creation. The myth of the fall of Adam and Eve symbolically expresses with great clarity this relation of the structure of creation to its evil: in that story evil came "after" creation and not with it. What is said in this old story is permanent and valid: evil is an "intruder" into a good creation, and not a necessary aspect of it. It is the result of what finitude did with itself in freedom, not the result of finitude as such.

This insistence that evil of every sort is an "intruder" rather than an essential part of creation reaches its climax in the biblical presentation of weakness, suffering, and death as the results, not of our created finitude, but solely of the Fall. Nothing expresses so strongly as this the Christian apprehension of the goodness of creation and the historical character of evil. This understanding of evil is, then, the foundation for the Christian confidence that however much an essential aspect of things evil may now appear to be, it is never necessary and so need not be everlasting. As a perversion of nature rather than a part of its essence, evil can be removed. This is the deepest meaning of the idea of the good creation.

It follows from this understanding of evil that for the Christian mind evil is a mystery not to be fully resolved by any intellectual answer. It appears from "nowhere" in a creation whose totality came from and is dependent upon God. To find a rational explanation for evil would be to find a natural cause for it. But this would be to transform this whole Christian understanding of the nature of evil from a perversion into a necessity; and it would be to locate its source essentially within the necessary and impersonal structure of things rather than in the mystery of freedom. If sin is genuinely an act of freedom, then it is not subject to external determination, although it may be subject to external temptation. But this is a very different matter, since temptation implies freedom and not necessity. If, then, sin is not externally determined, *ipso facto* no reason can be given for it. For the finding of a "reason" would mean the discovery of just those determining causes which the concept of sin as perverted freedom excludes. Again Augustine provides the classic source for the ultimate "unexplainability" of evil in Christian thought:

> What was the efficient cause of their evil will? There is none. For what is it makes the will bad, when it is the will itself which makes the action bad? And consequently the bad will is the cause of the bad action, but nothing is the efficient cause of the bad will.[6]

And a modern expositor of Christian doctrine agrees:

> Sin, like freedom, is by hypothesis inexplicable, since moral action presupposes freedom in the sense of real choices . . . Any alleged explanation of the fact that all men sin is only a new determinism. If sin, universal as it is, is to be treated as a moral fact and not as a natural fact . . . it must remain inexplicable . . . Man's sinful will cannot be explained; it must remain as the one completely irrational fact in the world which God created, and saw to be "very good."[7]

Thus in all the explanations Christian theology has offered for the presence of evil, two aspects essential to its own basic understanding have been underscored. First of all, it stressed the historical "event" of the Fall when evil originated. It thereby emphasized that the source of evil is radically differentiated from the source of finite being. And secondly, it personified that event into a dramatic action, the fall of Lucifer and the fall of Adam, to emphasize that the ultimate seat of evils lies in the mystery of freedom, rather than in the essential structure of existence. These symbols are, as critics quickly point out,

---

[6] Augustine, *The City of God*, Book 12, Chapter 6. It should be noted that by thus stating that evil has no efficient, but only a "deficient" cause, Augustine is defending the biblical conception of evil as arising from freedom, not the Neoplatonic conception of evil as arising directly from non-being.

[7] Whale, J. S., *Christian Doctrine*, The Macmillan Co., 1946, pp. 49–50.

not "explanations." If they become explanations they destroy the Christian understanding of evil. Then the theological explanation of evil merely replaces the philosophical explanations, and evil becomes necessary "because Adam fell," rather than because of matter or of individuality. In either case, evil has ceased to be a mystery that permeates our existence, and becomes a problem that we explain rationally. Above all, it ceases to be a perversion of our freedom for which we are responsible, and becomes the necessary fate of our finitude. Christian symbols, such as the devil and the fall of Adam, are not attempts to rationalize evil. Rather they are symbols which seek to point to and to express the mysterious possibilities of human freedom, which we cannot fully explain but which we can in part understand. And they use language appropriate to the ultimate nature of that mystery, the language of event and of freedom.

On the other hand, what the orthodox Christian understanding of evil has lacked in explanatory power it makes up for in other respects. The Christian sense that evil has an "accidental" quality which renders it intellectually mysterious created the Christian confidence that evil could be removed and conquered through the power of God. Those very facets of the idea of creation which made evil absolutely inexplicable, the transcendent power of God, the goodness of creation, and the love of God, were the ultimate principles according to which the fear and dread of evil were conquered in Christian spirits. For Christian faith, because God is the transcendent source of all, the evil that men experience has no power and reality comparable to the power of God. The evil forces that seem to control an individual's destiny are in turn controlled by God—and thus the victory over evil is assured. As Paul so triumphantly proclaimed: "Nothing in all of creation can separate us from the love of God"—no evil is so essential an element of the structure of things that God's power cannot conquer it.

Secondly, because finitude is good, so that evil is a perversion and not a fulfillment of its essential structure, there is the possibility of a "new creature," which is the fulfillment of man and not his negation. Since no aspect of our nature is essentially evil, sin arises from our free spirit in turning away from God, not from our essential being. But the very freedom that permits us to turn from God, opens the possibility that we may return again to Him. And with that return to our Creator, our creaturehood is fulfilled and its goodness realized. In no alternative philosophical "explanation" of evil can the condition of creaturehood be separated from the condition of evil. In Christian faith, however, they are separated, for the "new creature" is the symbol of a finitude freed from its burden of inward sin and its fear of outward evil. Finally, it is the loving will of God that makes most baffling the presence of evil in God's world. And yet it is this uniquely Christian conviction which became for Christian believers the great rock upon which the Christian hope for fulfillment rested. Neither God's power over all "principalities and powers," nor the essential possibilities of man's life portrayed in the picture of Jesus, were the real sources of Christian confidence and courage—for that power may be indifferent to us and that perfection too transcendent for our capabilities. But because the early Christian community knew God's almighty power as forgiving and restoring love, their confidence and hope in the victory over evil burst into contagious flame. They were given a hope, a confidence, and a courage in the face of actual evil that the ancient world never knew. Those very aspects of the Christian understanding of evil that made it a mystery to philosophy made it also a conquest to the spirit—and Christian joy and hope were born.

The Causes of Natural Evil

In this chapter we have noted an important distinction between two sorts of evil in our experience. 1) There is evil which proceeds from "natural" causes uninfluenced by human motives and actions, such as insanity, disease, famine, flood, death, and the pervasive conflicts and cruelties of animal life. 2) There is that which seems to come from human freedom, and which can be included under the general category of "sin." We have seen how philosophy has tended to explain human sin in the terms which it found helpful in understanding natural evil—and also the problems of despair which that approach raised. Also we have seen how Christian theology has viewed the misuse of freedom as the most basic form of evil, and the insight into man's nature and the hope for man's redemption which that approach has fostered. In fact, Christian thought has been so conscious of freedom as the source of all evil that it has attempted to explain natural evil as the result of sin: suffering, weakness, and death have been regarded as the punishment of God for the free act of sin. To modern Christians, however, this understanding of natural evil is no longer convincing or desirable. Dependence, weakness, and mortality are too evidently parts of the structure of finitude to be conceived as results of sin. Rather they must be regarded as products of God's creation and understood, if at all, in that light. Secondly, few contemporary Christians can conceive of the Fall as a past historical act of Adam, for which God punished the entire race. Their conceptions both of primeval history and of God forbid such an understanding of the Fall and its effects.

A modern Christian understanding of natural evil, therefore, must seek to use the methods both of philosophy and of theology. First of all, it must try to uncover those aspects of the structure of God's creation which give rise to both its potentiality for goodness and the possibility of its tragedy. But secondly, it must use this method of philosophy only in such a way that the Christian understanding of sin as a result of freedom is not compromised. In thus understanding natural evil as a result of creation rather than of sin, Christian thought is not thereby reducing the power and hope of its Gospel. For the Gospel has never claimed to eradicate natural evil from men's lives: what it has offered is the conquest of sin, and in that victory the eradication of the fear and the meaninglessness of natural evil. Let us see, then, how natural evil may be partially understood to arise from the structure of God's good creation.

One of the important corollaries of the Christian idea of creation is that created beings are in their essential structure dependent and yet real. Since no creature causes itself, none can stand by itself independent of all else. All creatures are therefore dependent parts of the system of causal interrelationships which is our world: every creature is dependent on creatures beyond himself for his being and for his fulfillment. This mutual interdependence of all creatures is the natural basis for the human values of life. Not only our existence itself, but also the human capacities for knowledge, for community, and even for personality itself, arise out of our essential relations of dependence on nature, on society, and on those we love, and would be inconceivable without that original dependence. But this same interdependence of all creation that gives each entity existence, and makes of man a self, makes each creature vulnerable in turn to outside influences, to insecurity of life, and ultimately to destruction. The contingent dependence of creaturely life is the basis both of its creative power and goodness, and of its capacity to suffer from natural evils. God in His goodness has, therefore, willed the interdependence of all beings on each other as the possibility of the intelligibility and value of their creaturely life, but He does not necessarily will all the "evil" results of that interdependence as it works itself out in nature and history.

In turn, the reality of the finite means that each entity has been given in creation a definite nature, an essence or structure of its own, or as Richard Hooker said, a law which determines its mode of being and of action. While all creatures remain dependent on God and on others for their being, nevertheless each finite creature reacts and acts according to its own nature and the modes of behavior that govern that nature. This structural integrity of each creature is, moreover, the basis of its possibility for fulfillment: for the goodness of all creaturely life is the realization of the excellence of which each nature is capable. If a man seeks to act either as an angel or as an animal, he will fail to realize his potentialities. It is only when his life is a fulfillment of his human powers and capabilities that he can experience the goodness of his existence. Thus the inherent reality and value of creaturely life imply the presence throughout creation of definite structures of finite being and definite patterns of behavior on the part of all creatures. But the fact that creatures thus follow the laws of their natures is also the main source of natural evils. Living cells grow according to the dynamic structure which they possess as cells, and given certain conditions they will grow into malignant cancers; and the pressure systems of our weather develop according to the structure of meteorological forces, and given certain conditions they will bring forth tornadoes, floods, and droughts. The natural evils of disease, destruction, famine, and death result, therefore, from the structural integrity of a relatively independent creation which operates according to its own God-given patterns of development. God in His goodness wills His creation to have these definite natures and patterns of behavior; He does not directly will all the effects of this structural character of creation.

Now the main point is that in each case the goodness and meaning of created life involves also the possibility of natural evil. These evils result from the whole system of interdependent causation which proceeds according to the dependable modes of behavior, of action and reaction, which finite things possess. And yet without this orderly system the world would be unintelligible and chaotic. If causes which acted in one moment would fail to act similarly in the next, then no relations among finite things would be dependable, and all life would be impossible.

If, for example, to breathe air is not to live and to breathe water not to die, then no man could exist at all, let alone remain sane. And in such a chaotic world all moral action would be impossible: I could not help my neighbor if to feed him bread at one moment is to nourish him, and then in the next to poison him. In a real sense, the goodness of creation as an intelligible and meaningful arena for natural and human life requires that God create and uphold the integrity of orderly causation, the very element in existence which makes possible what we call natural evil. But in thus creating a world of orderly interdependence, a good God does not will directly all the effects resulting from the inner workings of this world. What His goodness wills is the ordered structure of our existence, which is the possibility alike of its value and of our experience of natural evils. In the next chapter we shall see how a deep faith in God can pluck out the good of our creaturely life in commitment and service, and be immune to its possibilities of evil, so that even natural ills are to us by no means necessarily evil. Meanwhile we must recognize that this understanding of natural evil as the result of the systematic structure of our world only explains why what is called natural evil is an aspect of our *given* world. It does not tell us why God gave us the world He did, i.e., why He created natures of such a character that their systematic interactions result in tragedy. In that sense natural evil remains ultimately unexplained in God's creation.

The Christian Understanding of Sin

In our attempt to make natural evil partially intelligible we found it helpful to analyze the structure of creaturely existence in order to see how out of that good creation natural evils arose. In seeking to understand the second form of evil, human sin, we shall find the same method provisionally helpful. Although sin arises from the freedom of man and so is not a necessity to his life, nevertheless sin can only be understood in relation to the structural necessities of man's nature as a creature of God. For this reason the idea of creation is an unavoidable presupposition for the Christian interpretation of sin, and no theology of sin and grace can be coherent or intelligible without a prior analysis of man's essential being as a creature. As in the doctrine of God, therefore, so here, a sound Christian ontology is the basis of a coherent biblical theology.

The fundamental structure of creaturehood is, as we have seen, that it is dependent yet real. Man is a creature who shares fully in this basic character. He too is "made out of nothing," and thus he is not the source of his own existence but is dependent on things beyond himself, and especially on God, for his being. Like all other creatures, therefore, man is contingent and temporal, subject to outside forces and, without grace, destined finally to be overcome by those outside forces. Man is also, like other dependent creatures, a real being who has a definite structure which determines his mode of action and of reaction within the finite world. In man this structure is his freedom and self-transcendence, what is often called his "spirit." These words refer to that capacity in man to be a centered self; from this capacity come his powers of knowledge, of creativity, and of personal communion with others, and on it depends his personal uniqueness. But this same freedom forces upon men the necessity, and often the burden, of decision about the character and direction of his life. Whether he wishes it or not, man as a free creature must pattern his life according to some chosen ultimate end, must center his life on some chosen ultimate loyalty, and must commit his security to some trusted power. Man is thus essentially, not accidentally, religious, because his basic structure, as dependent and yet free, inevitably roots his life in something ultimate.

These two fundamental aspects of man as a creature, his dependence and his freedom, are intimately united in his nature. They interpenetrate each other within his whole being so that he is free and transcendent even in his creaturely dependence, and yet utterly finite and conditioned in his freedom. The dependence of man's being is, as in all creatures, total and unconditioned: his whole existence in space and time comes to him immediately from beyond himself and other creatures, and ultimately from God. Thus the total structure of man's being as a creature made out of nothing roots his life beyond himself in the transcendent source of his existence, in God his Creator and preserver. Now man's capacity for self-transcendence and for free decision, his "spirit," shares completely in this radical dependence of creaturely life. The spirit of man cannot be the self-sufficient center of man's life, for the intellectual, moral, and spiritual capacities of man are not "divine" powers set arbitrarily within creaturely flesh. On the contrary, man is a total unity, and so his spirit, like his flesh, is a creaturely, dependent spirit. Thus the human spiritual powers of mind, of trust, of commitment, and of love, as capacities of a dependent creature, can fulfill themselves only when they point beyond themselves to God, the ultimate source of man's existence. The wholeness and excellence of man come when his freedom is in unity with his creaturely dependence, when his spiritual capacities find their rootage in God, as his existence finds its source there. The first commandment, therefore, expresses not only the obligation of man to God; it expresses as well the law of man's essential nature as a free creature dependent upon God for his being: "Thou shalt love the Lord thy God with all thy *heart* and *soul* and *mind.*" In the fulfillment of that commandment man is in unity with God and with himself: with God, because all the powers of his free spirit are then rooted in God the source of his being; and with himself, because then the freedom of his spirit reflects the dependence of his basic nature in finding its center beyond itself in God.

In such unity both man's dependence and his freedom are creative and good. His contingency and temporality, which are the source of his greatest fears and anxieties, are by his unity with God stripped of their terror. Through faith in God's providence and God's love, the

fears both of meaninglessness and of death are transmuted into the security of a life made meaningful by
God's purposes and made everlasting by His love. And
positively our dependence on others, instead of being a
source of fear, becomes the occasion for creative service
in human community. Under the conditions set by the
first commandment, the second becomes possible: instead
of the fear of our neighbor on whom we are dependent,
we may now love him as ourselves. If the security of our
spiritual life is rooted in God, as our existence is, then we
are inwardly united and serene, and so able to love the
neighbor on whom we depend.

Secondly, the finitude of man as a creature, the inescapable fact that each of us is partial, a mere segment of
the whole of humanity, with only limited powers and with
only a restricted perspective, suddenly loses its demonic
character and becomes creative. For this particularity
and partiality are the sources of our personal uniqueness
and value, as well as of our bias and our narrowness; and
under God this uniqueness can find its own special vocation, for which just *this* particular personality was created.
If the spiritual meaning of our life is rooted in God, as
our limited finite being finds its source there, then we
are content with our little fame and our relative achievements, for they find their completion not in our works but
in God's sure purposes. Like our contingency and our temporality, our essential finiteness becomes creative rather
than destructive in union with God. The goodness of
man's being, then, appears only when the freedom
of man recognizes its creaturely character and finds its
center in God, as man's existence finds its source in
God. Then all the potentially demonic aspects of his
creaturehood become the creative powers of love, and all
the deadly fears of his transitory life are transmuted in
the security of faith and hope.

Correspondingly, the perversion and distortion of man's
nature which we call sin occurs when this union between
man's dependence as a creature and his free spiritual life is

broken. Although man knows well that his bodily existence is contingent and temporal, dependent on forces beyond himself, nevertheless he experiences through the power of his mind and the freedom of his will his own spiritual transcendence over himself and the world around him. And thus he is tempted to regard himself as independent in his spirit, as he is not independent as an existing creature. Then he attempts, through the power of his mind and will, to become the spiritual center of his own existence: to establish his own security despite his manifest contingency, to carve out the meaning of his life despite his weakness and temporality, to attain through his own thought to the truth despite his finite partiality. He tries, in other words, to be his own God, to replace the true source and center of his being by his own creaturely powers. This effort of the dependent creature to declare his spiritual independence from God is sin, and its results are devastating for man's total being.

The first result is, of course, that a personal break between man's spirit and God appears. There can be no corresponding ontological break between man's existence and God's being, lest man cease to be. But man's freedom means precisely the capacity to lose his spiritual contact with God by spiritually centering his life around himself rather than around God. When this occurs, however, man loses his relation to an unconditioned and eternal security and meaning in God's power and love, and he is left with merely his own contingent, temporal, and finite powers around which to build his life. Sin is, then, first of all defiance of God's lordship over our life. But immediately its second result is the radical distortion of our own being, for as dependent creatures we cannot be our own gods without destroying both ourselves and those around us.

Man's existence is perverted by sin because his creaturely powers that could be creative if his spirit were rooted in God become destructive and disrupted when he is centered in himself. As a creature "made out of nothing," and so ultimately dependent beyond himself for his security and significance, man without God becomes prey to all the terrors of non-being: of the ultimate loss of existence, of significance, of purpose, and of eternal life. Then his radical dependence on forces beyond himself becomes an increasing source of anxiety for his existence; his life is haunted by fears, and he desperately tries to secure himself against all conceivable dangers and from all conceivable competitors. His essential temporality and weakness come now to threaten the meaning of his life, and he either despairs or else seeks too desperately to achieve meaning and significance at the expense of others. His finitude and partiality become a source of continual uneasiness, and he claims that his own point of view is the only truth to which others must conform. Inwardly his life is disrupted by anxiety, restlessness, alienation, and hostility, as he searches throughout the contingent creation for the ultimate security and the ultimate meaning which he has lost in losing God; and all his hope for inward unity, serenity, and fulfillment has vanished.

Outwardly he destroys the order of God's creation and his own needs for human love and community. By raising his own contingent and finite life to the status of God, he changes his finitude from a creative particularity in God's world to an evil partiality against all the rest of God's world. If God is not the center of his life, then his creaturely need for security, meaning, and ultimate commitment drives him to make something else that center: his career, his nation, his race, his lusts. In every case his life is devoted to a false creaturely loyalty, and not to its true universal center, God. This means inevitably that man's life becomes destructive instead of constructive. To love one's self or one's group inordinately is to lose all love for those outside the immediate object of loyalty. To worship what is partial is to seek to destroy all that is not included in the partial interest. Man's sins against his fellow man spring ultimately from his defiance of God and from the false centering of his existence around self or around

his group, which that defiance inevitably brings. Thus the
God-given freedom of man makes it possible for him to
destroy both the divine purpose and the divine harmony
of creation. That purpose was for the fulfillment of each
creature rather than its destruction, and that harmony
was an order of communal love rather than a disorder of
conflict. Both are thwarted by sin, which is therefore unequivocally contrary to the will of God. In this way the
relative dualism between God and the created world, implicit in the idea of creation and realized in the laws of
nature, is by human freedom raised to the absolute dualism between the Holy God and the sinful world of history.
Although it comes from God, history reflects the human
rebellion against God and stands under His judgment.

Our conclusion is, therefore, that man's total existence
as a dependent and yet free creature must reflect the lordship of God over all his existence, both as the source of his
being and the center of his spiritual trust, commitment,
and love. For in God all aspects of our creatureliness
are truly blessed; without Him every facet is wretched.
This intimate relation between the transcendent goodness and sovereignty of God, the essential nature of man as
a creature of God, and man's consequent fulfillment in
God and perversion in sin, is expressed by Augustine:

Accordingly we say that there is no unchangeable
good but the one, true, blessed God; that the things
that He made are indeed good because from Him, yet
mutable because not made out of Him, but out of nothing. Although, therefore, they are not the supreme good,
for God is a greater good, yet these mutable things
which can adhere to the immutable good, and so be
blessed, are very good; for so completely is He their
good, that without Him they cannot but be wretched
. . . and since this is so, then in this nature which has
been created so excellent, that though it be mutable
itself, it can yet secure its blessedness by adhering to the
immutable good, the supreme God; and since it is not

satisfied unless it be perfectly blessed, and cannot be thus blessed save in God—in this nature, I say, not to adhere to God is manifestly a fault.[8]

The actuality of human sin, therefore, can only be understood on the foundation of the idea of creation. For, as Augustine says, only if man is so made as to be essentially dependent on God can we say that separation from God is a perversion or fault of man's nature. Otherwise sin is merely the defiance of an external law imposed on an essentially independent creature, and we cannot but sympathize with the rebel against such a tyranny.[9] Moreover, only if an ultimate dependence upon God is the created structure of man's existence, are faith in God and obedience to His will the restoration of human life rather than its new subjugation. The promise of the Gospel that "he who seeks to gain his life will lose it, and he who loses his life for my sake will find it" depends directly on the affirmation that we are creatures of God, made out of nothing for life with Him.

Only on the basis of the Christian idea of creation, therefore, can we begin to understand the baffling mixture of good and evil that is God's creature, man. The purpose of God's creation of man is personal fellowship between God and man, the relation between Creator and creature in which the loving sovereignty of the one realizes the fulfillment of the other. This personal fellowship as the goal of creation requires a created nature that is free, that must fulfill itself in decision rather than through necessity. Such an essential structure of freedom involves, as we have

[8] Augustine, *op. cit.*, Book 12, Chapter 1.

[9] This reveals the difference between the Christian myth of the Fall and the Greek legend of Prometheus. While the order which Adam defied was the law of his own Creator and so the law of Adam's own created nature, Prometheus, the Titan, was not the creature but the adversary of Zeus. Consequently, the law of Zeus was to him the law of a tyrant, not of a father, for it represented an order externally imposed upon Prometheus rather than the inherent law of his own being.

seen, the risk of perversion. Sin is that perversion. But spiritual perversion, like a bodily disease, reveals the structure of health. In the same way the character of human evil as sin reveals the essential structure of God's good creation; for only a child of God could sin through idolatry of self, and only a creature made to love God could destroy himself by his false loves. The possibility and the fact of sin, therefore, do not deny the idea of God's creation of a good world. On the contrary, the experienced character of sin presupposes that idea throughout, for only on the basis of a belief in our Creator can we hope to understand our own experiences of responsible freedom, of inward disruption, and of outward injustice.[10] And only on that basis could we hope for a rebirth of self in the love and power of God.

How Could God Create a World with Possibilities of Evil?

It is clear, however, that all our questions about evil have not yet been answered. Having seen how both natural and spiritual evil can arise out of the fundamental character of God's good creation, we are driven to ask a further question: why has God so created finite natures that their actions can lead in this way to natural and above all to spiritual evil? At this point we should note that our questions have been raised to a different level.

[10] Augustine vividly expresses this point in the following: "And indeed evil had never been, had not the mutable nature —mutable, though good, and created by the most high God and immutable Good, who created all things good—brought evil on itself by sin. And this its sin is itself proof that its nature was originally good. For had it not been very good, though not equal to its Creator, the desertion of God as its light could not have been an evil to it. For as blindness is a vice of the eye, and this very fact indicates that the eye was created to see the light . . . (for on no other supposition would it be a vice of the eye to want light) so the nature which once enjoyed God teaches, even by its very vice, that it was created the best of all, since it is now miserable because it does not enjoy God." Augustine, op. cit., Book 22, Chapter 1.

We are no longer seeking to understand how evil arises out of the given world of interdependence and of freedom that we know. What we are now asking is a more fundamental question: why was this sort of world created, a world with these immense possibilities for evil? For the Christian, therefore, there is ultimately no escape from a baffling dilemma: how could a good God have created a world that contains the possibilities of such evil? Is it possible to make intelligible why God's will chose just this creation?

Many attempts have been made in the course of Christian thought to resolve this problem. Principal among these has been the effort to show that creation is, despite its evil appearance, a perfect harmony, the best of all possible worlds, if not from the human point of view, at least from God's. We have already seen in the first part of this chapter how this explanation for evil ultimately results in a distortion of the Christian understanding of God and of the meaning of human life. Within its logic the Christian God becomes as impersonal and loveless as the Absolute of philosophy. More constructive are the efforts, of which the above is merely an illustration, to show that the conditions that make the actualization of evil possible are the very conditions which make personal and moral life possible, namely the interdependence of all creaturely life, the integrity of natural laws, and the reality of personal and moral freedom.[11]

In the end, however, these justifications of the ways of God are never more than partially successful. They can give us some understanding of the irrational fact of evil in God's world, but they can never make its presence completely intelligible to the mind of faith. And the reason is clear enough. If such justifications seek to show logically why God chose this world with its possibilities

[11] An especially helpful discussion of this subject is found in Hazelton, R., *God's Way with Man*, Abingdon, 1956, pp. 63–64.

for evil, then they are attempts to comprehend the plan
which the Creator had in His mind at creation, efforts to
see finite being through His eyes and with His end in
view. And such a divine perspective upon the goal of finitude is surely impossible for a creature immersed in finitude. In pushing the problem of evil to its utmost reaches,
we have, therefore, encountered a mystery quite beyond
our understanding. Our human intellects can inquire into
the character and structure, the possibilities of good and
evil, which are involved in the world that God has chosen;
and our faith can through revelation know something of
the nature of the will that has made the choice. But, as
creatures, we cannot so transcend our finite experience
that we can describe the thoughts and motives in the divine mind or explain to ourselves the logic of ends and
means in the divine decisions.

As we discovered in our discussion of God, one of the
important corollaries of the idea of creation was the transcendence of God to our clear and complete comprehension: we can know in faith that God's will is love, but we
cannot think the divine thoughts after Him. The same
divine transcendence that made the structure of the
world contingent to human science, makes the divine
choice of this world a mystery to us. The goodness of the
world is, then, an affirmation of faith based on our knowledge of God's will as love, not a matter of knowledge
based on a clear understanding of why God chose this
world. Perhaps, as Luther hoped, in a "theology of glory"
we shall be able to see the ultimate coherence that we
believe to characterize the divine purposes: how evil con-
tributes to good, how the character of our world reveals
God's love, and how God's justice is united to His redeeming grace. But now our origins, far beyond the web
of finite relations, are shrouded in mystery. And in this
case, as in so many, if we seek too persistently to make
this mystery perfectly logical and clear, we shall have to
deny one of the two certainties of Christian experience,
either the goodness of the Creator's will, or the reality of

evil. Clear and intellectual understanding can, therefore, only take us to the edge of our experience where finitude first appears. It cannot take us beyond that edge to make completely coherent our source.

Most modern philosophy recognizes that our minds must stop their search at this question.[12] Whitehead has argued that in philosophical inquiry we cannot ask "Why this world rather than another one?" because our minds deal with the given world and cannot therefore ask about the conditions out of which that given world has come.[13] Christian thought agrees with this philosophical principle, as far as our clear and rational understanding is concerned. On the other hand, it affirms that the mystery of our origins does not remain totally dark to us. At the source of our existence there is not "blank nothingness" for our minds and spirits; our life does not proceed ultimately from absolute arbitrariness, nor is the primordial form of our world, as Whitehead said, an "ultimate irrationality."[14] Although we cannot understand fully or rationally why the world is as it is, nevertheless the mystery of our origins has been clarified greatly for the Christian. For to him that mystery which lies behind all things has in part made itself known. The transcendent God who created all is also the God who has revealed Himself to men in history. Thus while we do not know specifically why this world was chosen, the Christian does know the character of the will which determined the choice. That will has been found by all who are confronted by revelation to be a will whose nature is love and whose purpose is salvation. With this knowledge of the will which determined creation, the Christian can face any adversity or evil with

[12] Cf. Lovejoy's excellent account of the history of the attempt to make creation "rational" and the ultimate failure of this attempt. Lovejoy, A., *The Great Chain of Being*, Harvard University Press, 1948.

[13] Whitehead, *Science and the Modern World*, Macmillan, 1925, Chapter XI, pp. 249–51.

[14] *Ibid.*

courage, confidence, and serenity, for hereby he knows evil
to be an intruder that can and will be conquered.

The understanding of evil, therefore, which Christian
faith offers is more creative of spiritual strength in the
face of actual encounters with evil than it is productive of
intellectual solutions to the problems of evil. But this is
just the sort of understanding that fits our real condition.
It is in its existential rather than in its intellectual form
that the problem of evil is most oppressive. Although these
intellectual dilemmas are genuine and must be overcome,
the intellectual aspects of the problem of evil are really
mere reflections of the living sin and suffering that characterize our actual lives. Kierkegaard has reminded us that
the real problems of life are crises in our existence, rather
than contradictions and puzzles among our thoughts; and
that their solutions are to be found through decisions of
freedom and courage, and through choices between right
and wrong, rather than through intellectual formulas. Thus
while man as a thinking being must achieve some intellectual understanding of the central intellectual puzzles
in his life, it is still more important for the meaningfulness of his individual existence that he have some hope
for and some realization of a victory over the actual evils
that threaten him. And it is on this score that Christianity surpasses those philosophies which can provide
only intellectual answers to the problem of evil. For Christian faith deals with the evils of life not so much through
an intellectual understanding of their origins as with the
hope of their actual resolution and of their ultimate redemption. In the Christian Gospel, Christ is grace as well
as truth, the power to overcome sin and death as well
as the clue to the understanding of life's dilemmas.

The Three Faces of Evil

What, then, is the power of evil over our actual lives
from which this Gospel saves us, and how does the Gos-

pel effect this conquest? In answering these more basic questions about evil, it is helpful to make a different distinction than that between "natural" and "human" evil, namely that between "manageable" and "unmanageable" evils. For, as modern culture has discovered, much of the suffering of our human life is manageable by human intelligence and good will. The Christian, as well as the humanist, recognizes the manageability of many forms of evil, for it is a part of the faith of both of them that finite entities, be they the forces of nature or of society, have definite natures and modes of behavior which can be studied, understood, and often controlled. Many evils arise in life because we do not understand and so control the factors at work in our physical and social environment. Consequently such things as plagues, disease, floods, economic dislocations, even personal feuds and wars, can be diminished by an increased knowledge of these finite realities that surround us. Perhaps the most impressive single feature of recent modern culture has been the confidence, the selflessness, and the skill with which thousands of scientists and public servants have embarked upon the conquest of manageable evils. We have tried to show that the Christian conception of an orderly and meaningful finitude, as well as the Christian sense of responsibility and love to our neighbor, have been largely responsible for this creative activity of Western culture.

The Christian, however, knows that not every evil is easily manageable by a frontal attack, however advanced our science and however devoted our wills. For evil is a mystery as well as a problem. It encircles and infiltrates those of us who are seeking to combat it, weakening and diverting and thwarting us. As we try to turn and face its concrete forms, other facets of evil outflank us from our rear, enter unrecognized into our souls, and destroy us from within. We are overcome from the inside, for in fighting evil we often become part of the very evil we sought to destroy. We seem driven by powers beyond our control, both outside and within us, to contribute unwillingly to the sum of tragedy. No sensitive soldier who fights tyranny, no political leader who has to choose between hopeless alternatives, no statesman who must balance power with power to protect his country, fails to feel this mystery of historical life. We intend to destroy evil and promote good, but our very efforts often involve us in the conflicts we seek to end, and in actions that cause not only immediate suffering and anxiety, but have unknown and possibly tragic consequences further down the corridor of time. In such experiences we have ceased to be merely the victims of evil, and have to our horror become its active perpetuators. We can no longer control evil, because now it seems to control us. And at this point evil appears to us much more serious and baffling than did the external problems of disease, droughts, and floods, terrible as they are. This mysterious form of evil, which baffles us because it is beyond our easy control, has been present to man since the earliest times: it is the theme of his profoundest thoughts and the object of his most terrible fears. This mystery of evil has revealed itself to man in the three guises of fate, sin, and death, which, as we can see, are closely related to man's structure as a contingent temporal creature, and yet also closely related to his own responsible freedom, to his sin.

The first guise of unmanageable evil is that of fate. Fate is the blind arbiter of our destiny, the cruel manipulator of historical and social forces—that power of time and history which beyond all our individual intentions seems to breed situations that almost necessarily lead us to self-destruction, to wars, to depressions, and to social conflicts. What is it that in one historical period unites all the economic, political, and social factors into a situation that produces conflict? What is it that so determines the forces of history that all these puny individual wills are gathered into one aggregate aggressive national will? What is it that so manipulates our economic relations that all the nation's shopkeepers are marshaled into a panic; what is it that creates social conditions that transform decent people of one race into segregationists? What is it that drives our science and technology remorselessly forward so that they create weapons that can annihilate us in a twinkling, so that, with planes poised in the air to attack, we stand on a veritable brink of destruction dependent for our existence solely on the unpredictable whims and passions of men? This is the most terrifying form of "fate" to us today. These are the great social and historical forces that both defy our wisdom and good will and manipulate our individual destinies. We cannot control them because they form the context within which we act in history. They are not created solely by immediate human decisions; rather they set the conditions for our historical acts, and therefore cannot be directly changed by them. Our decisions can in part counteract, divert, and possibly stay for a moment these great forces of history; but no decision of man can either create or destroy them.

Can aristocrats, by an act of even intelligent and forceful will, bring back a lost society of social ranks and privileges; can Englishmen will to return to their vanished position of imperial power; can the West overcome the tarnish of its imperialistic history and by any act of diplomacy and power become the welcomed leader of colonial peoples; can Americans by any policy divest Russia of its growing power or of its fateful appeal to dispossessed nations; can scientists or politicians will that the nuclear weapons not be developed to greater and greater efficiency? Each of these questions points to forces within history—political, economic, intellectual, and technological forces —which determine our historical policies and acts, and are not totally determined by them. Because these forces beyond our control are so crucial for our fulfillment or destruction, we are not the full masters of our own historical destiny. Our fundamental contingency and temporality has made union with the consequences of our past creativity and sin to form a historical fate for our lives that seems to move us either to glory or to destruction. Thus men ask themselves with haunting anxiety about this historical destiny upon which their fulfillment depends: will the forces of our time bring increasing power and security to democratic ideals as they did in the last century—or will they move against us to decrease our power, to weaken the appeal of our ideals, and to raise our enemies to dominance? Will these forces, whatever they are, help to achieve victory over *us*, as they helped so recently to build our victory over the Nazi foe? Will these forces lead to an atomic war that will blot us all out? If so, then are they merely blind and purposeless, raising some groups to prominence only to dash them again into oblivion? Are we and our Western ideals of truth, democracy and justice to become "one with Nineveh and Tyre"? These are the questions of fate that contemporary Western man anxiously asks, and if no answer is found, then a despairing sense of helplessness and meaninglessness is the only possible human response. This is one guise of the unmanageable evil which threatens the potential goodness of our life.

The second guise of evil is the most important contributor to the external fate of history. It is the internal fate of sin, a baffling irresistible force that subtly twists each of our acts and intentions into a glorification of self, that turns the self in on itself, so that all it does is done for its own glory and security. Despite the fact that it arises from our freedom, this is also a mighty force which we cannot control. We cannot control it, not because it is beyond our power, but because it *is* our power. It is we ourselves who are our own fate here; it is *our* wills that are self-centered. But a will cannot will to change itself; a self that is diseased cannot provide its own health. If the center and source of our acts and intentions is tainted with self, then all that springs from that center is so tainted, even our efforts to become good. The result is that men involved in the conflict with sin do not really want to win this battle with their own selfishness. As Augustine realistically prayed: "Grant me chastity and continency, but not yet."[15] Sin, therefore, is a mystery of evil beyond our control, because it has captured us from the inside, and so here again we cannot conquer evil by our own power.

The final guise of evil that threatens our life and yet is beyond our control is death. This seems at first the foulest face of evil: in countless individual lives it wipes out all possibility of fulfillment when death comes long before its time, and if it is the last word for all of us together, then all our human creativity seems ultimately unfulfilled. And yet, on further thought, it is fate and sin that give to death its "sting." In the first place, it is when death is arbitrary that it becomes unbearable. A heroic death that is related to a clear purpose, and that has manifested self-transcending integrity and courage, is tragic—but it is certainly not evil. And secondly, it is sin more than anything else that makes us despair of a life beyond death. A pure, immortal personality of infinite value, about which we often hear at Easter, may be capable of both immortality and happiness—at least the Greeks thought so. But an alienated, self-centered, fearful, and lonely self is a different matter entirely. And we who know this to be *our* own reality do not know which we dread the more about death: the extinction of this self or its eternal continuation. The three guises of evil in our lives, fate, sin, and death, are therefore strangely interrelated.

We might say, with a host of philosophers, that these three forms of the mystery of evil are intelligible as aspects of the essential structure of finite manhood, and that they are, therefore, necessary as a part of the inevitable lot of mortal man. Our origins are unknown, and our few days here are hemmed in and dominated by these three. No man escapes their power, and no life triumphs completely over them. What meaning, then, can mortal man, for all his intelligence and good will, find in the finitude that is crushed by these three? And so we return in our analysis of evil to the question asked by the earliest

[15] Augustine, *The Confessions*, Book VIII, Chapter 7.

Greek poets about the goodness and meaning of life. Is there any possibility that these forces beyond and within us that rule our lives may be in turn conquered? Is there a creator and sovereign who rules over these powers that rule over us? This is the ultimate question of our life, and its answer is the Christian Gospel.

Chapter 8

CREATION AND THE GOSPEL

In the last chapter the evil that hems in and threatens our life was pictured as having three guises: fate, sin, and death. Before these three grim figures man finds himself helpless. His own sense of creative power and dignity is outraged by this situation; one part of him, therefore, cries out like Prometheus against an order of existence that crushes him outwardly and perverts him inwardly. And yet his own deep realization that he himself is to blame for his predicament permeates and weakens his very rebellion against his fated lot. He feels himself to be both victim and cause of his destiny of cruelty, conflict, and suffering. But above all he experiences frustration: he is bound, captured, the willing yet unwilling servant of the power of evil that he abhors—and yet which lures and fascinates him. This sense of slavery, of being fettered in a fallen existence, permeates the world's literature and philosophy, just as does the sense of order and intelligibility we discussed earlier. The ancient myths and poetry of early cultures, the dramatic tragedies of Greece, the Promethean and Faustian themes in literature, the grotesque art of both primitive and sophisticated man, the universal religious message of salvation and redemption, and a great deal of contemporary literature—all express this sense of capture by evil and imprisonment by meaninglessness.[1]

[1] Apparently while some ages and cultures see the world in terms of its essential, created structure of orderliness and harmony, others can only see its disrupted, fallen character. Both a good creation and a fallen existence are thus valid aspects of man's experience of his world.

The answers of despair, resignation, and retirement from life we have discussed in earlier chapters. Now let us turn to another answer.

The Gospel of Jesus Christ was received by early Christian believers as the good news of God's victory over evil, and over evil in just the three forms we have outlined. The literature of the early church, from the letters of Paul right through the writings of Augustine, is filled with the sense of rescue and release: God had in Christ come into a world that was willingly and yet unwillingly captured by evil, and had freed us from our bondage. All the powers that rule over man's life—fate, sin, and death—had been captured at last, and man was free, born again, a new creature. With the coming of Christ, therefore, the new age had dawned and a new humanity had been created. Christ had become the sovereign Lord of man's life and of history, and through Him all things had been made new. The dominant theme in the writings of the early church was a chorus of exultation at a realized victory over evil in all its forms. In a variety of symbols: of light coming into darkness, of the Savior victorious over the devil, of ransom and release from capture, of reconciliation and rebirth, Christians expressed their joyous realization that through the power of God the tyranny of evil in their lives had been conquered, and that man had been re-established in his true being and had been given back his true destiny with God. Instead of being a gloomy group suffering from a failure of nerve, the early church, as both its courageous active existence and its literature plainly show, was filled with the ecstasy of freedom, of confidence, and of hope. Had our modern skeptical layman approached an early Christian with his worried question, "what do you do with the problem of evil?" the Christian would have answered with a burst of joy "I believe in the Gospel." And he would have meant by his answer that in the coming of Jesus Christ the evil that threatens men had been actually conquered for all who believe in Him. Its threats and terrors were gone; it had lost its power and control—life was made new, and joy was unbounded. The Gospel came into our world not as a quavering answer to the intellectual problem of evil but as a tremendous victory over the power and the reality of evil.

The Fundamental Christian Proclamation

We cannot, within the scope of this book, attempt to give a complete analysis of this Gospel of good news that transformed the ancient world and laid the foundations for our own cultural and religious life. It is, however, important for our purposes that we deal in two ways with the total positive affirmations of the Christian Gospel. First, because we have raised the issue of meaning and of evil, we will want to see in what general ways the Christian Gospel answered that problem and established Christian confidence in the "good creation" by God. Secondly, since the positive message of salvation in the Gospel presupposes the belief in creation, it is of interest for us to see just how these two Christian affirmations are related. In fact, the ideas of creation and salvation are mutually dependent in the most intimate way; neither one can be made intelligible, or even affirmed, without the other. The Gospel, therefore, is itself a central part of our study of the idea of creation. Let us, then, see what the main elements of this "good news" were to a world which, very much like ours, was oppressed by its bondage to fate, sin, and death.

There are probably many different ways in which the essential elements of the Gospel can be summarized. However, if we ask: "What was the central theological structure of the Gospel as men proclaimed and defended it during its first four hundred years, and what theological motif gave unity and power to the Christian victory over 'evil' in the ancient world?", there can be little doubt of the answer. The fundamental theological affirmation in the Christian proclamation was that Almighty God had come to save men, that He who had created all existence, the Maker of heaven and earth, had in the last times acted decisively in Christ to rescue men from evil. The identity of God the Creator and God the Redeemer, of the almighty power of existence with the love of Christ, is the theological axis of the Gospel of good news.[2]

This theological conjunction is perhaps the most fundamental affirmation of the Old and the New Testaments: in the Old, God, the Maker of all things and the Ruler of history, is the Lord of Israel who is coming soon to save; and in the New, this great event is proclaimed to have happened in Jesus Christ. It is also the heart of the theological battles of the early church with the Gnostics, the Arians, and the Manichaeans; and it is the dominant concern of the whole Christological controversy of the fifth century. The three great creedal statements that came out of this period, and that laid the foundation for all subsequent Christian theology, affirm in one way or another the fundamental conjunction of creation and redemption through the one Lord of all. 1) The belief in the creation of the world by God, the Father of Jesus Christ, was the

[2] Consider, for example, these clear statements from Irenaeus and Athanasius: "And that the whole range of the doctrine of the Apostles proclaimed one and the same God, who removed Abraham, who made to him the promise of inheritance, who in due season gave to him the covenant of circumcision . . . that He was the Maker of all things, that He was the Father of our Lord Jesus Christ, that He was the God of glory—they who wish may learn from the very words and acts of the Apostles, and may contemplate the fact that this God is one, above whom there is no other." Irenaeus, *Against Heresies*, Book 3, Chapter 12, Section 11.

"We will begin, then, with the creation of the world and with God its maker, for the first fact that you must grasp is this: that renewal of creation has been wrought by the self-same Word who made it in the beginning. There is thus no inconsistency between creation and salvation; for the one Father has employed the same agent for both works, effecting the salvation of the world through the same Word who made it in the beginning." Athanasius, *Incarnation of the Word of God*, Section 1. For New Testament passages reflecting the same theme, special reference is made to John 1, Romans 5, Colossians 1:15 f., Hebrews 1.

earliest dogma which the Christian community established as orthodox against its denial by the Gnostics, and became the first affirmation of the Apostles' Creed. 2) The Nicene Trinitarian formula (A.D. 325) was based on this conjunction, since its central confession was that the Son of God, He who is "of the same substance" with the Father and Source of all, has been present with saving power in Jesus. 3) The Chalcedonian Christological formula (A.D. 451) affirmed that in Jesus Christ, who is our Savior, both very God and very man are present and united. Each of these creedal formulas stated, in one way or another, that, in the act of divine redemption which founded the Church and to which it directs its life and worship, it is the God who created all things that is at work for our salvation. The great message of early preaching and theology alike was that in the person and loving deeds of Jesus Christ, God the Creator and Lord had revealed Himself. On this basis, then, we can understand the reason for the early Christian sense of release from all evil. Since it is the Lord of all life who has acted for man in saving love, no evil can finally maintain its power over man.

It follows that the identity of God the Creator and God the Redeemer, expressed most explicitly in the classical doctrine of the Trinity, is not merely the result of the Greek love of speculation, as Unitarians frequently imply. The Trinitarian doctrine has had a long and often confusing history, and it is the result of a protracted discussion of many often unrelated problems.[3] Nevertheless its permanent theological importance is that it represents an intellectual formulation of the very heart of the Church's faith, and that the Christian confidence in victory over the power of evil is based on the Church's certainty of its truth. For the fundamental import of the idea of the Trinity is a twofold theological concept of great religious

[3] See the clear and honest exposition of these problems in Cyril Richardson's recent little book, *The Doctrine of the Trinity*, Abingdon Press, 1958.

importance. On the one hand it affirms that the mystery of God is to be defined by means of the character of Jesus Christ. When we wonder about that mysterious power that has brought us into being and that determines our destiny, the answer is that the character and the "will" of this power is revealed in the love which shines from the face of Jesus Christ. And on the other hand, it asserts that the love which we see in Jesus Christ, and experience in the Holy Spirit, is one with the eternal power and being of Almighty God. When we ask about the ultimate status and significance of the selfless love and forgiving mercy which speak to us in the teachings of Jesus, through his death on the cross, and in the sacramental signs of our baptism and the Last Supper, the answer is that this same love is the will of the Almighty Lord of all existence and of all time. The basic religious affirmation of the doctrine of the Trinity is that the love of Christ and the grace of the Holy Spirit manifest and represent the love and grace of the power of all being and of all existence.

Now, if this conjunction of the power of all being with the love of Christ is not made, the Christian Gospel—and one could say all hope in life itself—falls apart. For then the almighty power of existence remains a cold and forbidding mystery, and life is dominated by fate, by sin, and by death. Correspondingly, the love that reveals itself in Jesus has only the pathetic frailty of a defeated liberal. In fact, if one removes the dubious concept of inevitable progress from Unitarian Christianity, one must arrive philosophically at the pessimism of Greek naturalism, salted only with reverence for a dead Socrates. The Trinitarian affirmation that God is both Creator and Redeemer is, then, no mysterious formula hatched by priests and professors. It is the very heart of the religious faith of all confident Christians, whether they think themselves Trinitarian or not. Modern centuries which have questioned the "religious value" of this idea were already imbued with Christian presuppositions based squarely upon it: namely, that God the Creator is love. Thus they took it for granted that existence was by its nature benevolent, and that the love of Jesus represented something eternal in the nature of things. Only in such a cultural milieu could it have been conceived that the Trinitarian conjunction of power and love in God was an outmoded speculative dogma, peripheral to Christian faith.

The astounding union in God of creative power and redeeming love, which the Christian faith proclaimed in its Gospel of Jesus Christ, was the basis for the Christian confidence in victory over all forms of evil, and so for a new sense of the creativity and meaning of human life. It was not that the three forms of evil were banished out of human experience: man still lived a contingent, unpredictable existence, tempted and tortured from within by hostility and self-love, and subject to suffering and death. People he loved and causes he revered still suffered defeat; his social existence was still immersed in conflict; and his understanding of his life was still cloudy and often ambiguous. Nevertheless, while real vestiges of fate, sin, and death still remained, the power, the necessity, and the terror of these evils was transcended. The things that happened to us that were unpredictable and even tragic no longer appeared as an irresistible and menacing fate. The naggings of self-love were no longer those of a necessary and unconquerable tyrant. And death was no longer the final word on our brief existence. All of these guises of evil had been for the Christian set in an entirely new framework provided by his belief in the power and love of God. We might say that they became the faces of mystery, not the guises of evil; even perhaps, as Luther called them, the "veils of God." They remained elements in our existence not yet fully understood, and by no means fully eradicated; but certainly they were not something to create either terror or despair in our souls.

In fact, for Christian faith, each "guise of evil" opened the possibility of a new and creative existence: fate became the call of providence, sin was transformed into a forgiven and redeemed freedom, and death became the seal of faithful integrity. "In all these things we are more than conquerors through Him that loved us,"[4] does not mean for Paul that sin and death are gone; it means that through the power and love of God their evil is transformed into a mysterious possibility for good, so that their sting is gone. What had been evil has become instead the mysterious residue in an existence that henceforth has an ultimate meaning and security beyond the residual power of fate, sin, and death—and so evil can now be faced and conquered with God's help. Our question then becomes: how in detail did this historic Gospel identification of power and love in God bring about this victory over evil?

The Transformation of Our Values

Certainly the most important element in the victory of the Gospel over evil is the complete transformation of values that this conjunction of God's power and love effected, and still effects wherever life becomes genuinely Christian. For in Christ the power of all life is revealed in history as suffering love; and this, if believed, radically changes all our values. Because Jesus Christ, the Son of God, humbled himself to death on the cross, the path to the eternal security of God's unconditional power must in this world be the path of powerlessness, of self-surrender, and even of suffering. This was a strange doctrine to the ancient world, as it is to men of any age, and for very good reason.

When man becomes aware of his own contingency and temporality, and without God confronts the three guises of evil that beset him, he will naturally conceive of the perfection and good of life to be an invulnerability to these evils. Quite reasonably, he feels that the "good" is a state of "changelessness" in the face of unpredictable threats, heedless passion, and mortality. Since without God he must provide his own protection against evil, he marshals

---

[4] Romans 8:37.

all his available defenses to make himself invulnerable. Perhaps he tries to fortify himself against fate by massing power and wealth; or, more profoundly, he retires into an inner citadel of unmoved, passionless indifference, where the buffeting of outward events, of inner passion, and the fear of death touch him not at all. This very human re-action to the threats of evil was powerfully expressed in the Hellenic idea of perfection, in which the excellence of the gods and the salvation of men consisted in a changeless invulnerability, a pure existence beyond all motion, affec-tion, and decay. For the Greeks, divinity meant that which was by its changelessness impervious to suffering and death.

Now when the Gospel proclaimed that the power be-hind all existence *loved,* and that Deity Himself had in Jesus Christ entered time, and finitude, and even suffered pain and death, this whole identification of perfection with security and invulnerability was rejected, and perfec-tion took on an entirely new meaning. As Irenaeus put it: the perfection of God is not (as the Greeks had said) denied by God's suffering love; it is especially evident there. And correspondingly, the perfection of man, as Christians understood it in Jesus Christ, was not compro-mised by the scandal of his suffering on the cross, but re-vealed precisely there. It is obvious that in the figure of the God-man on the cross, the vulnerability to suffering which is involved in loving others, and in submission to fate and death, can no longer be seen as "ultimately evil." For the message of the cross was that the perfection of God in history, and the perfect obedience of man to God, are revealed by just that suffering love, even in the face of death. To the amazement of all, the disciples and the en-emies of Christ alike, the divine power reveals itself in precisely that which is most vulnerable and powerless: self-giving love. Truly here was one of the most radical trans-formations of values in all historical experience: not the avoidance of suffering, but its willing acceptance in love, became the deepest clue to divinity.

Does this transformation mean, then, that for Christians divinity had *ultimately* resigned its power, so that suffering and death have the final word, even over God? Has the divine perished completely on the cross, so that all changeless security has been swallowed up in helpless love? Christians never concluded this from the surprising weakness and passivity of deity in history. First of all they knew that ultimately God remained invulnerable to fate, sin, and death; as the Creator and Lord of existence, the God of the Hebrews, like that of the Greeks, could not be overcome by any power within existence.[5] Secondly, through the concrete event of the Resurrection, and its promise to all who believed, the divine power had manifested itself beyond suffering and death. The ultimate security of God's eternal power which was sought by the Greeks is, therefore, promised in the Gospel. The means to this ultimate security are, however, very different: we can find rest and peace, not through the amassing of our own security, but through the loving acceptance of our own insecurity in dependence on God's power alone. Thus the victory of Easter over suffering and death was not negated but, strangely enough, made possible by the love-in-suffering of Good Friday. In this paradox is contained the whole transformation of the meaning of life effected by the Christian Gospel of God's power and love.

The classic texts in Scripture for this transformation of values are Jesus' words, "he that loseth his life for my sake, shall find it,"[6] and Paul's promise that "if we have been planted together in the likeness of his death, we shall be also in the likeness of his resurrection."[7] To understand

[5] Here is the deep religious root for the rejection of the monarchian heresy of Patripassianism, which maintained that, so to speak, all of God suffered and died on the cross. This threatened the gospel of salvation as radically as did the Arian claim that the love of the cross was in no sense divine. The difficult formula of the Trinity is an attempt intellectually to state a Christian position midway between these two misinterpretations.

[6] Matthew 10:39.

[7] Romans 6:5.

these texts theologically, we must recall our analysis in the last chapter of the nature of human fulfillment, and correspondingly of human evil. We found that God, as the source of the being of all creatures, is the sole source also of the ultimate fulfillment and serenity of His creatures. Thus, when the whole existence of man expresses its dependence on God in faith and love, such creaturely life is "good." On the other hand, when a man lives independently of God and in sole dependence on himself, then the entire being of that man becomes inwardly and outwardly evil. The fundamental fulfillment of the human self is not found in its earthly security of life, fortune, or fame; therefore threats to these relative values are not ultimately evil. The fundamental fulfillment of man comes when he is related to the source of his being, when his security is rooted in the power and the love of God. Thus perfection for man means communion with God, and ultimate evil for man means the loss of that communion. The relationship to God, rather than the security of the self, becomes the seat of value.

All this is expressed vividly in Jesus' words, "Fear not them which kill the body"—fate and even death are no longer ultimately evil; "but rather fear him who is able to destroy both body and soul in hell"[8]—alienation from God is the only real evil. And it is even more vividly expressed in his own life and death, where in obedience to God and in love for men, he willingly accepted temporal suffering, and thus retained his communion with God.[9] If God had

[8] Matthew 10:28. The same concept that surrender to God is the only true good, and separation from Him the only evil, is powerfully expressed by Luther's willingness to "be damned for the glory of God."

[9] Augustine has expressed this transformation of values inherent in Jesus' life and death: Jesus "exhorts His servants that they should not flee those who kill the body, but are not able to kill the soul." . . . "because man strove more to shun that which they could not shun, *viz.* the death of the flesh, than the death of spirit . . . the Mediator of life, making it plain that death is not to be feared, which by the condition of humanity cannot

associated Himself with finitude, with suffering and even
with death, and if the perfect man had done the same,
then clearly whatever fate or death could do to a man was
no longer really evil. If they were endured for love and in
relation to the divine purpose, they could become elements
of a meaningful life.[10] In Jesus' life and death it is clearly
revealed that the full meaning of human life is found in its
devoted and faithful relation to God, rather than in care
for the security of the self. And this means that the whole
natural human view of what is good and what is evil becomes radically transformed.

As the life and words of Jesus also reveal, moreover, the
means of profound communion with God involve the positive willingness to accept suffering and death. It is not that
these are themselves positive values—nothing in the Gospels would indicate that mortification is a good in itself.
Rather the reason is that the creature can find its true being in God only if it relinquishes its desperate hold on
creaturely being in itself. For God is both Lord and love;
as Lord He is the only true center of the life of each creature; as love His will sends each man to serve not himself
but his neighbor. Thus the communion of man with the
source of his being requires that man cease to be the source
of his own security and cease to determine his life by his
own will. And this continual act of trust in God alone, and
obedience only to God's will, involves self-surrender all
along the line. Communion with God, therefore, means on
the one hand humility, the surrender to God of the self in

---

now be escaped, but rather ungodliness, which can be guarded
against through faith, meets us at the end to which we have
come [death], but not by the way by which we came [sin]."
Augustine, *De Trinitate*, Book IV, Chapters III and XII.

[10] These words of Paul in Romans 5: 3–5 clearly express this
new understanding of the place of suffering in Christian life:
"More than that, we rejoice in our sufferings, knowing that suffering produces endurance, and endurance produces character, and
character produces hope, and hope does not disappoint us, because God's love has been poured into our hearts through the
Holy Spirit which has been given to us." (RSV).

all its glory and security, and on the other obedience, a willingness to serve God's purposes in any situation.

What separates us from God is our concern for ourselves, that false centering of our life around our own fortunes which we have called sin. The real evil of human existence then is self-glorification, the attempt to create by our own powers a self that is secure, invulnerable, and meaningful. Thus the efforts of the natural man to escape insecurity, suffering, and death by enlarging and defending the self, in fact remove him from his true fulfillment and security in God. Correspondingly, communion with God can only come when this whole enterprise is given up in repentance and humility, when the self realizes the futility and the evil of its own efforts to amass security, and accepts temporal insecurity as the price of its security in God. As Paul says, "We must die to self if we would rise with Christ." For it is only thus that our life can be directed by God's will for us. Union with God through trust in Him alone and through love for our neighbor requires, therefore, the inward death of the self. Our ultimate security comes to us alone through God's power, not our own—and that means the continual inward renunciation of our own glory that we may glorify God alone in our life and work. In this sense, no one can follow Jesus into the eternal security of God's kingdom unless he is willing in the present to take up his own cross in insecurity and love.[11]

The revelation through Jesus Christ of God's power as self-giving love meant, therefore, the paradox that man as a child of God could only relate himself to the ultimate security of the Creator through the insecurity of selfless

[11] The lowly acceptance of insecurity as the condition of ultimate security in God, is again well expressed by Augustine: "Therein is our true peace and firm bond of union with our Creator, that we should be purified and reconciled through the Mediator of life . . . For as the devil through pride led man through pride to death, so Christ through lowliness led back man through obedience to life." Augustine, De Trinitate, Book IV, Chapter 10.

love—through forgetfulness of his own fate and death, through personal humility and outgoing love—not through his own greatness and strength. This message is still strange and radical to most of us, and yet it is validated continually by our human experience. For in separation from God's power over fate and death, we are merely contingent and transient creatures, subject to the terrors of the external events that determine our lives, and completely destroyed by the death which ends our feeble creaturely power to exist. And separated from the divine love, we are unable to love: anxious about our insecurity, fearful of other creatures, our lives are self-centered, lonely, and hostile. The attempt to fulfill ourselves by ourselves subverts our fulfillment: the inner peace of faith, the communion with others in love, the hope for an eternal destiny, are alike stripped from us. When we seek to gain our own life we do in truth lose it, for we are only dependent creatures and cannot be the source of our own blessedness.

The Conquest of Fate

Reunion with the Creator who reveals Himself as love is, then, the basis for the Christian Gospel of salvation from evil in all its forms. For in that reunion fate, sin, and death have lost their power over us. Fate, as the blind determiner of our life, which destroys the achievement of all our private projects, is now quite unreal. Since God is the Almighty Lord of nature and of history, there is no power which blindly rules over man's life and can prevent the fulfillment of his created nature and purpose. Because God has revealed Himself as love, asking only faith and love from man, there is no situation that cannot call forth responding faith and love—and so there is no situation wherein a man cannot at once fulfill himself in communion with God and in love of his neighbor. Whether a man finds himself in a concentration camp, in poverty, in sickness, or even facing death, he is no further thereby from what God asks of him for his own fulfillment. Love of his neighbor and the building of God's kingdom can be accomplished even in those most unlikely spots. Since God is Almighty Power, no situation, however apparently removed from Him, and no action of commitment or trust, can fail to be incorporated by God's providence as a part of God's transcendent purpose. And however the causes we hold dear, and the culture we value, may seem to be threatened by the menacing powers of history, we know that nothing in them which embodies the divine purpose of love can be finally overpowered, because God is the only sovereign Lord of history.

We do not know when we shall be called in this life to face possible failure, defeat, suffering, and death. But no Christian in adversity doubts that the love of God can be revealed there through us, and that the power of God is present there for the unfolding of God's purposes. Thus determination by fate ceases to be an evil and becomes a mystery of providence—the God-given opportunity to which we can give a creative response of faith and love. And dependence upon other things, especially upon people, becomes the call to co-operation and community. In this way one of the most painful aspects of finitude, man's utter contingency, loses its haunting fear and becomes the basis of man's vocation on the one hand, and of his deepest ties with his fellows on the other. Both Augustine and Calvin made plain that the identification of God the Almighty Creator with God the loving Father completely destroyed the concept of fate, and freed man for a creative life within the conditions of historical finitude:

> 'Tis wonderful that the astrologers, by believing Christ's words, endeavor to convince Christians that Christ lived under an hour of fate. Well let them believe Christ when he sayeth, "I have power to lay down my life and to take it up again . . ." Is this power then under fate? Let them show us a man who has it in his power when to die . . . and let them not, because of these words, be

imposing fate on the Maker of heaven, the Creator and Ruler of the stars. For even if fate were from the stars, the Maker of the stars could not be subject to their destiny. Moreover not only Christ had not what thou callest fate, but not even hast thou or I, or any human being whatsoever.[12]

Finally whenever we call God the Creator of heaven and earth, let us at the same time reflect, that the dispensation of all these things which he has made is in his own power, and that we are his children whom he has received into his charge and custody, to be supported and educated . . . that our hope may depend on no other . . .[13]

If this conviction of the power of God were deeply seated in our hearts, we would not be so much alarmed, and would not be disturbed by any calamity whatsoever.[14]

These are powerful assertions of the way the Christian knowledge of God as power and as love conquered the power of fate and freed man from its fear. In Christ we know that man's fulfillment, his good in life, comes to him through his commitment to God, and through the love and service that follows therefrom. "Fateful" events cannot disturb this good, but only give it new opportunities. Thus in no situation can a man be separated either from the power of God, which guarantees the efficacies of His purposes, nor from His love—and in that faith no situation is any longer a fate to man. The importance of such trust in God as creative and providential power and love in times like

[12] Augustine, *Lectures or Tractates on the Gospel according to St. John*. Tr. by J. Gibb, Edinburgh, T. & T. Clark, 1873, pp. 23–24.
[13] Calvin, *Institutes*, Book I, Chapter XIV, Section 22.
[14] Calvin, *Commentary on the Book of the Prophet Isaiah*, Edinburgh, Calvin Translation Society, 1852, Volume 3, pp. 217–18.

these, when the purpose and goodness of life are menaced by a sense of meaninglessness and of blind necessity, cannot be overemphasized.

The Victory over Sin

The Gospel of God's power and love was, however, especially directed at the conquest of sin—since, as we have seen, separation from the power and love of God was the essence of man's bondage, and this above all was the work of sin. Again it was faith in God as both Creator and Redeemer that effected the victory over sin.

Paul's experience of being "captive to the law of sin" was no new one for mankind, although in him perhaps its intensity was new. Men had always felt bound by inward forces of evil, perverted from their true life by powers acting within themselves which were beyond their control. In late Hellenic culture, for example, men had thought this inward evil came either from the influence of the stars or from the passions and lusts of the body: in either case, something outside man himself had captured and perverted his inward life. Since this captivity was external and necessary, there was no hope of freedom unless man escaped from the influence of the stars or from the encumbrance of his body. As we have seen, however, with the faith in God's creative power, human evil was no longer regarded as a function either of stellar fate or of the essential structure of things. It became "sin," a result of the misuse of man's freedom. In rebelling against God's authority over him, man had destroyed the real meaning of his creaturehood. In this way man had bound himself in his own captivity, because he had perverted and twisted his own essential nature. Sin, therefore, was no external necessity victimizing man; it was rather the result of man's own freedom in separating himself from God. Like fate, then, it could be conquered through reunion with God: God as Creative Power meant that human evil had become no longer necessary but a consequence of sin, an act of freedom and therefore conquerable.

It was, however, the love of God that effected the conquest. Since separation from God is the ultimate form of evil, the love of God, which reconciles us to Himself, has always been the main element of Christian proclamation: "God so loved the world that He gave His only begotten Son,"[15] and "God shows His love for us in that while we were yet sinners, Christ died for us."[16]

The love of God accomplished this victory over sin in two ways that correspond to the two devastating effects of sin. The first and primary effect of sin was man's separation from God, his existence under God's wrath and judgment, and therefore his inability to be reunited with God. Corresponding to this primary effect of sin is the first victory of love: through the reconciling love of God revealed in the atoning death of Christ, though he be a sinner, man has been forgiven and returned to favor, to sonship with God. However variously the Church has understood the mechanics of the Atonement, it has always known that our assurance of reconciliation with God, despite our sin, has been sealed by Christ's death on the cross. Through that act there radiated to all Christians a love which, as Paul said, re-establishes us into a relationship of sonship with God—not through our merits, but solely through the grace of God in Christ. This love in turn calls forth in us a response of trust and gratitude, and our reunion with God is made possible. Since, then, separation from God is the ultimate source of evil—creating fate out of man's contingency, sin out of his freedom, and mortality out of his finitude—this reconciliation through God's forgiving love is truly the central pivot of the Gospel's victory over evil. Through the re-establishment of his relationship of dependence on and trust in God, a man is given back the essential structure of his existence as a creature, and there

15 John 3:16.
16 Romans 5:8.

are opened up to him immense possibilities of creativity and meaning. For this reason, the Reformation was surely right in making justification by the grace of Christ, through faith alone, the absolute norm and center of the Christian message.

For the Gospel, however, the conquest of sin includes more than this. Although it is never completely eradicated in this life, the second effect of sin, namely its destructive power in man's life, is also "healed" by God's loving grace. "But if Christ is in you, although your bodies are dead because of sin, your spirits are alive because of righteousness . . ."[17] Sometimes termed the work of the Holy Spirit, and sometimes of "the Christ in us," this healing grace of God is closely associated with the forgiving grace of God. For the healing of man's disrupted life comes to him when his existence finds its center again in God, through God's loving mercy. Thus it is the forgiving love of God which creates and always recreates man's communion with God in trust. For at no point are we ever perfect enough to establish that communion by our own merits or fidelity. Our relation to God is always a gift of grace, dependent on His forgiveness for our continuing sin.

In establishing our communion with God, however, the love of God also begins to make of man "a new creature," a being whose essential nature is in the process of being restored to health because it is reunited with God and with itself. In this union with God through God's love, therefore, man's nature is fulfilled, not enchained. God's grace does not constrict or destroy personal integrity and freedom, as if the lordship of God in our life was something essentially alien to us. Rather, since man is a creature of God, his spiritual strength and freedom are fulfilled in God and lost without Him. What subdues and binds by an alien tyranny is the evil that grace destroys: the isolation and destruction of sin. Thus our life in grace is a restoration, not a destruction of creation, a fulfillment of our es-

---

[17] Romans 8:10 (RSV).

sential nature as free and loving persons.[18] It re-establishes the relation to God on which our whole being as finite creatures depends, and it begins the restoration of that serenity and outgoing selflessness that alone can create internal peace and outward community. As the loving Creator of our being, God achieves through grace a victory over our inward disruption which no other force, within or without us, could conceivably accomplish.

The Conquest of Death

Most dramatic of all is the Christian victory over the terror of death—although, like the other two, this victory must be re-established in each person and in each generation. The fear of death was broken for Christians because behind this "evil" there stood God: God who represented in Himself two forces more powerful than even the ultimate threat of death to end existence. The first of these was the power of God that had brought each creature into being from non-being, and so could grant to His creatures an everlasting victory over the non-being of death. And,

[18] On the relation between grace and free will, let us listen again to Augustine: "Do we then by grace make void free will? God forbid! Nay, rather we establish free will . . . so free will is not made void through grace, but is established, since grace cures the will whereby righteousness is freely loved." Augustine, *On the Spirit and the Letter*, Chapter 52. And the following quotation from Hazelton: "It is not that my own will retires while God's will occupies the space left empty. The vitality and spontaneity of my freedom still find full expression. 'I live, yet not I' wrote Paul; and this may be transcribed theologically by saying that God's grace transforms itself into the motive power of my freedom, not by breaking personal integrity but by enhancing it and releasing it. There are not two actions, God's and mine, but rather one, my own made good by grace . . . Again and again Christians have joyously confessed not that taken over and manipulated by God, but that they *found* themselves in Him . . . To say 'For to me to live is Christ,' is more than anything else to understand the very meaning of my life." Hazelton, R., *op. cit.*, pp. 84–85.

secondly, there was God's unconditional love which had, like a shepherd, sought out the lost to rescue them. In the teachings and life of Jesus Christ this love for each individual being had been evident; in the historical event of his Resurrection, this power over death had been vividly revealed. Accordingly, no Christian doubted that beyond death there was, for those who loved God, an eternal destiny in which the fulfillment of man's being would be completed. Death, therefore, ceased to be the final word about man's brief life; he was no longer "condemned to die." On the contrary, since nothing could separate him from God's love and power, death was no threat to that on which the meaning of his life depended—his relation to God. And that relation to a loving and eternal power was clearly one which could raise his corruptibility to incorruptibility and everlasting life. This confidence and serenity in the face of death is well expressed in the great words of Paul and of Athanasius:

For whether we live, we live unto the Lord;
And whether we die, we die unto the Lord:
Whether we live therefore, or die, we are the Lord's.[19]

Now, when we die we no longer do as men condemned to death, but as those who are even now in the process of rising, we await the general resurrection of all, which in its own time "He shall show," even God who wrought it and bestowed it on us.[20]

Thus through the Gospel of God's almighty power and His redeeming love, all three of the guises of evil were stripped of their terrors. All that was beyond man's control and understanding ceased now to threaten him. What did threaten him was within the area of his freedom, his relation to God. When he had trust and faith in God, then

[19] Romans 14:8.
[20] Athanasius, *On the Incarnation of the Word*, Section 10.

neither fate, sin, nor death could destroy him, and his life was therefore confident, serene, and creative. When he rejected such faith, then these three became enemies again; and suddenly his precarious and finite life became for him once more a thing of dread.

This is the deeper meaning of Paul's great phrase: "We know that in everything God works for good with those who love him . . ."[21] It does not mean that through faith and love we will be miraculously relieved of misfortune, sin, or death—as many who in our day speak of "faith" as the "key to success" insist. Rather it affirms that through faith and love, what was evil in creation ceases to be really evil. For now each man has a vocation of love and service which gives a present purpose to his life in every circumstance of fate; he has a real foretaste of healing inwardly; and he has the hope for the future of an eternal destiny. For such a man the precariousness and mortality of finite life hold no terrors. He can find his contingent, dependent existence in time and space meaningful because of the power and love of God. For such a man the partiality, the ignorance, and the lusts of the flesh of individual life are no condemnation; in Christ he knows he is forgiven his sins, and that in God's will he can find a purpose that transcends his own partiality and error. His own poor works are perfected in the majesty of God's purpose, and forgiven in the depths of His divine love—and so he can never despair about himself. Thus finite creation with all of its mystery, which can so easily become evil, is to him "good," because his life is related to its own transcendent and loving source. When, therefore, a man patterns the life of his free spirit on the structure of his creaturehood, when the meaning and fulfillment of his life are rooted in God's love and power as his existence is grounded there—then that man can experience the conquest of evil in finite existence, and the restoration of a "good" creation.

[21] Romans 8:28 (RSV).

The Relation of Creation to Redemption

In this chapter we have sought to show how the Christian Gospel effectively conquered the evils that threaten life's meaning. Since the central motif of this powerful Gospel of salvation was the identity in God of unconditional power and unconditioned love, it is plain that the ideas of God as Creator and God as Redeemer are intimately intertwined in Christian experience and thought. Nevertheless, it might be well to spell out more precisely that interdependence of creation and redemption, as in the preceding chapter we showed the intimate relation between the Christian conceptions of creation and of sin. For this is the center of our argument that the idea of creation is essential for any full understanding of the Christian faith, and ultimately for any secure confidence in release from the power of evil. We might summarize this interdependence as follows: it is because of the knowledge of the love of God gained in Jesus Christ that the meaning and purpose of creation are known, and it is because of the power of God as Creator that redemption through Jesus Christ can be effected and our faith in Him made valid.

Throughout our discussion three ideas have been uppermost in our minds: 1) the transcendence of God, and the consequent mystery of His nature and will to our minds; 2) the reality of the experience of evil and meaninglessness in human finitude; and 3) the stubborn insistence that despite this evil, creation is good and potentially filled with great meaning. Now, it is plain that the first two ideas make a problem for the third. If God and His will are mystery to us, and if we experience evil, then we may well ask: "How is creation *known* to be good?" Christians have always stated that it is, and we have analyzed the contents of that statement. Is it merely because one of the opening verses of Genesis states that "God saw that it was good"? If not, then what is the foundation for the Christian belief that creation is good? Does this certainty come from our general experience of nature and of history, or from revelation? And if from the latter, how is it "revealed" to us?

Certainly if we merely look around us in the natural universe, we can find no certain basis for confidence that created existence is by nature "good." Nature simply does not reveal an answer to the question: "Why are we here? Is it for good, is it for ill—or for no reason whatsoever?" To scientific inquiry our ultimate origins are a total mystery; we appear within the bosom of nature apparently for no other reason than that preceding "causes" have pushed us into existence. And when we look at the workings of nature we see that the same impersonal causes have indifferently produced and destroyed countless individuals and species. Only from our human point of view does this natural process of coming to be and passing away seem to indicate a progressive development culminating in the appearance of man. Whether Nature herself knows or cares about this development, or is capable of perpetuating and fulfilling it, we cannot on the basis of scientific inquiry say. In herself, Nature seems sublimely indifferent to her products and their welfare. No answer to this question: "Is it good for us to be?" is forthcoming from the soulless flux of natural forces. The Hindu god, Siva, lord of creation and of destruction alike, who joyfully brings each creature into being and joyfully hurls it out again, seems the most fitting symbol for Nature as we know her. And so, in looking around us in the natural universe, we find neither assurance nor promise of fulfillment: evil and good seem balanced in Nature, and no final confidence in the essential goodness of life is possible.

Likewise when we look at history we are faced with baffling ambiguity. At some periods history clearly seems to reveal a good purpose and a coherent structure: are not truth, goodness, and beauty progressing before our eyes in the development of democracy and justice, in the spread of education and the arts, and the increases of technology? The goodness of life appeared evident to the eighteenth and nineteenth centuries, which looked at the world from the crest of a high cultural wave. But in other periods of history our observation seems to show that these cultural values are threatened and even engulfed by apparently malicious forces. The hordes of barbarians who overran classical culture, and the modern totalitarian barbarians who threaten to engulf us, seem anything but harbingers of the goodness of life. In such times God's power and love seem totally "hidden" amid successful tyranny and unremitting conflict; the goodness of life is drowned out by the cries of the persecuted, the homeless, the hopeless, and the maimed. History seems to have lost its pilot and its sure direction, and we do not know at all whether in the next decades our values will strengthen their precarious hold, or be entirely submerged in the holocaust of atomic war or in the flood of Communist totalitarianism. The course of human history is much too ambiguous to provide a certain, dependable clue about the goodness of life—no more than nature does it reveal the ultimate mystery from which we come or the essential structure of our existence. Therefore, because of the transcendent mystery of our ultimate origins, and the pervasiveness of evil, it is a real question *how* one knows that creation is good.[22] The goodness of life is a mystery known only by faith: it is not an obvious datum of our experience. But this is well, for the meaning of life must be rooted beyond the obvious surface of existence if it is to withstand the human encounters with tragedy and evil. Whatever is deeply rooted is perforce hidden from view, and is not known until uncovered; so with a secure meaning—it cannot be easily discovered or simply proved.

As we have already indicated, the Christian confidence in the goodness of life is based on our knowledge of the will of God. It is this will that provides for the Christian

[22] As we have noted before, the many modern, secular philosophies that assume this goodness might well ask themselves why they do so. Probably the only answer is that they have taken over this precious certainty from their Christian heritage.

the clue of the meaning and fulfillment of life. As we saw in Chapter 6, each facet of life—its material, emotional, and intellectual aspects—was "good" because each of them was created in and for God's purposes; and our individuality, with its quirks, its flaws, and its small talents, was seen to be good as a result of God's creative will. Finally, that Christian victory over evil which alone made possible a real confidence in life's meaning depended utterly on the character of God's will. Surely it is plain that if this origin of all that we are is not concerned with our fulfillment but is merely indifferent, there can be no question of a "good" creation. But how *do* we know that God's purposes are good?

At this point the intelligent reader is probably thinking, "what a foolish question; every child knows that God is great and God is good." But has every child always known this? Is it obvious from our experience of nature or of history that the ultimate power of all is "good"? Is it perfectly plain that the ground of existence drives toward, yes, even intends, the fulfillment of creaturely life? Surely the history of religion, of philosophy, and of literature reveal clearly that the goodness of being has never been nor ever can be taken for granted. It is a surprising statement, considering the mystery and the evil of life—and it is only through the convention of our established religious faith that everyone can grow up assuming that "God is great and God is good." Actually all modern secular naturalistic humanism denies this affirmation, as did almost all types of nonbiblical religion.

Now the point of this digression is simply this: the knowledge of the goodness of God's will, on which is based the Christian belief in the meaning of creation, comes from the revelation of God's will in the prophets and in Jesus Christ. There God's sovereign will is known as both just and loving, seeking to save His creatures through both His judgment and His forgiveness. As we have seen, one central motif of Christian proclamation is this message that God's will is a restoring, fulfilling will, ready to go to

any length to recreate the lost and give meaning and fulfillment to men. The other central motif is that this loving,
life-giving will was precisely the power that brought everything into being: in the Christian Gospel, the ground of all
existence reveals its inmost nature to be love. Here, then,
is the basis for the Christian affirmation of the goodness
of creation. If the Creator's will is motivated by the same
love for man revealed in the words of Jesus and by the
cross, then the products of His will must exist for fulfillment, and not for mockery and destruction. It is, then, in
the face of Jesus Christ that the "glory of God" is seen by
Christians. Or, as Irenaeus put it, "the Father is the invisible of the Son, but the Son the visible of the Father."[23]
The mystery of our origins is not completely dark, for to
the Christian a visible and knowable event in history points
beyond itself to the heart of that mystery. In the personal
and immediate experience of the love of Christ, the transcendent will of God the Almighty is revealed. Through
the God-in-history is seen the love of God at the beginning
of time and of history. And thus because God is known to
be "good" in Christ, the world He made is known to be
"good" in creation.

Like all Christian ideas, therefore, the doctrine of creation takes its peculiar stamp from the character of Jesus
Christ. It is a "Christological" doctrine through and
through, and must always be understood in the closest relation to what we know of God in Christ. This is true, as
we have seen, in the important problem of the goodness of
creation. It is also supremely true in ethics. Every Christian knows that God created the world with a wide variety
of beings, including all kinds of men: black and white,
Aryan and Jew, talented and plodding, energetic and lazy,
male and female. Now if the Christian attempts to bypass
Christ in his search for the divine purpose behind all this
rich variety, he will find himself in serious trouble. For example, he may say: "God is the first segregationist; did He

[23] Irenaeus, *Against Heresies*, Book 4, Chapter 6, Section 6.

not create man originally black and white"? But by piously using the word "God," a man is not thereby necessarily being a good Christian; he becomes a *Christian* only when he understands and obeys God's will in and through Jesus Christ.

The wonderful variety of creation is certainly God-given, but when Christians ask about the meaning of that variety for their attitudes and behavior, they must look only to Christ for that meaning. This is ethically what being a Christian is, namely to understand Jesus Christ to be the only clear clue to the Father's will for us. For sin has intervened in the good creation, and made out of a bountiful variety an endless occasion for arrogance, domination, and conflict; men have dominated women, white men have dominated black, the Aryan has dominated the Jew. All through history sin has changed the richness of created variety into the tragedy of conflict. If, then, we seek to understand the meaning of this variety without Christ, we shall find only the message of man's sin there, rather than of God's purpose. Creation viewed through our own partial and biased eyes always sanctifies our own prejudices, and reveals to us that the security, preservation, or advancement of our own race, nation, class, or sex is the purpose of existence.[24] In Christ, however, we can see the original purpose of this created variety to be a harmonious community achieved through love and respect. In Him, brotherly love among those who are by nature "strangers" is the principle according to which conflicts are changed into a richer harmony. For in Christ, created differences never mean conflict, superiority, or dominion—or, let us note, the loss of that difference. They mean, rather, the opportunity for men to treat one another with respect and love, and so

[24] Calvin's conception of biblical revelation as the "spectacles" that clarify our perverted understanding of God in creation is relevant here. As biblical revelation corrects our mistaken views of the nature of God, so it corrects also our mistaken views of His purposes and will. See the *Institutes*, Book I, Chapter VI, Section 1.

to create a community richer because of its diversity, a community unburdened with the sins of man's dominion over man. It is in Jesus Christ that the purpose of God in creation is revealed to us, and so it is in Him alone that we can discover God's will for our attitudes and our behavior.

It is, moreover, in terms of the Gospel that the end or goal of creation is alone to be understood. Are creatures brought into being, we ask, to please God "for the glory of God," or to please themselves: for the fulfillment of God's purposes or for the fulfillment of their own happiness? Put thus abstractly, it seems that there is surely a conflict here: the "glory" of a transcendent God seems certainly to be antithetical to the fulfillment of His hapless creatures. But if we seek, as Christians should, to understand God's will and glory entirely from the point of view of the love which is known in Christ, this apparent contradiction is at once resolved.

Through Jesus Christ the ultimate purpose of God is revealed to be personal fellowship with His creature man. For this reconciliation with man, God has done all that He accomplished in Christ; and so, for Christian faith, the goal of the divine will is that man be reunited with God in personal fellowship, commitment, and obedience, and with his neighbor in love. Now it is precisely through this reconciliation with God in faith and love that God's glory is most fully realized. For it is through man's personal trust and obedience that God's rule over man and man's enactment of God's purposes are both achieved. Then man's inward life and his outward actions alike sing the praises of the Creator: the life of faith and obedience is a life in which the divine sovereignty is fulfilled, and in which God's rule over His creation is most perfectly accomplished. Moreover, as a being rooted in God, man fulfills his own essential structure only through personal fellowship with God: the creature becomes himself when he lives in total dependence upon his Creator. Only through faith in God is man able to love his fellows, and so to realize in his life the harmony of creation which is God's

own ultimate purpose in history. And it is only through reunion with God that victory over the real threats to human existence is achieved. In the personal fellowship of
faith, therefore, in which man responds to God's love in
trust, commitment, and obedience, both the glory of the
Sovereign Lord and the fulfillment of man are united. In
the reunion with God through the Gospel, man first learns
why he is created: for fellowship with his Lord, for communion with his neighbor, and for the consequent fulfillment of all his human powers. There is, then, no contradiction between the full glory of God and the true glory of
man. The purpose of the creation of man, and so man's
most essential glory, is a fellowship between Creator and
creature in which both the majesty and the love of God
are expressed and consummated, and in which the inherent possibilities of the created spirit are most fully realized. To be in subjection to God, said Irenaeus, is to find
temporal peace and eternal glory.[25] And as Calvinists repeated, the true end of man is to glorify God and to enjoy
Him forever.

All of this indicates, finally, that it is only through the
Gospel and its understanding of God that we can comprehend and describe the relation between the Almighty Being of God and His free and yet dependent creature man.
As we have seen, this strange relation is a continual puzzle
to the abstract language of philosophy. Philosophy can only
express this relation in terms of analogies drawn from the
impersonal relations between things; and so man is said to
be a part of the substance of God, or an effect of God, or
God is called the ground of man's being. For various reasons, we have found that these impersonal "ontological"
terms, while helpful at some levels of theological discourse,
nevertheless are not adequate to give final expression to the
relation between the transcendent God and His real creature. If, however, we use the concepts inherent in the biblical Gospel, perhaps we can understand much more closely

[25] Irenaeus, *op. cit.*, Book III, Chapter XX, Section 2.

how an unconditioned being may be "other than" His conditioned creature.

If God is love, and it is thus that we know Him in the Gospel, and if therefore the purpose of His creation of the creature man is that he may have personal fellowship with God, then the reality of a finite being alongside an infinite power becomes intelligible. Considered in the personal categories where He is most deeply known, God can be understood as a self-limiting Creator who desires to give being to another free person. For if it is God's will to be "Lord" in a personal sense, then this self-limitation of His almighty power and being is required. Personal fellowship only exists where that fellowship is consummated in free decision; and this means that a personal being who stands over against God, free to reject as well as to accept God's lordship, is an inevitable implication of God's creative love, if that love is understood as *personal*. It is, therefore, in terms of personal fellowship between free spirits that the relation between God and man can best be understood. In these terms, both the ontological dependence of the creature and his ontological separation from God are intelligible in terms of the personal categories of faith and freedom. The ontological dependence is the basis for man's spiritual need for God, which culminates in faith and love; the ontological separation is the basis for man's freedom, which alone makes this relation to God personal and deep.[26] What was unintelligible in the metaphysical cate-

[26] For an excellent discussion of this dialectic of independence from God in freedom and dependence upon God in faith, see Brunner, H. E., *The Divine-Human Encounter*, Westminster, 1943. And for the way in which an understanding of God in personal categories makes intelligible God's self-limitation of His power in creating a dependent yet real finitude, see the following: ". . . God limits Himself by creating something which is not Himself, something 'over against' Himself, which He endows with a relative independence. Thus it is God Himself who creates this limitation—hence He is also free to remove it. He creates it, He limits Himself in order that a creature may have room alongside of Himself, in whom and to whom He can reveal and impart

gories that deal in necessity and impersonality becomes intelligible as the lived relationship of personal religion. The goodness, the meaning, the goal, and now the relation of creation itself, are to be understood only through the revelation of God which we have in the Gospel of Jesus Christ.

Creation the Presupposition of Redemption

In the preceding section we saw how Christians, in contemplating the meaning and purpose of creation, look at it through the eyes of Jesus Christ, for there the nature of God's will for His creatures is revealed. Let us now reverse this proposition and see how in turn the redemption that God has wrought for men in Christ depends upon creation. For it is surely true that only the Almighty God who has created us can be the loving God who redeems us. Like the Christian doctrine of sin, the Gospel promises of salvation are rooted in the idea of creation. We can understand this most clearly if we see how the unconditioned nature of God as Creator is required for the Gospel victory over each one of the three guises of evil.

As we have already shown, the Christian sense of victory over fate depended entirely on that significant conjunction of power and love in God which the Gospel proclaimed. The fear of fate is the fear of being subject to powerful forces of nature and history which blindly determine man's destiny. These inscrutable powers that men fear can be infinitely various: to some ancients they were the sightless stars; to others a host of potent demons. To some modern men they are the impersonal and arbitrary forces of economic and political development, which raise men's

---

Himself . . . But this limitation is freely self-imposed; God wills the existence of an independent being alongside of Himself; thus in the last resort this limitation springs from the love of God . . . and it is a limitation of the power of God based solely on His will as Creator and Preserver; which thus not only does not infringe His freedom, but on the contrary asserts it to the full." Brunner, *The Christian Doctrine of God*, pp. 251–52.

fortunes high and then dash them down again; to others they are the blind urges of nature in the unconscious, or the determining power of heredity and environment, which control and manipulate our life. Whenever men feel their fortunes and lives to be subject to such purposeless, irrational forces beyond their control, then the fear of fate arises.

Now this fear will be broken only if man can find a meaning and a purpose to his life which is related to the power that rules over these forces. The promise of God in the Gospel to bring men to fulfillment is "good" only if God is the ultimate maker of the powers that seem to rule our life. No one, said Luther, trusts the promise of one who is unable to perform what he promises. And God cannot receive our unconditional trust if the powers of nature, of culture, and of time itself are not instruments in His providential hand, used by Him to develop His purposes. A God in the "grip" of these impersonal forces, cannot save us from fate; He himself will need help if His purposes are to be achieved. Thus the promise of the Gospel that nothing can separate us from the love of God depends upon the belief that all powers in nature and history are, as we are, creatures of God and so subject to His will. Only a creator of all can be the guardian of man's destiny.[27]

In the second place, the victory over sin which is

[27] For example, see this powerful quotation from Luther: "If God can, from a small drop of water, create the sun and the moon;—can He not defend my poor body against all enemies and against Satan himself? —Can He not, after that poor body is laid in the tomb, raise it again to another and a new life? —Wherefore we are to learn, from this book of Genesis, the *power* of God; that we may accustom ourselves to doubt nothing of those things which God promises in His word! For in this glorious and marvelous creation *work* is there laid a confirmation of our faith in all the *promises of God:* —that there is nothing so difficult, nothing so seemingly impossible which God cannot do and perfect by His word. For all this is here proved by God's creation of the heaven, of the earth, and of the sea, and of all that they contain." Luther, Martin, *Commentary on Genesis,* Genesis 1:20.

achieved through the forgiving and healing grace of God
is possible only if God be the source of our existence.
We have seen how the Christian understanding of sin presupposes the idea of creation; equally the Christian conception of salvation, the most intensely "personal" level of
our faith, depends as well upon the unconditioned nature
of God as the source of our being.

Christian salvation turns upon the ideas of God's righteous judgment on man's sin, and God's forgiving grace
that rescues him from sin. Both these elements of salvation imply creation. It is, for example, essential to biblical
religion that God's judgment of man for his sin is "righteous" in the sense that it is "God's business" to do this;
He is not interfering in matters which do not concern
Him, when He judges us. The absolute claim of God on
man, reflected in an infinite number of distorted ways in
man's experience of "conscience," is the presupposition of
the experience of God's judgment. For it is only if God
can validly claim us as His own, that He can righteously
judge us for our rebellion against Him. The validity of the
claim of God on man is founded on His creation of man:
"we are not our own, but His," said Calvin,[28] and so He
can require our obedience, and judge us for our disobedi-
ence. Correspondingly, an experience of this claim is one
of the deep sources of our certainty that we are created by
God. The law, then, that man has disobeyed is God's law,
one He has established and one He upholds by His righteousness. Now for Christian faith this law is not alien to
man's nature, as if a tyrant had imposed on man for his
own pleasure a set of requirements totally unrelated to
human needs. The law is expressive of man's own essential
structure: its fulfillment represents the fulfillment of man,
and its defiance is the perversion of man's nature.[29] The

[28] Calvin, *Institutes*, Book III, Chapter VII, Section 1.
[29] This is the *theological* error that many psychologists, especially Erich Fromm, make when they write about Christianity as
if God's law were an "alien yoke" imposed on man "heterono-
mously." However Christians may have erred in practice,

law of God, then, according to which God judges, is the law of creation, the structure according to which things are, the *logos* or natural order of existence itself. If, then, God rightly judges man when he defies this law, God does so as the Creator who established and upholds the structure of His creation. Thus even the highly "personal" judgment of God implies God's ontological status as Creator and man's status as creature.

Furthermore, the message of God's forgiveness through grace alone involves the idea of creation. In this message it is declared that despite man's continual failure to follow the law of God and of his own nature, yes, even despite his defiance of that law, God through Christ forgives him and accepts him back into personal fellowship as a "son and co-heir." This conception of forgiving grace, therefore, implies God's transcendence even over His own law. God is "free" in mercy to forgive those who have defied His law. Now, as we have seen, this law represents the natural order of creation, the essential structure of man, and of nature. Thus implied clearly in the concept of God's forgiveness beyond the law is the concept of God's transcendence over the structure of the world. God does not, in other words, merely represent the order of things which "punishes" or destroys whatever defies that order: He is not merely, as many liberals claimed, the spiritual counterpart of natural physical laws. If He were, then the sinner could never approach His presence with anything but absolute terror.[30] On the contrary, the "good

---

Christian thought has always insisted that the law represents the essential nature of man and is therefore in no sense fundamentally external to him. Only because man is in sin separated from his own essential nature, does the law come to him from the outside, as an "enemy"—but psychological health also appears at first as an "enemy" to neurotic patients who likewise are "separated" from their true selves, and who similarly resist the loss of their neurotic defenses.

[30] For example, consider the prophet's feelings of terror expressed in Amos 5, Hosea 4 and 5, Isaiah 6:5, and also the early agonies of Luther, at the prospect of facing a God who merely represents the law of life.

news" about God is that He can transcend the structure of His own creation in mercy, as well as uphold it in judgment. This transcendence of order by the freedom of God's love seems to the philosophical mind to be anthropomorphic and chaotic. To the Christian who has experienced the reality of sin and judgment, it is the most fundamental basis for hope and meaning in life. The only hope for a life that knows its own sin and waywardness is that ultimately we have to do, not with an inflexible moral order, but with a God whose transcendent freedom is such that He can meet us in mercy beyond the law.

Perhaps nothing in Christian faith points so surely to the unconditional transcendence of God as this personal word of forgiveness. For here the structure of existence, the law of life, is an instrument in the hands of a God who can in grace, as Paul and Luther said, "free man from the law"; and here the meaning of life is dependent, not on the iron firmness of its order, but on the love that abrogates that order that thus it may be fulfilled. Only the transcendent Creator of the structure of life could both uphold that structure in judgment and transcend that structure in grace.[31] This is perhaps the most funda-

---

[31] See the following quotations expressing this point from three very dissimilar theologians. "God's omnipotence is particularly shown in sharing and having mercy, because in this it is made manifest that God has supreme power, namely that He freely forgives sins. For it is not for one who is bound by the laws of a superior to forgive sins of his own free choice." Thomas, *Summa Theologica*, Part I, Question 25, Article 3.

"The revelation of the Atonement is precisely a 'final' word because it discloses a transcendent divine mercy which represents the freedom of God in quintessential terms: namely God's freedom over His own law. Yet this freedom is not capricious. It is paradoxically related to God's law, to the structure of the world . . . The final majesty of God is contained not so much in His power within the structures as in the power of His freedom over the structures, that is over the *logos* aspect of reality. This freedom is the power of mercy beyond judgment." Niebuhr, Reinhold, *The Nature and Destiny of Man*, Charles Scribner's Sons, 1943, Volume II, pp. 67 and 71 respectively.

mental reason why belief in a finite God of order, rather than in the free transcendent God of all being, cannot provide the framework within which the gospel of salvation by grace through faith can live.

As we have emphasized throughout this chapter, Christian salvation means the fulfillment of man's nature, not its destruction. Jesus Christ reveals not only the love of God but also the perfection of human existence; and man's trust and obedience to God and love for his neighbor represent, not the constriction or stifling of human powers, but the sole conditions for their creative use. Salvation, then, is in Christian faith the restoration of creation, not its destruction; and the created self is enhanced and perfected, not overwhelmed, by grace. Now only if God is the source and ground of our being can a relation of dependence on Him restore rather than disrupt our existence. If God is not our Creator, then His domination of our existence is, as some psychologists say, an external tyranny that stifles our powers. But if He is our Creator, then our essential nature is to be in relation to Him, and so it is in freedom from God rather than in subjection to Him that we lose ourselves. Thus, again, the uniquely Christian conception of salvation, as both a gift from God and also the fulfillment or perfection of man, requires that the God who saves be also the God who has brought us into existence.

Man's final enemy is death; and here above all, as the early church realized, the unconditioned creative power of God is needed if we are to hope for victory. Only the power of existence and of life can fulfill the promise of continued existence with God in everlasting life. Only if God has at first brought us into being out of nothingness, can He at the end bring us into life after death. As Ire-

---

"The highest manifestation of the freedom of God takes place where He sets the sinner free, where He, the king, gives to the rebel soul the life which had been forfeited. He proves Himself as Lord, who stands above the law which He Himself has laid down." Brunner, *The Christian Doctrine of God*, p. 148.

naeus and Athanasius emphasized over and over: "To change the corruptible to incorruption was proper to none other than the Savior Himself, who in the beginning made all things out of nothing."[32] Many contemporary Protestant theologians insist that God cannot be described at all in "ontological" language, and that in theology we should reject all concepts of existence or being, and understand God only in the personal terms of Judge and Father. And yet these same theologians will assert their faith in a divine promise of resurrection and of eternal life. They overlook the fact that only the source of existence, who has brought us into being, can maintain us in everlasting being. No merely personal being, floating about the universe like some benevolent pagan demigod, can grant eternal life to anyone, even to himself. The promise of victory over death through God's power is vain and ridiculous, and our only hope is in the perpetual power of our immortal souls, unless God is the unconditioned source of all existence.

In the case of every major promise of the Gospel, therefore, the unconditioned power of God the Creator stands as the foundation on which Christian confidence is based. As a response to this Gospel, Christian life is a life of trust in God; it is the commitment of the spirit to God, because in God is known to lie the ultimate security and fulfillment of that spirit. The Gospel, therefore, would be able to make no meaningful promise, and Christian faith would be a delusion, unless the God who is proclaimed there were the Creator and source of all finitude, unconditioned and transcendent in His being and eternal in His existence. The transcendent majesty of God is not just an abstraction dear to the theologian's mind; it is the sole ground of faith and trust for all who believe with Luther that God is a "mighty fortress," and for all who through faith in Him look forward to the fulfillment of His prom-

[32] Athanasius, On the Incarnation of the Word of God, Section 20.

ises. The idea of creation provides, therefore, the only framework in which the Christian Gospel can be preached effectively and believed intelligibly. The knowledge of God that we have in historical revelation is, it is true, the sole basis for our understanding of the purpose and meaning of creation. But the God revealed there as our Lord and Savior is inescapably He who infinitely transcends His creation in power and glory, and so who must be understood, not only as a personal Father, but also as the self-existent ground of all being.

Proclamation — Statement Not has to make
Sense!

Chapter 9

CREATION AND TIME

Time and Modern Man

Perhaps the question of "time" will seem to the average churchman to be an abstruse and even irrelevant issue. Before his mind come vague thoughts of "relativity," "the fourth dimension," and other puzzles of modern scientific speculation. And he will wonder what such problems have to do with his own life. "My only time problem is catching the eight-fifteen each morning, and getting my wife to parties somewhere near the right hour," he will say testily. "Beyond that I prefer to leave time to the astronomers and physicists." This is, in its own way, all right with us too; we shall also leave many of the puzzles of time to the scientists and philosophers. It seems to us, however, that certain aspects of time do play a large role, often menacing, often creative, in the layman's life. They impinge upon us as mysteries in our ordinary existence, rather than problems for our inquiring minds. And these may well be worth our discussion. In this chapter, then, we shall deal with another facet of the mystery of our finitude, that of our existence in time. Like the question of contingency, it raises baffling problems for our life, problems which continually interact with the various forms of evil we have discussed. And, like the mysteries of contingency and evil, the mystery of time can be resolved only by the gospel of God's power and love.

Perhaps we can see some of these "nearer" aspects of time if we call our subject "temporality." One of the

things which we all *are* is temporal. Like dependency and
contingency, this is an inescapable structure and character
of our existence as finite beings. As we have seen, our dependency and contingency largely determine our inward
existence, often creating in each of us the sense of being
the victims of blind forces beyond our control, and therefore quite unable to fulfill our lives meaningfully. In much
the same way, the other major aspect of our finitude, our
temporality, can dominate and menace our inward existence. Time is not something that merely moves the hands
of our clocks and regulates our external comings and goings. It is also something that pulses through our own essential being, graying our hair, shortening our wind, sof-
tening our passions, and ultimately ending our existence.
We use time for all our purposes, organizing through the
means of time our life of work and play: "By means of
time I am able to plan my campaigns, husband my re-
sources, gather in my harvests . . . am I not continually
remaking time, rather than being remade by it?"[1] But,
strangely enough, time also seems to use us, pushing us
before we are ready into youth and adulthood, and then
sending us careening unwillingly into old age and death.
In this role, temporality plays with us like puppets, bringing us on to the stage of life, moving us ever more rapidly
across it, and then relentlessly jerking us off when it so
chooses. This is no abstruse problem for the physicist: it
is one of the fears that haunts every human being.[2] A

---

[1] Hazelton, *God's Way with Man*, p. 93. The whole discussion of time in this excellent book is one of the most perceptive
and helpful that has been written in recent years.

[2] Psalms 39 and 90 express this haunting sense of temporality:
". . . Lord, make me to know mine end, and the measure of
my days, what it is; that I may know how frail I am. Behold, thou
hast made my days as a handbreadth; and mine age is as nothing
before thee: verily every man at his best state is altogether vanity.
. . . Surely every man walketh in a vain shew: surely they are
disquieted in vain: he heapeth up riches, and knoweth not who
shall gather them. And now, Lord, what wait I for? my hope is

major problem of serene and creative living, then, is so to understand and appropriate our own essential temporality that it ceases to be a source of anxiety to our life and becomes the condition for courage, creativity, and zest in the face of the new—even the new that may displace us.

The painful awareness of temporality comes to us all in many experiences, but there is one especially that with increasing power menaces our sense of meaning in life. This we may call the sense of vanishing reality, the feeling that our existence is slipping ever more rapidly away from us into nothingness—and we can do nothing about it. The man who finds an ever greater number of gray hairs in his beard as he shaves, and realizes with a shock that he is no longer a "promising young man"; and the woman who with increasing terror discovers ever new wrinkles on her face, both are experiencing temporality with deep anxiety. We cannot seem to stand being merely temporal animals who live and die. When we experience our temporality, it goads us into overcoming it by some means or other. Man knows he is mortal; but he struggles continually against this awareness.

Our reactions to these experiences are varied, but each one has a dominating influence on our whole personality. Some of us try to disguise the wrinkles under new layers of cosmetics, and to hide the years in coy lies and coquettish attempts to retrieve a vanished youth. Some of us hazard the role of "perpetual undergraduate," living for stag parties and boisterous reunions in a desperate attempt

---

in thee. . . . Hear my prayer, O Lord, and give ear unto my cry; hold not thy peace at my tears: for I am a stranger with thee, and a sojourner, as all my fathers were. O spare me, that I may recover strength, before I go hence, and be no more."

". . . For a thousand years in thy sight are but as yesterday when it is passed, and as a watch in the night. Thou carriest them away as with a flood . . . The days of our years are threescore years and ten; and if by reason of strength they be fourscore years, yet is their strength labour and sorrow; for it is soon cut off and we fly away . . . and establish thou the work of our hands upon us; yea, the work of our hands, establish thou it."

to keep ourselves, not in college as such, for we care little about learning, but in *youth*. This is a losing and self-destructive battle: the wrinkles do keep coming, and the middle-aged collegian never really succeeds in bringing off his wild oat. Each of these reactions can, it is true, have creative elements of gaiety and joy if behind them lies a deep courage and serenity despite the real facts of one's temporality. But if such courage is absent, and if these struggles against the reality of temporality stem solely from anxiety, then these are the most pathetic and transient of human reactions, stripping life of both dignity and satisfaction. When the real joys of maturity are refused, then age and fear peep through the thin veneer of recaptured youth.

Another way entirely of conquering the anxiety of our temporality is to try to balance the decline of our youth and our powers with a corresponding increase in our status, influence, and prestige. When we see these gray hairs multiply, we are sent into a flurry of professional activity. Our hope is that the anxiety of ceasing to be young will be overcome by the satisfaction of becoming important. Here personal significance tempers the inevitable chronology of human life. We can stand the onrush of maturity and old age if we feel that our life and work have accomplished something—be it a good book, a successful business enterprise, or a large family. But grasping for significance is just as ambiguous as is clutching after youth. Unless it is tempered by deep inward serenity at the prospect of personal oblivion, and unless it finds its significance in a cause beyond the self, it can lead to a ruthless quest for personal fame, power, and prestige. The anxiety of never being anything at all joins with the growing apprehension that soon all our opportunities to become something will be gone, and these two together push us along a path of personal glorification. And as the lives of those who reach too desperately for "success" so vividly reveal, the man who only out of anxiety wishes to become great or powerful uses friend and foe alike for his own glory. This attempt to cheat time leads inevitably to personal hardness, self-centeredness, and ultimate loneliness. We humans cannot conquer the threat of temporality by our own greatness without destroying the only chance for greatness we have.

Every culture and religion has produced some answer to this deep problem of temporality, of coming to be and passing away, of being "in time."[3] The best and most characteristic answer of the modern age has been that of finding an important "cause" beyond ourselves which can lend significance, permanence, and meaning to our own transitory life. Thus many men and women have been able to bear the threat of the loss of their powers and their existence, because the work of their lives has been a creative "vocation" or calling. In such cases a transitory life is given significance because it has become the partial cause of some aspect of man's progress toward a fuller, more secure, more prosperous existence. One thinks of the great figures of a nation's history, of the leaders of a growing science and medicine, of the founders and developers

[3] The worst answer of our culture to the problem of temporality has been the attempt to overcome the anxiety of mortality by sedatives compounded of sensuality and deception. Thus in typical mortuaries we try to soften the hard extinction of death with clever cosmetics, satin coffins, sylvan groves, and appropriate music. It is, however, futile to hope that these sensual effects can in the least mitigate death, which is the total loss of the sensual. Since only the subjective feelings of the mourners can possibly be affected by these sensual devices, the deception lies in the impression that it is not merely the sorrow of the bereaved that is overcome, but the hardness of death itself. Probably some useful activity or a happy family party would be a healthier way of dealing with sorrow, and certainly only faith in God's power can deal with the fact of death itself. Even more confused is the effort to achieve "eternity" by physical means: as when expensive coffins are advertised as lasting "forever," and cemeteries promise "perpetual care." My theologian friend, Roger Shinn, has remarked that this conjured up in his mind a strange picture of the cosmic end of the world, when all else had been burned to a crisp by a rampaging sun except for a thousand bronze coffins left whirling in space and attended by a few faithful morticians.

of our artistic, educational, and civic life. Each one is an example of a life made significant and more permanent through its creative influence on the development of some aspect of civilization in its widest sense. The service of important historical causes beyond one's self has provided the dominant motivation and meaning to most of the great figures of recent modern culture.

This has been a noble creed. If realized, it is a mode of life able to conquer the feeling of futility and insignificance without succumbing to the demonic aspects of the naked search for personal glory. Countless men and women have selflessly given themselves for causes larger than themselves, and have not thereby destroyed themselves through selfishness. On the other hand, the intimate biographies of great men reveal how difficult it is to combine selflessness and significance in one soul. Temptation never ceases to challenge the reality of our dedication, and threaten to turn our "cause" into a vehicle for our personal glorification. And further, this avenue to personal significance helps only those persons fortunate enough to have outstanding creative talents. For most ordinary mortals, whose lives are lived in oblivion and whose works are not of "world-historical importance," this creed offers no more than the Egyptian faith that the pharaohs were gods. Nevertheless it is true that in finding a vocation of service, many men and women have been able to achieve inward serenity in the face of their own temporality, without falling victims to the sins of pride and self-glorification.

The most significant aspect of this modern, humanistic answer to the problem of personal temporality, however, is that it forces each man who lives by it pell-mell into the question of the nature and direction of time itself. Even the practical man, who thinks that the philosophical problems of "time" are esoteric puzzles but who centers his life around some worthy social or individual cause, has thereby involved himself in the most far-reaching affirmations about the pattern of history. For, let us note: the moment a man finds the meaning of his life in a cause beyond himself, he cannot avoid asking in turn about the permanence and stability of that cause. If his "vocation" is to rescue his transitory life from the meaninglessness of extinction, it must itself be related to something beyond extinction. Consequently his anxiety about his own temporality has been shifted to a similar anxiety about that of his cause. Is the cause of progress to which he has devoted his life to remain strong and free in the course of history, or is it to be overwhelmed by new and demonic turns of culture? Are the political rights he has helped to establish to grow, or to be destroyed again by some returning tyranny? Are the justice and good government, perhaps the peace itself, he has aided through his work, to be strengthened by historical developments, or are justice and peace rare luxuries in history, easily snuffed out by new atomic conflicts? These questions about the relation of his cause to the qualitative pattern of history are unavoidable and crucial.

In so far as a man's life is rooted in a cause, in just so far is the significance of that life dependent utterly on his confidence in the future of that cause. If he really believed that remorseless time would see the extinction of his cause and all its influences—if he felt that it was temporal as he himself is temporal—he could not build the significance of his life upon it. Instead of being the power that lifted his temporality into significance, it would crumble into the oblivion that threatens him. Temporality cannot overcome temporality. Just so, causes that are mortal and sure to die cannot provide a vocation that rescues my temporal existence from extinction. Behind every dedicated life is the implicit assumption that this cause, be it a national, scientific, industrial, cultural, or religious cause, is somehow related to the very structure of history, and through history to eternity itself. Back of every meaningful vocation lies a philosophy of history which relates the immediate causes of a man's life to the deepest dimensions of history.

No man, then, who looks with some anxiety at the gray

hairs on his temples can escape the question of the nature of history and of time. The anxiety about the significance of our temporal lives leads us to ask about the direction and purpose of history itself. Time as a ruthless destroyer, time as that sheer, relentless chronology that ages us more each day, drives us to affirm something about time as purposive and qualitative. If our lives are not to be mere victims of the scythe that claims us all, they must be rooted in a pattern of historical time that can give to our life's work the status of a vocation—a purpose and a significance that temporality cannot destroy. Human temporality reaches inevitably for eternity; it can be redeemed only because eternity has in turn reached down and reunited itself with our temporality.

Correspondingly, that faith in personal significance through "progressive causes" which has given its characteristic drive to modern culture depends in turn on a certain view of history and of time which is unique. It has not always been easy for a man to regard his short life as significant because it seemed to add something to the onward march of humanity. Other views of the character and pattern of time have made it quite impossible to derive significance from activities in history of any sort. It has only been where time and history have been viewed as moving toward a goal that what happens to democracy, education, science, or industry in the 1950s can be understood to have real and lasting significance. The modern answer to the anxiety of temporality depends upon the modern view of history as a progressive development. This is one reason why in our own day, when the theory of unbroken progress is so widely questioned, our sense of anxiety and of insignificance has so greatly increased. It is also, however, the basis of our claim that the average man, for all his indifference to "esoteric problems," is vitally concerned with the origins and foundations of our faith in the meaningfulness of historical time. The question of time may be the question on which his own personal confidence or despair turns.

The Endless Cycles of the Greeks

The view that a man's local and transitory activities in history could give his life permanent significance and meaning would not have occurred to a typical man of the Hellenistic culture that preceded Christianity. This is because he saw the pattern of time, and so of the historical events in time, in a very different framework than our own. The classical view of life was based, as we saw in Chapter 5, on a vision of nature as a "cosmos," a realm of natural order. The whole of nature possessed an immanent harmony which permeated every sphere. For the Greek soul it was the perfection of order and rationality that gave meaning and intelligibility to existence, not the achievement of moral purpose. What enthralled him in the world around him was the harmony and the order of the heavens, the regularity of the seasons, the invariable coming to be and passing away of vegetable and animal life. But, above all, his delight lay in the perfect and eternal realm of ideas, where the mind could come to rest in the contemplation of timeless truth. The ideal to the Greek was the perfection of form and the order inherent in form. Sheer perfection, therefore, was that of eternal changelessness and necessity, where nothing varied because everything was completely controlled by its inherent and rational order. The divine was for Hellenic man, therefore, the perfection of necessity and changelessness. Now in the natural world of things in space and time there was, of course, a great deal of change and movement, and even a goodly measure of unexpected variety; nothing in nature was perfectly changeless, and unique and unusual events often upset the regular and orderly occurrence of forms. But, on the whole, the cosmos could be said to share in perfection because each natural object in it, and each human community, illustrated a recurrent and identifiable type. In the world of change, then, the perfection of harmony, changelessness, and necessity was approximated by the secondary but nevertheless orderly perfection of recurrence. If there must be change, said Aristotle, the circular, ever recurrent change is the nearest to the divine changelessness.[4]

Now the Hellenic mind perceived that, as one of the major aspects of the moving, changeable natural world, time shares in this secondary perfection of all else that moves. In the Greek view, therefore, it is the circular character of time that gives to time its intelligibility and meaning. For a cycle of recurrence is the closest that changing nature and history can come to the perfection of changelessness which is the divine. Whatever time brings into existence, therefore, recurs over and over again, and this harmony of repetition and recurrence gives to the inevitable changes of history an order and a meaning. Of course, since there is no absolute creator, there can be no beginning to this movement of nature and history. Hence the recurrent motion of the world, and the cycles of time which accompany it, are everlasting. All that has been has recurred an infinite number of times, and will return again in an infinity of repetitions. By eternally repeating itself in a cycle, time both mirrors the static perfection of eternity and illustrates the immanent harmony of all nature. In this way, the classical emphasis on natural order and rational harmony led inevitably to the cyclical view of time,

---

[4] "Now 'being' . . . is better than 'not-being': but not all things can possess 'being,' since they are too far removed from the 'originative source.' God therefore adopted the remaining alternative and fulfilled the perfection of the universe by making coming-to-be uninterrupted: for the greatest possible coherence would thus be secured to existence, because that 'coming-to-be should itself come-to-be perpetually,' is the closest approximation to eternal being.

"The cause of this perpetual coming-to-be, as we have often said, is circular motion, for that is the only motion that is continuous." Aristotle, *On Generation and Corruption*, Book II, Chapter 10, 336b–37a.

which was assumed almost universally by the ancient world.

This view of time as composed of ever recurring cycles is well illustrated by Aristotle and especially by the Roman Stoic, Marcus Aurelius:

> Further, since time is continuous, movement must be continuous, inasmuch as there can be no time without movement. Time, therefore, is a "number" of some continuous movement—a "number," therefore, of the circular movement.[5]

> These two things then thou must bear in mind; the one, that all things from eternity are of like forms and come round in a circle, and that it makes no difference whether a man shall see the same things during a hundred years or two hundred, or an infinite time; and the second, that the longest liver and he who will die soonest lose just the same.[6]

> All things are change, yet we need not fear anything new. All things are familiar to us; but the distribution of them still remains the same.[7]

> All things are the same, familiar in experience, and ephemeral in time, and worthless in the matter. Everything now is just as it was in the time of those whom we have buried.[8]

And both writers draw the inevitable conclusion about the significance of historical events and of one's participation in them. Time is cold chronology, mere coming to be and passing away, and has therefore no positive relation either to eternity or to a permanent purpose:

[5] Aristotle, op. cit., Book II, Chapter 10, 337a. See also Physics, Book IV, Chapter 14, 223b.
[6] Marcus, Meditations, Book 2, Section 14.
[7] Marcus, ibid., Book 8, Section 6.
[8] Ibid., Book 9, Section 14.

For time is by its nature the cause rather of decay, since it is the number of change, and change removes what is. Hence plainly things which are always are not, as such, in time, for they are not contained by time, nor is their being measured by time.[9]

Soon will the earth cover us all; then the earth, too, will change, and the things also which result from change will continue to change for ever, and these again for ever. For if a man reflects on the changes and transformations which follow one another like wave after wave and their rapidity, he will despise everything which is perishable.[10]

Of human life the time is a point, and the substances in flux, and the perception dull, and the composition of the whole body subject to putrefaction, and the soul a whirl, and fortune hard to divine, and fame a thing devoid of judgment. And, to say all in a word, everything which belongs to the body is a stream, and what belongs to the soul is a dream and a vapor, and life is a warfare and a stranger's sojourn, and after fame is oblivion. What then is that which is able to conduct a man? One thing and only one, philosophy.[11]

It is abundantly clear from these quotations that for a man like Marcus, and for his whole culture, participation in historical causes had little or no creative significance or meaning. One's inner philosophy might require that one act in society with justice and in accordance with the dictates of duty and conscience, but the historical events in which one acts are themselves meaningless, for in its onward rush time destroys, creates, and then destroys again every natural object, historical person, and event:

[9] Aristotle, *Physics*, Book IV, Chapter 12, 221b.
[10] *Meditations*, Book 9, Section 28.
[11] *Ibid.*, Book 2, Section 17.

How many a Chrysippus, how many a Socrates, how many an Epictetus has time already swallowed up? And let the same thought occur to thee with reference to every man and thing.[12]

There could, therefore, be no significance or meaning in helping a person, an institution, or a community to "develop," since, like our own brief life, that development will soon turn into disintegration; and in any case the entire development and decay has already happened over and over again.

While for the classical mind there was a pattern in historical time, it was a pattern which was antithetical to human purposes and meaning. Human purposes aim at a goal which has not yet been achieved and which, when achieved, will not completely vanish again. At each point a circular concept of time denies this: nothing has as yet been unachieved; and, once achieved, nothing will remain. Time has been understood entirely in terms of natural change, as chronological repetition, and as the eternal circling of the shadow on a sun dial. It has been entirely separated from a qualitative understanding of time as moving toward a new and irreversible goal which accords with human purposes and with a meaningful development in history.

All this is not to say that the great classical thinkers had no answer to the problem of graying hairs. They were sharply conscious of our temporality, of the corroding influence of time on our being and powers, and in large measure their philosophies were attempts to find a serene and untroubled answer to the question of the changes that will finally remove us all. What is significant is that in each case they found this answer in some sense out of time. Because time itself spelled out mortality, everlasting coming to be and passing away, it could not give significance to mortal life. Thus Marcus found peace in the inner citadel

[12] *Ibid.*, Book 7, Section 19.

of the soul completely removed from the comings and goings of history. Plato, Aristotle, and, later, Plotinus found the real significance of man's life beyond time and change in the unchanging world of eternity. Inward indifference to time and change and upward ascent from time and change were the twin goals of classical serenity and meaning. Because time merely repeated automatically a meaningless round of occurrences, eternal significance was completely separated from the moments of time and the events of history. It is clear that a "vocation" in time, which through creative historical action gives lasting significance to this transitory life, was not possible in later Greek culture.

The Christian View of Time

One of the most significant and dramatic turning points in the development of Western culture was the victory over this deadly view of circular time achieved by the biblical understanding of history. As important culturally as the destruction of the pagan gods was the overthrowing of the endless cycles: for on nothing does the modern sense of life depend so directly as on the Christian view of time. The contrast between these two conceptions of time was absolute; and only a faith as virile and certain as that of early Christianity could have so uprooted the ingrained sense of temporal meaninglessness that permeated and deadened the ancient world. Let us see how the potent words of Augustine express this victory over circular time and then analyze the basic Christian ideas involved. We shall find our subject, the idea of creation, very prominent here:

> . . . They have therefore asserted that these cycles will ceaselessly recur, one passing away and another coming . . . the things which have been, and those which are to be, coinciding. And from this fantastic vicissitude they exempt not even the immortal soul that has attained

wisdom, consigning it to a ceaseless transmigration between delusive blessedness and real misery.[13]

Having in this way expounded the classical view, Augustine denies its validity on the basis of three fundamental Christian convictions:

1) Far be it, I say, from us to believe this. For once Christ died for our sins; and, rising from the dead, he dieth no more. "Death hath no more dominion over him," and we ourselves after the resurrection shall be ever with the Lord.[14]

2) For how can that [soul] be truly called blessed which has no assurance of being so eternally, and is either in ignorance of the truth, and blind to the misery that is approaching, or knowing it, is in misery and fear? Or if it passes to bliss and leaves miseries forever, then there happens in time a new thing which time shall not end.[15]

3) For, though Himself eternal, and without beginning, yet He caused time to have a beginning; and man, whom He had not previously made He made in time . . . God, without change of will, created man, who had never before been, and gave him an existence in time.[16]

The three fundamental Christian ideas that were in direct conflict with the conception of endless cycles were in their order of importance: 1) the eternal God sent Jesus Christ into the world and time, to save men from sin and death, and for an eternal destiny. This was a completely new event in history and had results for men which were both new and eternally significant, not to be rescinded by any further turns of the wheel of time. 2)

[13] Augustine, *The City of God*, Book 12, Chapter 13.
[14] *Ibid.*
[15] *Ibid.*
[16] *Ibid.*, Book 12, Chapter 14.

Men are in the course of history really saved, and thus to each of them, as to history as a whole, a new, irreversible, and eternally significant event can occur. 3) God, who is eternal, has created time with a beginning and an end. Time is thus finite, giving to each of its moments the possibility of being unique and unrepeatable. Time is, moreover, "going somewhere": from its beginning in creation it moves toward its end or goal, and its moments are meaningful because they lead to this eternal goal.

Let us now look a little more closely at the implications of these three ideas. The first two ideas together made it impossible for any Christian to feel himself the victim of a cycle of endlessly recurrent blessedness and misery. The event of the incarnation and death of Christ was of such a character that it established a new relation between eternity and time which broke the power of the cycles and, so to speak, flattened the cycles of time out to become the linear stage of God's purposes.[17] No longer was eternity related to time through the cyclical pattern of time; with the event of Jesus Christ, eternity was related to time through that one series of moments which made up His life, and which to the Christian was filled with an eternal content. This meant that those moments could not be endlessly repeated; as moments in which eternity entered time, they could not be subject to the cycles of time. Thus they were unrepeatable, unique, "once for all." Neither an event that was merely temporal nor an eternity that was unrelated to time could so pluck a few brief historical moments from the endless meaninglessness of the cycles of natural time. But the eternal content of the Incarnation raised that one series of moments above all natural repetition and gave them a new and unique status: that of an unrepeatable event whose effects were for eternity. Correspondingly, any subsequent historical moment

[17] In the Old Testament the corresponding event of the Exodus almost certainly did the same for the Hebrew religion. Thus Augustine inherited from the Jews much the same view of time which he found implied in the fact of Christ.

in which a Christian by faith and love became related through the Christ event to eternity could not be a *merely* temporal moment. Its relation to the eternal God through Christ raised that moment of Christian experience beyond the passage of time and above "coming to be and passing away"; as the locus of a relation to eternity, that moment of time possessed an everlasting significance and effect. The entrance of eternity into time at one moment of the past gave to the future moments of time an entirely new meaning: they were now under the power of God, not of the cycles, and thus their own divine content could be unique and irreversible.

Thus Augustine could argue that because of Christ and because of the salvation He brings, the cycle of recurrence had become inconceivable. To a person who had known these historical moments filled with eternal content, time was an arena filled with unique and unrepeatable events, each of which could, under God, have a permanent and irreversible significance. For in those moments men could make decisions that related them to the eternity that transcends the cycles of time. In fact a new kind of society, the Church, was coming to be in time through this divine activity and through the human response to that activity. This temporal community of God was a historical institution related to eternity, and yet entered through temporal decisions and lived in by temporal people. Moreover, this divine community gave to the onrush of time a consistent and permanent meaning, for despite the "mortality" of cultures which come to be and pass away, this society of God will last throughout time's span, since its growth and purification are the inward purpose of history itself. Time was, therefore, filled with an eternal content. In each of its moments a man could, through Christ and through entrance into His body, the Church, come into living relationship with the eternal God and with His purpose that guides the moments of time toward their culmination in the perfected community of God. Thus man's historical life, where concrete decisions of faith and obedience to

God, and of love toward God and man, are made daily, became the crucial center of human concern. And as Augustine's great works the *Confessions* and *The City of God* so vividly illustrate, both the personal history of the human being and the grand history of the entire race appear for the first time as objects of immense interest.

Finally, this new view of time was made possible because of the new framework for time which the idea of creation established. As Augustine insisted, at creation time itself began. This meant first of all that from that point onward every moment in history was in a real sense new, occurring for the first and only time. Since the time series began at a definite point, there was no infinite extension of moments behind men; thus each succeeding moment added a unique event to a finite series. Time, therefore, was not an endless round of cycles but a finite line with a beginning, a direction, and an end or culmination. It was "going somewhere" besides where it had been. The future held for men the promise of something new. Thus past and present could have significance because they were building toward that new future. The content of the "new" future toward which God's history was moving was, moreover, a resolution of the frustrations and tragedies of man's previous historical existence: for in the Church was to be found a new kind of human community, characterized by truth instead of doubt and error, by love of God and man rather than love of self, by peace rather than uneasy conflict, and by the hope for eternity rather than the fear of death. The inward character of history was, therefore, developing toward a new kind of history, and man's existence in time could look forward to a genuine rebirth, both in time itself and in an eternal destiny with God. Gone completely, therefore, was the classical feeling that ten thousand years from then all will be the same. For Christian minds the future moved toward a culmination, and man's decisions in time were relevant to that development. With this concept the sense of the dynamic freedom and creativity of history, as creative of both the new and the better, conquered the power of the repetitions of nature, and history is given significance because the events in which men lived build toward a culmination of history.

Time and its development were, moreover, within the power and purposes of God, because it was God who had created and begun this linear time series. Time was not an enemy to meaning, nor alienated from God's eternity. Rather it was the intentional creature of God, made by Him and directed and controlled by His will. Thus the culmination of time to which all events point was not merely of temporal significance; it was even more the fulfillment of God's eternal purpose, and signaled the beginning of an eternal life for men of faith. Time was, therefore, a linear movement related to eternity at every point: it was the creation of the eternal God, it was guided and redeemed by His will, and it would culminate in His glory. While in this view eternity was not identified with time, nevertheless because time was the creation of God, the scene of His mighty acts, and the locus of the fulfillment of His deepest purposes, eternity and time were held in the closest possible relation. The events in time that contained and revealed the divine gave content and form to eternity; in turn eternity, by filling and directing the events of time, gave meaning and significance to temporality.

This Christian understanding of time completely broke the power of the relentless cycles, and put in its place the sense of time that has given our culture its buoyancy and confidence. The moments of a man's life are no longer meaningless because they have been and will be infinitely repeated, and because they cannot build toward anything. Consequently the energies of a man's life need not be expended in escaping from the content of these moments in order to find an eternity outside or beyond them. Rather the moments of a man's life, where in the midst of the people of God he hears the Word of God and responds in faith and obedience, enable him to make contact with the eternity that has appeared in Jesus Christ, and with the community whose growth is the ultimate purpose of history. His temporal decisions of faith and his daily decisions of commitment to God thus continually relate him to the eternal God whose love and power can uphold his finite and mortal life. It is in time, then, and not out of it, that the terrors of man's creatureliness, the terrors of fate, sin, and death, are stripped of their power. This experience of eternal grace, and of a personal relationship to God in time, is the most important treasure that time can hold for the Christian. Through it his finite life is transformed and recentered in a new and selfless direction, through it he becomes a member of the eternal people of God, and through it his mortality assumes the immortality of his eternal destiny.

The immediate contact with eternity in time, however, is not the only meaning which the moments of time have in Christian eyes. Despite the importance of eschatology, and of the community of God in which the Christian life is bred and lived, the Christian is not only a wayfarer on earth with his feet in the Church and his eyes on heaven and the end. He is also a man intensely concerned with the secular world around him, and so with the historical content of the moments of his life. The health and security, both physical and spiritual, of his own home, the economic development, social welfare, and political justice of his community, the advancement of education and the arts, the wider struggle against poverty, ignorance, inequality, and war—these are historical issues that impinge inescapably on every thoughtful Christian, demanding his attention and active participation. The condition for a Christian's creative participation in these "causes" of his historical period is certainly that in the temporal event of Christ he has become personally related to eternity. But one of the goals of that reunion with God is that he shall thenceforth have a "vocation" in some one of these purely historical activities. The saving acts of God in time have as their purpose not only that men may find eternity at the end of time; they also intend that men live creatively in secular history, and participate thereby in the wider divine purposes of history.

There is, therefore, for the Christian a horizontal as well as a vertical, a secular as well as a sacred, significance to the moments of time. And this is possible because the moments of secular history are also the creatures of God, which are upheld and directed by His sovereign providential will. Because time is the finite creature of God, all of its moments form a line that moves toward the divine end. Thus each historical day, with all of its varied activities, comes to a man from a past that has built towards this unique present. Consequently that new day's work faces each man with an opportunity for participation in the ongoing movement of the present toward a unique and significant future. And because these developing moments are under the sovereign lordship of God, this movement in a definite direction is a movement subordinated to the divine purposes. The future toward which this present day moves is the future under God. To participate in this movement of time through creative historical activity is therefore to relate one's daily work to the underlying current of history itself, which has an eternal significance. For the Christian, therefore, "today" is more than just July 22, 1957, a little piece of cold chronology preceded by a day, a week, and a year which it meaninglessly repeats. "Today" has a unique and qualitative content, given it partly by the past that created it and partly by the opportunities for the service of God that it presents. To discover the quality and challenge in each day is therefore to escape within time the transiency and anxiety of time; it is to find a divine and eternal significance within the moments of life.

This service of God which gives eternal content to the moments of time is infinitely varied. It may involve the more obviously significant works of cultural creation, since the advancement of civilization is one of the good gifts of God's creation and providence. Thus, provided their lives have been touched with the grace of selflessness, the great

and the famous among men, those who creatively advance
our political, economic, artistic, scientific, and educational
life, can be the servants of God's creative purposes. However, it is clear that since God wills humble love more than
greatness, His purposes are more often fulfilled by the
quiet love for a neighbor, the inconspicuous relieving of
suffering, and the unknown and often unacclaimed struggle for justice than by the fanfare of historical greatness.
The powerful movements of civilization on the surface of
history, on which ride history's leaders, may not be
the vehicles of God's ultimate purposes; and, as Christians know, their defeat does not signal the defeat of
the divine purposes. Faith and commitment can discern
that by the most obscure life and in the most dis-
couraging circumstances, God's opportunity is presented
each day; and in a response to that opportunity, an eternal
significance in history is offered to an humble life that
genius may never achieve. Thus any life, whatever its talents or fortunes, may find a divine vocation in time. If in
some moments of his life a man hears God's word ad-
dressed to him, and responds in faith, commitment, and
love, then his concrete situation, his daily round, can become a "calling" to him to serve God, and in that calling
his life relates itself to the eternal God, who upholds the
course of time itself.

The Christian belief that God has created time and directs its movements gives to concrete, finite existence a
meaning it never had before. The chronological aspect of
time, which seemed to drain each temporal life of significance, is thereby united to a qualitative purpose in time
that can lift each life into eternity. And this is possible
because God is the Creator and Ruler of chronological
time as well as of eschatological time. Thus the purely
chronological act of "catching the eight-fifteen" each morning can now be related to the deeper significance of serv-
ing God's purposes in history. And the chronological fate
of growing to maturity can become an increasing opportunity for a creative service that has an eternal reference

and goal. Under God, a divine purpose, in which our lives may by grace participate, runs through the chronological sequence of time. And because of God's love and power, no evil, whether of fate, sin, or death, can permanently separate our lives from that ultimately significant service.

In Christian faith, concrete finite existence is given an eternal meaning which does not absorb but enhances the uniqueness of an individual person. A finite individual person, with all his peculiar talents, is not only freed from the terrors of contingency, the distortions of sin, and the fears of transiency, but also he is used creatively for a significant work in his actual situation. As a creature dependent on his Creator, each man's life in time can become good and meaningful. It is, therefore, finally through his faith in God as redeeming love, and his obedience to God's calling as providential Ruler, that the Christian can experience and understand the real goodness of God's creation. And the concrete meaning of his own creation as a unique individual person is revealed to him only when he finds that unique self restored to its Creator and called to its own peculiar task in God's history. Then at last the agonizing questions with which we began: "Why am I here?" and "Why am I as I am?" and "Who has put me here and for what purpose?" are answered. In our vocation under God we understand the meaning of our creation; for our commitment to our destiny fulfills the purpose for which God created us as we are.

Modern Problems

It is clear that the Christian faith generated the powerful interpretation of time and its character that completely transformed our Western world. On its basis the whole latter-day edifice of the belief in historical progress was fashioned. Having dispensed, however, with its religious foundation on the rock of the divine eternity, the divine creation, and the divine providence, this edifice has proved too shaky. Based now solely on the sand of historical observation instead of the rock of faith, it has no deeper foundations on which to stand in the recent storms of history, and threatens to collapse. It is also clear that the doctrine of creation provided the fundamental framework for this understanding of time, as it had already done for the Christian understanding of finitude, of sin, and of the Gospel. Modern Christians, however, feel certain serious problems with this traditional interpretation of creation and time, and these we must briefly discuss now.

The problems center especially around one aspect of the relation of creation and time which has always been a part of the traditional doctrine. This is the idea of an absolute beginning of time. By this is meant that the moments of time began to be with creation. God's act of creation came, therefore, "just before" the beginning of the world or at that beginning, because among the things that God created was time. Thus at creation the first moment of time appears in existence. Time itself has an absolute beginning; the series of moments in time is finite, going back to a first moment, before which are no other moments, but only God's eternity.

This identification of the idea of creation with the beginning of time has meant that the "originating" activity of God has had two distinct meanings for most Christians: 1) in the deeper sense we have emphasized, namely that by creating God originates the *existence* of each creature out of nothing, whatever its position in the time scale. But also it has meant 2) "originating" in the sense of founding and establishing at the beginning, starting the whole sequence of things at a first moment. For most Christians, creation lies not only at the base of the existence of things; it also lies *back there* in time, at the beginning of the time series. Creation was an act done "once and for all" at the beginning of the universe: it was the first event in the history of the world.[18] For this reason many people think

18 Thus a typical history of the world, as for example that of Sir Walter Raleigh in the early seventeenth century, always had as its first chapter a description of the divine creation of the

of the Christian doctrine of creation as the religious story of what happened when the world came to be, of how the earth, sun, and stars got themselves made, rather than a deeper affirmation that all that is, however or whenever it came to be, comes from the power and love of Almighty God. For them, therefore, creation concerns the early events of our universe more than its later events. Consequently those early events have a specially "sacred" quality about them, as the direct acts of God. It is clear that this interpretation of creation has helped to cause the familiar conflict with scientific descriptions of our origins. Until the nineteenth century, almost every Christian thinker accepted this dual implication of the doctrine of creation: God had long ago brought the world into existence out of nothing at a first moment of the time series. To all of them it seemed the clear message of the first verse of Genesis: "In the beginning God created the heavens and the earth," and for that reason it was seldom questioned.

Two new factors have, however, entered the theological scene to question this older interpretation of creation as an absolute beginning. In the first place, modern science has revealed beyond any real question of doubt that the universe did not, as our Christian forefathers believed, originate complete and full-blown in its present form with its present kinds of things. On the contrary, its character

---

world. These two ways of regarding creation are distinguished very clearly in Flew's interesting analysis:

"Perhaps it would help to define two senses of the word 'creation.' In the first, the popular, sense questions about whether the world was or was not created are questions to which the latest news from the science front is relevant. Because if the world was eternal and had no beginning; then there would be no room for creation, in this sense. In the second, the theological, sense, questions about creation are questions about an absolute ontological dependence to which particular scientific discoveries are simply irrelevant. This distinction is important: but difficult, because almost everyone—including St. Thomas—who has believed in creation in the second sense has also believed that the world had a beginning, and that it was in the first sense, also, created." Flew, *op. cit.*, p. 174.

has developed gradually over countless years; its form and its content have been changed during the process of time. Thus, if the form of the present world and especially if the emergence of the new into existence are aspects of God's purposive creation, Christians must reinterpret their understanding of the relation of His creative act to time. If God can be said in any sense to have "brought into existence" the world we know, then He must be said to have created not only at the beginning of time but also *in* time. In preserving over the duration of the moments of time the universe which He created out of nothing, God has at the same time been continuously bringing forth new creations. God's creation and preservation of the world are, therefore, not activities separated by time, as if He created first, and then began to preserve. They are, on the contrary, different aspects of the simultaneous activity of God, who continually gives to all that arises existence and form, molding the new as well as preserving the old.

> The more we take into account the fact that the various forms of life did not all arise at the same time, as we must certainly do on the basis of our present knowledge, the more unavoidably are we led to this thought. God did not create everything at once; He is constantly creating something afresh.[19]

[19] Brunner, H. E., *The Christian Doctrine of Creation and Redemption*, p. 34. See also Hazelton's interesting use of this idea:
"Yet neither does the world merely refer back to God, as an effect implies cause; it does not come ready made from God as furniture or automobiles from a factory. No, it is constantly in the making, being made and remade, becoming what it is and being what it is meant to become. Time, therefore, is of the essence of existence; it belongs to the very character of God's creative act." Hazelton, *op. cit.*, p. 107. The difference between this modern and the traditional interpretation of creation can be seen by comparing this with Augustine's insistence that creation could not be in time but was an instantaneous act "outside of" time, and Augustine's attempt to understand the relation of the "new" in time to God's single, past act of creation through the conception of the *rationes seminales*.

In so far, then, as the traditional theology implied that creation was "at the beginning" and not within the process itself, the idea of creation has to be rethought. It may be that creation began the time series and thus was in the beginning; but God's creative activity impinges as well on each succeeding moment, bringing something new out of the process He preserves in being.

A second problem is even more challenging to the older concept of the absolute beginning. An essential element of this concept was the idea that the universe began at a certain moment, which means that time extends backward to a definite point beyond which there is neither a universe nor time. We have seen how this idea of the beginning of time helped effectively to break through the cyclical view of time, and to establish a view of time as purposive and developing. The problem involved here, however, is simply this: can the knowledge of the finite extent of time, of a first moment of the universe, be a part of theology and of Christian faith? And it must be admitted that it is difficult to conceive how any kind of knowledge could inform us on this point. First of all, it is not easy to see how there could be a scientific hypothesis concerning a first moment of the total universe. Since science presumably would have to assume that there was "something there" out of which that moment arose, albeit an existence in a very different form, science could not include the concept of an absolute beginning of process itself. Equally, theology could not include such a concept. The first moment of time, if there was such a moment, is a cosmological fact about the natural world. Therefore, only if revelation and religious truth inform us of cosmology, of the size, form, and age of the universe, could Christians possess this sort of knowledge through the means of their faith.[20]

[20] Thomas Aquinas was very clear on this point, namely that only through a revealed proposition accepted by faith could it be known that the world had an absolute beginning. As he indicates in the following, the issue between an eternal creation and an absolute beginning cannot be settled by a philosophical (or a

As we have indicated, however, revelation and religious truth concern God and His relation to the world. They point to and reveal the divine dimension which undergirds the natural order. They do not impart "facts" about that order, or inform us of its character or its constitution. Thus the early Christian belief that heaven was "up there" and hell "below" have rightly been challenged by our modern astronomical understanding of what is really up there and below. We now know that no space ship can ascend to heaven, nor can a tunnel dig down to hell; and we recognize that these mistaken views of the spatial constitution of the universe are deposits of early pagan cosmology, not aspects of divine revelation. We are certain that valid information about the observable facts of the sensible world is derived only from scientific inquiry, not from religious faith. Correspondingly, it seems that the knowledge that the universe began at a moment, since it is a cosmological fact about the universe and not a theological affirmation about God, cannot be a part of religious truth. Our di-

---

scientific) examination of the present state of the world. If, then, they were to reject (which they do not do) belief in propositional revelation, Thomists would agree that it is not possible by any means whatever for us to know about an absolute beginning of the world.

"That the world did not always exist we hold by faith alone: it cannot be proved demonstratively . . . The reason for this is that the newness of the world cannot be demonstrated from the world itself. For the principle of demonstration is the essence of a thing. Now everything, considered in its species, abstracts from *here* and *now*; which is why it is said that *universals are everywhere and always*. Hence it cannot be demonstrated that man, or the heavens, or a stone did not always exist.

Likewise, neither can the newness of the world be demonstrated from the efficient cause, which acts by will. For the will of God cannot be investigated by reason, except as regards those things which God must will of necessity; and what He wills about creatures is not among these, as was said above. But the divine will can be manifested by revelation, on which faith rests. Hence that the world began to exist is an object of faith, but not of demonstration or science." Thomas, *Summa Theologica,* Part I, Question 46, Article 2.

lemma, then, seems serious. On the one hand we have shown that the idea of a beginning to time has a great theological and cultural value; but on the other hand we have been forced to deny that there can be for theology any factual content to this idea.

We may note first of all that this same dilemma dogs the heels of every major theological idea. Every doctrine of Christian faith expresses the paradoxical relation between the transcendent God and the world of facts. For the essence of Christian faith is that this transcendent, eternal God has come into the time He created, to redeem, to direct, and to fulfill it. Each doctrine must on the one hand point men's minds and faith beyond the world and its history to God, and on the other it must point to the facts of the world and of history into which God has come. If religious ideas stay wholly within the world of fact and experience, they lose that saving content which is the transcendent power and love of God—they then can tell us only of the world which is God's creature, and all theology and religion cease. If, on the other hand, they transcend the world entirely, and if they describe God in the purely negative and impersonal terms of speculative philosophy, that relatedness of God to the world of which the Gospel speaks is lost. Theological truth must maintain a dialectic or tension between God's transcendent eternity and the finite world of change and time, if it is to express the Christian Gospel of God's salvation. It must continually relate to the facts of our experience what transcends fact; for what theology seeks to formulate is the activity of God who transcends our experience, impinging upon that experience in creative power, in judgment, in love, and in His call to our commitment. Out of this situation, intrinsic to Christian theology, arises our present dilemma with regard to the idea of creation. As a religious idea, creation points beyond the world to the God who created it; but as a concept expressing God's relation to the world, it makes contact with fact, and thus is always in danger of moving into the legitimate area of science. One of the basic problems of theology, then, is to express the relation of eternity to time as Christianity understands it, without on the one hand competing with our scientific knowledge of the origins of the natural universe of space and time, and without on the other losing all positive relation to the world of actual experience.

Now it is through what the theologians have called "myth" that this tension between eternity and time is expressed in Christian thought. The word myth in theology is a technical term, not perhaps the best, but one adequate for its use—if its meaning is understood. It means to speak of the transcendent God in the language of history, to talk of eternity in the language of time, to understand what transcends man in the language of human action. Myth is, as it always has been, a "story about God." When Christians try to speak of what they believe about God's act of creation, they speak of it in the paradoxical language of myth. That is, they talk about that transcendent creative activity which establishes the world and time in terms of activity within time; they use temporal language to describe that event which relates eternity and time; they tell a story about an activity that lies behind all stories. For example, typical biblical phrases describing God's creative activity speak of this work of creation in the simple language of human work in space and time: "He that planted the ear, shall he not hear? he that formed the eye, shall he not see?"[21] "The sea is his, and he made it: and his hands formed the dry land."[22] "The heavens are thine, the earth also is thine: as for the world and the fulness thereof, thou hast founded them. The north and the south thou hast created them."[23] And when both creedal confession and theology, following the biblical model, say that God, who dwells in eternity, created in the beginning the world and

[21] Psalm 94:9.
[22] Psalm 95:5.
[23] Psalm 89: 11–12.

time because of His goodness and love—they describe, in the terms of a purposed act by an agent in time, an event that transcends time as its foundation. This is the language of myth. This language is paradoxical in essence because it is describing in the language of activity and time what is the foundation of all activity and all time, and so what transcends time.

When Christians say that the idea of creation is "mythical," therefore, they do not at all mean that it is something unreal, a fairy tale, a creation of the human imagination. Rather, by using the word "myth" theologians seek to raise our minds beyond all questions of this fact or that fact within the world order, to the deeper dimensions of all facts, to the relations of all facts to their eternal source and ground in God. Thus, although the myth of creation does not refer to a particular event, still it is true and not imaginary. It is a true, although not literal, affirmation about the relation of the whole system of facts in the world to their Creator God.

If, then, the meaning of the myth of creation is to relate the whole finite world of facts and of temporal events to the transcendent and eternal God, it does not concern the one fact at the beginning, any more than it concerns all facts everywhere and at any time. The myth of creation does not tell us about a first moment of time, any more than the myth of the Fall tells us about a first human being. What it does tell us is that every moment of time, like every contingent thing, comes to be from the creative power of God. The question of the first moment of chronological time is a question for the astrophysicist, not for the theologian, just as the question of the first Homo sapiens is a question for the anthropologist, not for the biblical scholar. The event of creation of which we speak in theology is not just an initial event within a first moment of time: rather it points to the relation of all events to their eternal source. It is a theological myth which speaks to us of God and of His deeds, not ultimately of the universe and its workings. But the question with which the theological myth does deal, namely that of the source and ground of our temporality and of time itself, is a crucial question for us all, more crucial by far for our existence than the intellectual puzzle of the extent of time. And in answer to that question, the myth of creation expresses the true and valid religious affirmation that all of temporal creation comes into being through God's creative will.

With the question of theological myth we have, however, moved into the new problem of how we are to talk and think about God. Why do we use this language of human and historical action when we talk about God; why do we speak of God's activities in terms of "events," and why do we "tell a story" about God? Do we not know that God transcends the world and time, and so cannot do a deed, as men in time and space do deeds? Can we speak of an event of creation that seemingly does not happen in a moment, a deed of God that has no date? These are important questions for modern theology, which wishes to preserve the traditional way of speaking about God's "mighty acts," and yet which realizes that all factual statements about the general character of the universe ultimately stem from scientific inquiry, and not from revealed knowledge. To these questions of language about God, therefore, let us now turn.

Chapter 10

SPEAKING OF GOD

In the preceding chapters of this book we have tried to understand the meaning of the Christian doctrine of creation. We have explored briefly what it implies about God, and we have in greater detail shown its relevance to the important questions of the meaning and status of our creaturely existence. In this process we have seen that the positive feeling Western Christian man has for his physical, individual life, his sense of victory over evil, and his faith that historical activities have significance, come largely from this conception, and from the Christian faith of which it is an essential part. Thus any hardy readers who have stayed with us, may by now be ready to give this conception a grudging nod of approval: it does make more sense than many had believed, and above all it gives to life the framework within which our own existence has positive meaning.

In our last chapter, however, we were left with a problem that must have nagged at the reader's mind. There we said that Christians think about God in "mythical" terms. That is, they speak about His self-sufficient, eternal being and its relation to our world in the language of time and of history. They talk about His "deeds," His "acts," His "intentions," His "will"; they speak of a God who transcends history and time as if He were within history and time; and as if the unconditioned source of all existence were a personal being within existence. Is this not a patent contradiction—to speak of the source of all being as a par-

ticular being who acts; to talk of the Creator of time as if
he were an actor on the stage of time? Why does Christian
theology hold to these clearly paradoxical anthropomor-
phisms?

This same question of our language about God may
arise for the thoughtful man in another form. When he
thinks of the idea of creation as Christian piety has understood it: of God willing a world into being with a good
purpose out of His boundless love—he cannot help but feel
extremely uneasy. Intelligible or no, is this not the worst
sort of wishful thinking? Is it really conceivable that a
humanlike will and purpose lie behind the vast impersonal
reaches of the universe, that there is anything like love out
there beyond the galaxies? Is it not, in all honesty, woefully
childish and immature to paint the magnificent otherness
of the cosmos in homely human symbols, as a child pictures a faraway land in the colors and forms of his own
street? The idea of creation, as we have expressed it, describes the origins of the vast, impersonal cosmos in terms
of the conception of a self, a person, with something like
freedom, purpose, will, intention, thought, and love. In so
doing, theology clearly takes one tiny aspect of experience,
our experience of a person living and acting in time, and
makes it the clue to the ultimate origin of all things. It
takes what is finite, conditioned, dependent, temporal, and
makes it infinite, unconditioned, independent, and eternal. Not only does this procedure seem childish, it seems
to make no sense at all. What can be meant by a "person"
without a body, a character with neither heredity nor environment, a self without a world around it? Is not personality the *most* dependent sort of thing we experience: dependent on our physical bodies, on a material and social
environment, on existence in time? Why, of all possible
analogies, do theologians pick *this* one? Is it not much
better to think of our origins in terms of nature and its
workings than it is in terms of man's personal life and its
decisions? All of these objections to the language about

God which the idea of creation has used are really asking the same question: Why do we talk about our remote origins, or God, in the categories of human action and history, with words which are appropriate only to personal existence?

The classical way in which religious thinkers have answered these important questions has been by "proving the existence of God" to the questioner. Through some train of intellectual argument the theologian shows the doubter that a supreme being with some personal characteristics really does "exist," and is responsible for the world as we know it. For various reasons, we do not feel that this is a useful way to deal with these questions. To prove God by philosophy is neither good philosophy nor good theology, and of no real help either to unbeliever or to believer. To the first, God is never actually proved; to the second, a proved God is never satisfactory—and both are right.

It is, in the first place, highly questionable whether the transcendent Creator of Christian faith can ever be "proved" by philosophy. Any valid proof exists within some recognized system of coherence, either a world system of causes and effects, or of logical implication. Thus the coercive logic of proof, e.g., that the world as effect implies God as cause, necessitates that both terms be included within this fundamental system of coherence. Behind and above such a God, therefore, there must exist a more ultimate term, the final coherence of reality which requires His existence, and which is the source of all meaning and coherence to everything within its scope. God then becomes one comprehended factor within the larger coherent world system envisioned by the philosopher—and not the transcendent and mysterious source of all being, coherence, and meaning which faith knows. Thus ultimately only a finite, immanent God can be proved. That such a God is not adequate for the Gospel, as we have understood it, is apparent from all of our preceding chapters.

This is not to say that the almighty power and eternity

of God are quite unknown to the "natural man." Both the universality of religion and the unending quest of philosophy for ultimate being, reveal that man, without special revelation, has an inkling, however dim, that his life touches upon a mysterious, transcendent, and holy reality. There would be no such things as gods in human history, and no such concepts as eternity and substance in human thought, if man were not aware, in some way, of a being or a reality beyond the contingent and temporal finite which he encounters in his everyday experience. Calvin remarked that "the eternal power and majesty of God are everywhere evident in creation," and he also added, in man's experience of himself.[1] However, because of man's alienation from God in sin, this dim awareness of deity never becomes an adequate understanding of God until it is clarified and corrected by God's revelation of Himself in history. Until that revelation, the almighty power of God is either worshiped as the "gods" of nature and of tribe, or contemplated as impersonal being. In special revelation these "idols" are shown to be products as much of man's vain imagination as of revelation, and the true God, transcendent to the world and yet creative of it, is at last known. If, then, natural theology is the attempt to reach God the Creator either through man's experience of the immanent coherence of the world or through his general religious experience, it can only uncover an idol, never the true God.

With these brief remarks on natural theology and "proofs" of God, let us begin our own defense of the idea of creation against these probing objections to our way of speaking about God. What we say will be largely a regrouping of ideas and motifs that have run throughout our total discussion. Our thoughts will revolve around four main words, each of which has appeared before: analogy and revelation, paradox and myth.

[1] Calvin, *Institutes*, Book I, Chapters 3–6.

Analogies and Symbols

Against the objection that creation "humanizes" the vast, impersonal reaches of the universe, let us recall that the transcendence of God requires that all our language about Him be analogical. Transcendence does not mean that "up there" there is a being like a large person who made all this world—such an interpretation of transcendence completely misses the point. Rather it means that our origins lie in deep mystery; that the source of our being is not "just like" us, but quite other than finite things; and so that whenever we say anything about that ultimate origin of creaturehood, we say it with a continual certainty that our words are feeble analogies, always transcended by the depths of mystery they sought to express. Christians are not people who claim to know all about their origins and their destinies. More than most secularists, they are conscious of the mystery surrounding both ends of their life. For they know the transcendence of God, more mysterious and more "other" by far than the stars and the reaches of space. To understand our existence solely in the terms of natural causation is in truth to bring its mysteries close to home, to reduce the deep dimensions of our life to the relations we can study in the laboratory or through the telescope. The modern naturalist is far surer he can understand everything in the terms of human thought, i.e., science, than is the Christian who knows of the transcendence and mystery of God beyond all our thoughts.

Second, it is not quite accurate to picture Christians as the only people who think fantastic or childish analogies about their ultimate origins. It has been a steady implication of our chapters that some sort of symbolic expression of this mystery is unavoidable. Every living person possesses, in some corner of his mind, a conception of the source and ground of his existence. The reason, as we have shown, is that the basic questions that men ask about the meaning of their life raise inevitably the question of the ultimate origins of that life. If men have any feelings at all about the fundamental goodness or the meaninglessness of life; if they seek at all to understand the nature and source of evil; if they try at all to penetrate the mystery of human sin; if they look for any sort of fulfillment; and if they seek any kind of significance—in all of these quests, men cannot fail to ask about that on which the being and meaning of their life depend. The existence of each of us is the embodiment of some view of life's meaning. Any life that a man lives, therefore, be it only a life of thoughtless pleasure, is a living answer to the existential question, "Why am I here?" and so implied in it is an answer to the further question "Whence did I come?" The answer may be that the vast sea of nature produces us, social environment and the id determine us, and the grave receives us; but within that seemingly sophisticated philosophy are a set of descriptions of our ultimate origins which are, like those of the Christian, aspects of our finite experience used as symbols to describe the mystery from which we come. Contingent and transitory existence raises the question of God. We men who are dependent creatures can no more escape describing, however misguidedly, the transcendent from whence we come than we who have weight can escape standing on something under our feet.

The question, then, for human thought is not whether or not we shall be naïve enough to describe the transcendent, but rather what analogies and symbols are most appropriate, meaningful, and illuminating for this description. Positivism notwithstanding, there is no human life that does not imply an ontology and a religion, and no consistent human thought that does not depend on a metaphysic and a theology. And ultimately any ontology or metaphysics leads us back to some transcendent origin, whether we call it nature, process, substance, the One, or God. The Positivist is not one who has seen the foolishness of philosophy and theology; he is merely one who refuses to look objectively and clearly at the inescapable implications of his personal existence and his thought alike.

Man's experience of his own existence, then, inevitably raises the question of the transcendent origin of his being. He cannot live without searching into the depths of life for its source and ground. In another chapter we have discussed the attempt of philosophy to satisfy this inescapable drive of human thought to reach and comprehend what transcends our ordinary experience. Because its materials are composed of this ordinary experience, philosophy always describes God either in terms of the world of our experience—and makes Him a part of the world; or else it describes Him in terms of the negation of that experience —and makes Him a completely transcendent, changeless absolute, unrelated to our world of experience. On the basis of his common experience of finitude, man cannot find an answer to his questions about the infinite; because of his sin, he does not wish to find the answer of self-surrender to God. Thus to his own mind the ultimate origins of a man's life remain dark, and all his efforts to comprehend them, to live in relation to them, remain unfulfilled. It is, therefore, not mere naïveté, but possibly an intelligent understanding of their situation, that turns men to other modes of relation to the transcendent source of their being, and to other ways of understanding that source. As the contingency and transitoriness of man's existence point his spirit in faith beyond the world to his eternal Creator, so the inability of his mind to uncover the mystery of his origins points his thought beyond philosophy to revelation.

Revelation

Christian faith is, therefore, founded upon revelation, and Christian thought about God is primarily determined by this source. God is to be known, if at all, by His own self-manifestation to us within the world, not by our intellectual ascent beyond the world to Him. The analogies by which we seek to understand God stem, therefore, from our special experience of revelation, rather than from the general experiences of our common life. Philosophy adds to and complements what we know of God in faith; but it is revelation that is the original and determining source of our knowledge of God, whether as Creator or as Redeemer.[2] If, then, our ultimate origins in God are to be known only by revelation, how does revelation "reveal" this knowledge of the transcendent, and on the basis of this knowledge, how is it best to speak about God?

By founding the idea of creation on revelation, we do not mean that this idea is based solely on those passages of Scripture that refer to God's creative activity: on Genesis I, on Second Isaiah, on certain Psalms, on John I, and Colossians I. This would be to return to theories of an infallible Bible, filled with propositions dictated by God, which we have already found quite inadequate. The foundation of the idea of creation, and of our thought about God as Creator, is certainly related to these passages of Scripture that speak of Him thus; but it is not exclusively based there. The belief in creation stands firm as an essential element of the Christian understanding of God, whatever the final exegesis of these particular passages may be.

By revelation we mean God's revealing and saving activity within history. Revelation refers, then, to those events

[2] For example, see Calvin's exposition of the relation of the knowledge of God in general experience to the knowledge of God in special revelation: "For as persons who are old . . . if you show them the most beautiful book, though they perceive something written, but can scarcely read two words together, yet, by the assistance of spectacles, will begin to read distinctly—so the Scripture, collecting in our minds the otherwise confused notions of Deity, dispels the darkness and gives us a clear view of the true God . . . [so] the Scripture discovers God to us as the Creator of the world, and declares what sentiment we should form of him, that we may not be seeking after a deity in a labyrinth of uncertainty." *Institutes*, Book I, Chapter VI, Section 1.

through which and within which God encountered, called, and fashioned His people, first His people Israel, and second the new Israel, the Church. In those events God made Himself known to His people so that a relation between Him and the community which responded was possible. Thus the history of revelation in the life of the Hebrew and the Christian peoples is also the history of salvation. In His "mighty acts": in the Exodus, at Sinai, in the upheavals and turmoils of Israel's life as interpreted by the prophetic word, in the Incarnation, in the Crucifixion, in the Resurrection, and finally at Pentecost, God was in a special way active within history, re-establishing His relation with men by revealing Himself and His will to them. The faith of the Hebrews which made them one people, and the faith of the Church which made it one community, the body of Christ, were each a response through the Holy Spirit to this revealing and saving activity of God. Likewise the witness of prophet, psalm, and preaching to those revealing events, was a human response to the divine activity. Thus the Scriptures, which contain history, prophetic writings, psalms, gospels and letters, are a human witness to revelation; they are not themselves the revelation, but its first and most lasting result. God reveals Himself in and through these special events; Scripture is the human telling of these events and the human witness to their meaning.[3]

[3] John Baillie and G. E. Wright have expressed this view as follows:
". . . All revelation is given, not in the form of directly communicated knowledge, but through events occurring in the historical experience of mankind, events which are apprehended by faith as the 'mighty acts' of God, and which therefore engender in the mind of man such reflective knowledge of God as it is given to him to possess." Baillie, J., *The Idea of Revelation in Recent Thought*, Columbia University Press, 1956, p. 62.
"Since God is known by what he has done, the Bible exists as a confessional recital of his acts, together with the teaching accompanying those acts, or inferred from them in the light of specific situations which the faithful confronted." Wright, G. E., *God Who Acts*, S.C.M. Press, Ltd., 1952, p. 85.

Now if by revelation we mean God's saving and revealing acts in and through historical events, strictly speaking creation is not a part of revelation. The Exodus and the Incarnation were events *in* history to which faithful men gave witness: the event is the revelation, known and experienced. as revelation by the responding faith of the Israelites and the disciples. By its nature, however, creation is not such an event *in* history, through which revelation and salvation come to men. Since these revelatory "acts of God" happen in history and are responded to by God's people, they presuppose the existence of history, and so the creation of nature and of mankind. Creation is, therefore, the presupposition of the saving historical events which are God's revelation. Correspondingly, the idea of creation is an inference from the nature of God as He is revealed in these events; it is not itself a part of revelation. In history God reveals Himself as the sovereign Lord of a real and yet good history, as the righteous Judge of a history characterized by sin and therefore by freedom, and as the loving Father, who seeks out the sinner in mercy and in healing love. This sovereign lordship, this judgment and this love are the immediate content of the great revealing acts of God within history, and thus they form the primary content of the Scriptures and of the Christian Gospel. But their unavoidable presupposition is the creative activity of the eternal God, who has brought all of finitude into real and yet dependent being out of nothing, and who upholds it with His power. The two aspects of God, as Redeemer and as Creator, are inseparable as message and as presupposition.[4] For, as we have endeavored to show throughout these chapters, God cannot be the sovereign Lord, the Judge and the Redeemer that Christians proclaim Him to be unless He is also the Almighty Creator. When, therefore, God is known through historical rev-

---

[4] "The Biblical doctrine of the Creator, and the world as His creation, is itself not a doctrine of revelation, but it is basic for the doctrine of revelation." Niebuhr, R., *The Nature and Destiny of Man*, Volume I, p. 133.

elation as Lord of the Covenant, it is realized that He is also the Creator; and whenever in his own experience a Christian confronts God, he realizes that He who claims, judges, and saves him is inescapably his own Creator.[5] Because of this, the status of the idea of creation is not dependent upon any particular passage of Scripture. The doctrine stands in all Christian thought as the necessary and essential background of God's historical activity, as the only understanding of ultimate reality within which the Christian faith can function and live.

It is not appropriate within the scope of this book to show in detail how the historical encounter with God through the events of Israel's history and the event of the Incarnation established the idea of creation as the essential framework for the message of the Gospel. It might, however, be helpful to summarize briefly some of the main motifs that went into that development. Within the idea of creation we have found that there are three important concepts. These are: 1) God is the unconditioned source of all that is; 2) finitude is real, separate from God and yet dependent; 3) creation is an act of the free, loving will of God. While the freedom and love of God follow easily and naturally from God's revelation of His will in saving historical events, we may well ask about our knowledge of the first two concepts. How, through our historical experience of God, in Israel and especially in Jesus Christ,

[5] "Because God has absolute power, He has the absolute right over us; and in the fact that He lays His absolute claim upon us, we perceive His absolute authority as 'Lord.' Since God lays His absolute claim upon *us*, who are parts of this world, He reveals Himself to us as absolute Power, the power from which all other power is derived. Only as this power—as the power of the Creator —is He able to assert an absolute right over us. We belong to Him unconditionally, because He has created us. But we do not at first know that God is Creator, and then, on the basis of this knowledge, acknowledge His sovereignty as Lord; but, because he manifests Himself to us as the absolute Lord, we know both truths at once: His unconditional claim (the Ideal) and His absolute power, His being as Creator (the Actual)." Brunner, *The Doctrine of God*, pp. 141–42.

is the unconditioned, transcendent creative power of God known, and how is the reality of the finite over against God known?

The answer lies in the character of the biblical understanding of God as He revealed Himself to men. In the Old Testament three concepts of God became increasingly dominant, and these three led inescapably to the conception of God as the unconditioned source of a dependent and yet real finitude. (1) The God of Israel was the sovereign Lord of all men and of all history. He appeared to Israel as the Lord who made an unconditioned claim on Israel's existence, and who was able to guide and rule not only her destiny but also the destinies of all nations and all men. As the prophets, especially Second Isaiah, declared, it is He who determines the course of all history, who calls Cyrus as well as Israel, who chastises all nations and uses them as instruments in His hands. The revelation of God's total sovereignty over Israel led to the insight that He was their Lord; and the further revelation of His sovereignty over all history led to the faith in His creation of all existence. God as the Almighty Lord, who claims, judges, and rules all men, was seen at last to be the Creator of all. (2) The God of Israel was the covenant God, who had chosen Israel among all the nations, and who had therefore a relation of "compact," of love and fidelity to Israel, rather than a relation of place or of blood. God was not the Lord of Israel because He was the deity of their region; He was their Lord through His own free choice alone. Thus in principle He was from the beginning a universal God, bound to no place, tribe, or force of nature. The idea of the free covenant led inevitably to the idea of God's free transcendence over nature and history as its sovereign Creator. (3) Although God dwelt "with His people," nevertheless He was never to be identified with His people: He was always a transcendent power that could "remove Himself" and "return." Also the covenant people could through sin be alienated from Him, even to the point where He could reject and destroy them.

In Israel, therefore, man is never a part of the substance of God; God is always "over against" man, who was regarded as independent and free enough to rebel against God. The history of the broken covenant implied inevitably the transcendence of God and the reality and freedom of the creature—as did the later promise of return and restoration. Only a transcendent God gives a deep enough dimension for the freedom of man's existence; only a God separate from our own reality, but creative of it, can be our Judge and Redeemer. Out of this biblical experience of freedom, of sin and of renewal, then, came the inference that God was the transcendent Creator of a real and yet good finitude.[6]

[6] See these instructive remarks on the rise of the Hebrew faith in God as Creator:
"Chronologically the creation myths are late in the history of culture . . . In Biblical religion the interpretation of the meaning of history is also much earlier than the interpretation of time. The principle of meaning for the history of the children of Israel is given by the idea of God's covenant with Israel. The idea of a covenant with a God who is not owned or chosen by Israel but who chooses Israel contains the germ of a conception of universal history which the prophets explicate. The ascription of the creation of the world to this God is, however, a fairly late interest in prophetism. The Second Isaiah is the first prophet to be particularly concerned to reinforce the concept of the divine sovereignty over historical destiny with the idea of the majesty of the divine creator of the world." Niebuhr, Reinhold, *Faith and History*, Charles Scribner's Sons, p. 36.
"Lastly it was through the prophetic realization that God is the Lord of History that there came about the recognition of God as the Creator of the universe; this perception would not have arisen had not Israel's God been discovered to be the Lord of all history and of all nations. The necessary corollary ensued that nature, the theater of history, was likewise subject to the creating, sustaining, and directing power of the one God (cf. Jeremiah 27:5). Thus we arrive at the fully developed Old Testament view of Yahweh as the Creator and Sustainer of the entire world, operating through His word, His fiat, which is at once the expression of His will and the executor of His power." A *Theological Word Book of the Bible*, ed. by A. Richardson, SCM Press, 1950, p. 90.

The Christian Church adopted completely the Hebrew belief that the God of the prophets, and now the Father of Jesus Christ, was the Maker of heaven and of earth. Their own experience of God in Christ, however, deepened and strengthened this conception so that it has become even more characteristically Christian than Jewish. This deepening process affected all the elements of the concept of creation. First of all, the Christian experience of the new birth of the individual and of the community, and of the power of grace to transform the living and to raise the dead, immeasurably strengthened the sense of God's power over all existence. The experience of God in Christ was an experience of recreative power, a power that could heal and make whole the created structure of human life. It was an experience of "new being," of a return to fellowship with the source of our being, and so a new birth which actualized our nature as it was intended to be. Thus one aspect of the divine which the Christian community found in Christ was the creative and unconditioned power of God: creative, because any grace which could refashion both individual and communal human life to its original possibilities must be the same power that has created that life; and unconditioned, because the victory of God's grace over fate and death showed that grace to be the absolutely sovereign power over all existence.[7]

Secondly, the sense of the distinction of the creature and his world from God was greatly enhanced by the heightened Christian awareness of sin. Through the experience of the cross, Christians were made even more conscious than Jews that man and God were alienated from one another, so that creatures were not "parts of God" but were made out of nothing. And finally, the experience of God's forgiving love revealed to Christians the absolute freedom and transcendence of God's will. Not even the fact of sin could prevent that love from coming to man;

---

[7] See especially the clear identification of the Creator and Redeemer in John I and Colossians I.

not even His own law could capture and restrict the freedom of God's love. As the creative *power* of God was revealed in Christ's resurrection, and in their own resulting new life, so the transcendent *freedom* of God was manifest in the mystery of God's reconciling love on the cross and in their own consequent experience of forgiveness. The victory of God's grace over evil was, therefore, the revelation of a love and power which could restore from nothing the meaning and goodness of a finite life. Such a loving power, unconditioned by anything beyond itself but creative of good, manifests because it reflects the free, transcendent love and power of God at creation.[8] If redemption is the restoration of creation, as Irenaeus said, then the experience of redemption revealed the God who created us. In this way, then, the covenant faith which culminated in Christ contained the revelation not only of the righteous and loving will of God, but also of His sovereign power to create and restore the entire creaturely realm. Through the events of history which revealed God to be the Judge and Redeemer of His people, God was

[8] The following are helpful comments on the relation of creation to Christian experience:

"The New Testament deepens this understanding [of God the Creator] in its even clearer recognition that the God of creation is one with the God of Redemption, that the creative word was one with the redemptive word incarnate in Christ; the Apostles had learned from the scriptures that God at the first creation had brought the world into existence through his word, but now they had themselves witnessed his mighty act in bringing into being through his incarnate Word a New Creation, the redeemed community, the Church of Jesus Christ." Richardson, *op. cit.*, p. 90.

"Creation is not an impressive theory, but it has its ground in divine revelation. Like the men of the New Testament we move back to the significance and reality of this first creation from the center of all history, Christ Himself. Through the faith which He gives to us and that new creation which He works within the lives of men, we affirm that through Him all things have come into being and that in Him all things cohere." Rust, E. C., *The Christian Understanding of History*, Lutterworth Press, 1947, p. 210.

also known to be the transcendent Creator of man and of nature. The idea of creation is an inference from revelation, from what is known of God through His acts in history; and it is validated over and over again in every vital Christian experience of the claim of God upon us, of the judgment of God over us, and of the renewing love of God toward us.

Paradox

We must discuss now the third word important to understanding how Christians speak about God: paradox. A paradox, which meant literally what was "contrary to expectations, to common opinion, to what seems to be," is not a simple logical contradiction. A contradiction occurs when two opposing, or different, things are said about a circumscribed reality: A cannot in the same respect be both B and not B. The contradiction obtains when A is a simple fact with no inherent diversity that could support within itself discordant predicates. For example, to say that John Doe is in age both old and young is contradictory, but to say he is old in body and young in spirit is not at all contradictory—here the distinction within the man between body and spirit resolves the contradiction. Contradictions, therefore, do not occur when the subject of our apparently opposed statements has either a width or a depth within which the opposition of the predicates can be resolved.

This gives us a clue to the meaning of paradox. Like a contradiction, a paradoxical statement is a combination of an affirmation and a denial; it describes something in apparently conflicting terms. But it does so on the assumption, not that these attributes meet and ultimately conflict at the same circumscribed point, but that beyond our knowledge they are resolved within the mysterious depths of the subject of our talk. Thus it is a paradoxical affirmation about John to say, "he is so old and yet so young." Here conflicting attributes are ascribed to John, not to contradict and cancel out one another, but to complement each other in order to describe the complexity of his total character, which reveals itself in some respects as aging and in others as fresh and vital. To try to describe John in completely consistent terms would be foolish, since it would mean leaving out some significant facet of the mystery of his unique personality. Paradox is the use of affirmation and denial ("old and yet not old") to express the depth or mystery of something unusual or strange, which could not otherwise be accurately described in its total impact.

Paradox, therefore, is necessarily used whenever the hidden unity of these experienced characteristics is beyond our grasp, when, in other words, we meet something individual, unique, or transcendent, and therefore not to be completely analyzed by our minds. And yet paradox reveals a relation to the object known, as well as a separation from it: it expresses real cognition and understanding of the strange, unique, or transcendent being before us. By our affirmations we show his continuity and similarity to what we know otherwise; by our denials we show his strangeness—and by their combination we express his own individual uniqueness. The mysterious unity of John's person has communicated itself to us in personal encounter: we know it is neither contradictory in itself nor utterly strange and unknown to us. But when we speak of it, we objectify this encountered unity into ordinary language which can express that unique and transcendent unity only by simultaneous affirmation and denial. Thus paradox is a way of speaking about what is unique, mysterious, or transcendent to our usual experience, and yet something which can be made partially intelligible in the terms of our ordinary experience.

It is not at all strange that this unusual way of speaking of the unusual should be commonly found in religious language about deity. For in all high religions the divine is unique, transcendent, and so beyond our clear comprehension. Thus talk about Him, or It, cannot be the usual consistent, clear, matter-of-fact sort of description which we use with familiar objects. It is more like talking about the mysterious depths of other persons, whom we know in part and yet do not know. In talking about God at all, we must assume He is like what we know in experience—lest He be quite ineffable and irrelevant; and yet we must indicate as well His transcendent strangeness and unlikeness —lest He cease to be God. Thus whatever we say of Him must be affirmed and denied at the same time. Moreover, we cannot hope to penetrate with our concepts to the mysterious essence of God, to discover how this likeness and unlikeness are resolved, for the ultimate cannot be put into a class of things which we can clearly measure, or adequately define. In the encounter of faith we do stand before Him; but in our theological language we can never grasp the inmost unity of His nature and being. Thus paradoxes are the only way of speaking about God: we affirm and deny things about Him, affirming something of God so we shall not be silent, and yet at the same time denying it so we shall not make of Him an ordinary object. In this sense, paradox, as a mode of religious language, includes the ways of negation and analogy we have mentioned; for every negation ultimately implies some affirmation about God, and every analogy must be negated in part if it is adequately to apply to God.

> The reason why the element of paradox comes into all religious thought and statement is because God cannot be comprehended in any human words or in any of the categories of our finite thought. God can be known only in a direct personal relationship, an "I-and-thou" intercourse, in which He addresses us and we respond to Him . . . He eludes all our words and categories. We cannot objectify or conceptualize Him. When we try, we fall immediately into contradiction. Our thought gets diffracted, broken up into statements which it

seems impossible to reconcile with each other . . . they [paradoxes] are inevitable, not because the divine reality is self-contradictory, but because when we "objectify" it, all our judgments are in some measure falsified, and the higher truth which reconciles them cannot be expressed in words, though it is experienced and lived in the "I-and-thou" relationship of faith towards God.[9]

Examples of paradoxical language applied to the ultimate are common in all high religions, even in those mystical faiths which are most hesitant to say anything at all about God. Indian religious speech about Brahman the ultimate beyond all clear understanding, abounds in paradoxes: at one moment Brahman is said to be described only by negation: "not this and not that"; and yet at the next It is called the most real, the most active, dynamic source of all things. At one moment Brahman is the unconditioned All underlying and so transcending all things, at the next It is identified with the universal soul of man:

Hence, now, there is the teaching "Not thus! not so!," for there is nothing higher than this, that he is thus. Now the designation for him is "the Real of the real."

[9] Baillie, D. M., *God Was In Christ*, Charles Scribner's Sons, 1948, p. 108–9. On the relation of religious paradox to the modes of analogy and negation, Casserley makes the following remarks: "Our analysis led us to the conclusion that the ways of analogy and negation are not, as has sometimes been supposed, two distinct, perhaps even opposed, ways of approaching the mystery of the Divine Being, but two aspects of a single way of approach which is profoundly paradoxical. The way of analogy cannot be pursued without denying the limitations inherent in the finite image it employs." Casserley, J. V. L., *The Christian in Philosophy*, p. 182. My only qualification of Casserley's excellent analysis of paradox is that he founds the need for paradoxes in speaking of God upon the "singularity" of God, rather than on His transcendent mystery to our knowledge. The word "singular" has the unfortunate connotation, not only of the unexpected and the mysterious, but also of a "singular" being—which is not quite "paradoxical" enough for God, who is also the "ground" of all singular beings.

There are, assuredly, two forms of Brahma: the formed and the formless, the mortal and the immortal, the stationary and the moving, the actual and the yon.

This shining, immortal Person who is in the earth, and, with reference to oneself, this shining, immortal Person—who is in the body—he, indeed, is just this Soul [Atman], this Immortal, this Brahma, this All.[10]

Perhaps the most fascinating use of paradoxes in religious language occurs in the Chinese mystical classic, the Tao Tê Ching—although the practical use of paradoxes in the training of the Zen Buddhists is also intriguing. In the Tao Tê Ching paradoxes tumble over one another in limitless profusion as the writer seeks to speak about the Transcendent and its relation to our life:

The Tao that can be told of
Is not the Absolute Tao.
The Names that can be given
Are not Absolute Names.
The Nameless is the origin of Heaven and Earth;
The Named is the Mother of All Things.

Therefore by the existence of things we profit.
And by the non-existence of things we are served.

Looked at, but cannot be seen—
That is called the Invisible.
Listened to, but cannot be heard—
That is called the Inaudible.
Grasped at, but cannot be touched—
That is called the Intangible,
These three elude all our inquiries,
And hence blend and become One.

[10] Brihad-Aranyaka Upanishad, Second Adhyāya, Third Brāhmana, #6 and #1, Fifth Brāhmana, #1 respectively. Found in Hume, R. E., *op. cit.*, pp. 97 and 102.

That is why it is called the Form of the Formless,
The Image of Nothingness.
That is why it is called the Elusive:
Meet it and you do not see its face;
Follow it and you do not see its back.[11]

In classical Christian thought the same sort of paradoxical religious language appears. The mystery of the
transcendent God is expressed in apparently contradictory
affirmations because His essential nature is beyond our
powers of definition; and so He can, in His mysterious
richness, only be described by an elaboration of the un-
resolved oppositions inherent in our experience of Him:

What, then, art Thou, O my God . . . stable, yet contained of none; unchangeable, yet changing all things;
never new, never old . . . always working yet ever at
rest; gathering, yet needing nothing; sustaining, pervad-
ing, and protecting; creating, nourishing, and developing; seeking, and yet possessing all things . . . And what
saith any man when he speaks of Thee? Yet woe to
them that keep silence, seeing that even they who say
most are as the dumb.[12]

Conscious that God transcends any consistent definition,
and that He combines what are, to our finite minds, the
apparently contradictory attributes of changeless eternity
with a dynamic, creative activity, Augustine can only affirm
apparently opposing attributes of God if he is to keep from
silence. God can be made partially intelligible, and so we
speak; but His unique unity transcends our understanding,
and so we speak in paradoxes. A finite thing that can be
clearly circumscribed, defined, and understood may be
either at rest or in motion, static or dynamic; but God,

[11] Tao Tê Ching, Sections 1, 11, 14. Translated by Lin Yu-
tang, *The Wisdom of China and India*, Random House, 1942,
pp. 583, 588, 589-90.
[12] Augustine, *The Confessions*, Book I, Chapter IV.

who transcends all our finite characteristics, reveals Himself as having both aspects, and thus must be spoken of in paradoxical language if He is to be described at all.

With this quotation from Augustine we have moved into the area of biblical religion, and here we find an understanding of God which is in a radical and essential way paradoxical in character. The Ultimate of mystical pantheism must, it is true, be spoken of in paradoxes because It transcends our ordinary experience, and yet is described; but this Ultimate never acts within certain events of history nor confronts us as a "Thou" over against our own real selfhood. The Christian, however, affirms that God, who is the sole source of all being, who is in all and beyond all, and who is therefore eternal and unconditioned, nevertheless is dynamically related to a real and separate creation, and what is more, active as a "doer of mighty deeds" of revelation and salvation at special times and places within its history. Here is the deepest paradox: the unconditioned acts in history, the eternal is creatively and redemptively at work in time, the changeless is involved in a changing world, the Absolute is over against His creatures in judgment and in forgiveness. Both sides of this fundamental paradox are essential for the expression of the Christian apprehension of God. If God be a conditioned part of the world, then no real salvation is possible; and yet if God is never related to the world, no salvation is known or experienced. To attempt, therefore, to "smooth out the paradox" is fatal to the meaning of the Christian message. For in the effort to achieve consistency at this point, either God's absoluteness is sacrificed and his deity lost, or else He is removed so completely from our historical experience as to cease to be the creating, ruling, and saving God of the Bible:

> It is impossible to bring the notions of absoluteness and relatedness into any kind of relation, precisely because the terms themselves preclude this. All it is possible to say is that both these principles exist in

God, and neither is prior to the other. It is a final paradox. But every attempt to compose it only introduces
confusion and inconsistency. The paradox can never be
overcome. . . .[13]

Paradox, then, the affirmation of both the unconditioned
and eternal and also the active, dynamic, related character
of God, is involved in any theological affirmation which
expresses adequately what is known of God in Christian
faith. For that faith is founded on historical revelation,
and yet the God who is revealed there is He who infinitely
transcends the world and history in His eternal being.

As we have noted, the idea of creation fairly bristles
with these paradoxes characteristic of every Christian affirmation about God. At every important point, it asserts
things about God that apparently contradict the *doxa*,
those fundamental opinions which are based on the whole
of our ordinary human experience.[14] We have said that
God "creates," and yet "out of nothing"; that He gives
being, but not His own being; that He is eternal, and yet
He founds and rules time; that He is infinite, absolute,
unconditioned, and self-sufficient, and yet that He limits
Himself by a dependent creature outside of Him; that
He is in all as their ground, and yet over against all as
their personal judge and savior; that He is good, and yet
permits the existence of real evil. Each paradox cries for
resolution; it seems to leave us with an intellectual conflict unsupportable by a rational mind. Why say "create"

[13] Richardson, C., *The Doctrine of the Trinity*, p. 38. See
also the following: "Faith cannot avoid the use of paradox in
speaking about God . . . Faith perceives God as the Eternal,
exalted above all temporal change; but also as the One who is
active in the changing phases of history and present in contemporary life. The resultant tension cannot be removed by an
application of the philosophical concepts of transcendence and
immanence without at the same time removing the living God
of faith." Aulén, G., *The Faith of the Christian Church*,
pp. 101–2.
[14] Tillich, P., *op. cit.*, Volume II, p. 92.

if you add "out of nothing"? Why say unconditioned and eternal, if you add active and personal; why say ground of being, if you add a "living, personal God"? In each case a consistent philosophy would demand that these affirmations be made mutually coherent; dualism and monism are such philosophical attempts to achieve a nonparadoxical understanding of origins. But by such "rationality" the meaning and significance of both God and of human existence known in the Christian faith are sacrificed. Paradox is the only way in which the Christian mind can express its knowledge, in faith, that the eternal God is the source of a good world. And it is the only way that what is known in experience, i.e., that both the meaning and the evil of life are real, can be understood without contradiction. The idea of creation is inevitably a paradoxical idea, because it seeks to express in human language a mystery known in the personal encounter of faith, a mystery too deep for a precise intellectual formulation, but a mystery which undergirds and supports all the more obvious coherences and meanings of our ordinary existence, and which is continually validated by them. To seek to unravel this mystery of faith would be, as we have shown, to lose both our relation to the God from whom all meaning comes, and our hold on these everyday coherences of life.

Myth in Christian Theology

We are now in a better position to understand how the word myth is used in Christian theology when, for example, we speak of the myth of creation. Myth is a form of religious language which unites the three concepts we have been discussing: analogy, revelation, and paradox, into one mode of speech about God. In mythical language about God, Christians use personal and historical analogies, but they use them paradoxically, in order to express in a dramatic story the understanding of God and of our life which faith has received in its encounter with God's revelation. Thus when Christians speak of God as Creator,

they tell a story of God's "act" of creation: "In the beginning (before all time) God created (out of nothing) the
world and time in a free act of love"—or, as the Bible puts
it, "He stretched out the heavens," "He fashioned the
mountains." When Christians speak of God's relation to
history, they also use "mythical" language: "God rules the
events of history," "He sends His son into the world," "He
fulfills His purposes in history," "He speaks through the
prophets," "He acts decisively in Christ, reconciling the
world to Himself," and so on. This "mythical" language is
analogical because it uses the analogy of human activity
in history to describe God and deliberately denies that
this language is to be interpreted literally. It is paradoxical
because this personal and historical language is in each
case used to refer to the source of all being. And, as we
have seen, this characteristic of biblical religion, to
speak of the Creator of finite beings as if He were Himself
a finite being in space and time, doing deeds and fulfilling
purposes, is highly paradoxical. Myth, then, is a way of
talking about the God who transcends history in the dramatic terms of an active agent within history.

In general there are two sorts of objections to the use of
"mythical" language in Christian theology. Stemming
from conservative religious folk, the first insists that theological ideas are quite literally and objectively true, and
describe factual situations in the same way other "truths"
describe factual situations. To them, therefore, the idea
of creation contains a literally true story about the earliest
processes in the universe, in which God was the primary
moving and molding force at work. Thus, in their minds,
to say that the doctrine of creation is "mythical" and not
"literal," seems to be implying that it is not true. We shall
try to answer this objection shortly.

Meanwhile, let us note that this conservative insistence
that theological doctrines have *some* relation to fact is
sound. The Christian faith is based on historical revelation
through concrete events in history. The theological doctrines of that faith are interpretations of the meaning of

these events, and inferences drawn from them. Thus
Christian theology is not a series of abstract ideas unrelated to any special events because it is equally related
to all; it is rather a system of concepts drawn from and
so expressive of the meaning of definite historical events.
Within this admittedly intimate relation between fact and
meaning, event and interpretation, however, two distinctions should be made. First of all we must distingiush between the factual and the "mythical" elements in the historical events on which Christian faith is based. In the
Incarnation, for example, there is an undeniable, essential
element of observable historical fact: the life and death of
Jesus of Nazareth. This historical fact is then understood
by those who encountered Jesus as the culminating revelation of God to man, as a fact within which God was
uniquely active for man's salvation. Those who responded
in faith interpreted this activity of God in and through
the life and person of Jesus in the symbols of the Incarnation of the Son of God, of His atoning death upon
the cross, and of His Resurrection and Ascension. This
interpretation is regarded by Christians as valid because
they believe that there was in reality this divine dimension to the historical facts so interpreted, that those events
did in fact have this divine meaning. However, this interpretation is also "mythical" because it speaks of God and
His activity in the analogical and paradoxical terms of the
"story" or the "drama" of a personal agent in history. Such
symbols as the descent and ascent of the Son of God, of
His personal decision to "empty Himself" and "take on
flesh," of His death as a ransom or a propitiation, and so
on, cannot be understood literally as if a large being in the
sky had been the chief actor in these events. These symbols
are analogical, and so "mythical," expressions of the
meaning that is discerned to be the deeper dimension
of the historical fact of Jesus of Nazareth. Now although
for faith these two elements, the historical facts and the
deeper, "mythical" meanings, are united in reality—since
God really *was* in Christ reconciling the world to Himself

—nevertheless a distinction must be made by the mind between the fact which is observable, and so describable by historical science, and the divine dimension of the fact, the activity of God, which faith discerns within it (as the Chalcedonian creed makes a distinction for the mind between the human and the divine "natures" of Christ, while insisting also in their real union in His person). The life of Jesus was a "literal" fact; but the divine dimension is described and interpreted "mythically"; and that description and interpretation, and its relation to the historical base, form the content of Christian doctrines about Jesus Christ. Thus even where Christian faith is most closely associated with fact, its doctrines have a "mythical" character. In faith and theology the fact, while remaining fact, is understood mythically; for the divine dimension and meaning of the fact, the activity of God within it, is described analogically and paradoxically in personal, historical, and dramatic terms.

The second distinction is between those revelatory events *in* history which are understood mythically, such as the Incarnation, and inferences from those events about God's "prehistorical" activity which are described mythically, such as creation. As we have seen, unlike the Incarnation, creation is not an historical event to which men responded in faith, and to which they witnessed in prophecy and preaching. No one observed the fact of creation, and then proclaimed its divine meaning. Rather, creation, which "precedes" history, is an inference from what is known of God in revelatory events within history itself; it is not a doctrine that comes to us through some event in history to which it is essentially wedded. Thus, like the symbol of the Fall, creation has no inherent and original factual content; its meaning is not intrinsically tied to any particular, individual event in history. It is, as we have seen, the valid expression of the deeper dimension and meaning of every fact, but it is not associated with any special fact, even the first fact, as are the revelatory events within history through which God is known. In both these cases, the language about God is "mythical," being language couched in the terms of a story about an active agent within history. But in the one case the divine action has its locus in a particular, observed, and known fact, while in the other it refers to the dimension of depth in every fact.

The second objection to "mythical language" in religion comes from the more sophisticated interpreters of religion. To them mythical language about God is *too* concrete and "factual." Agreeing that no descriptions of the ultimate can be literal in character, they draw the rational conclusion that all analogies drawn from personal and historical experience must be discarded when we speak truly of God. If God is the ground of fact, the ultimate reality, He cannot be involved in any special facts, nor can He have a will or purpose as do finite beings in time. Thus, for these thinkers, while concepts that picture God as a "person," doing deeds and fulfilling purposes, as judging, forgiving, and loving, may be helpful on a naïve level, true language about the Ultimate must move beyond "myth" into impersonal, ontological, and philosophical discourse. Again we are in partial agreement with this position: ontology is essential for Christian theology. But we cannot agree that the mythical should be superseded by the philosophical, that personal, historical, and dramatic categories should be interpreted in the terms of impersonal ones. Rather it seems that the language of myth is an essential and permanent, rather than a preliminary, element of theological discourse, and that this language should provide the determining and final concepts with which God is understood in Christian faith.

Let us now turn to the five reasons for this view of our language about God. The first two attempt to show, in disagreement with the conservative objection, why theological language about creation must be "mythical" (i.e., analogical) and not literal; the last three show, against the philosophical objection, why it must finally be "mythical" (i.e., personal, historical, and dramatic) rather than ontological and philosophical.

1. In the first place, it is surely clear why we can never regard personal symbols about God as literally applicable, nor our descriptions of His "deeds" as literal descriptions of finite events in space and time. God is the source of space, time, and being; He is not literally an actor within that context. Our words about Him are, therefore, symbols and analogies because, in the first place, the source of all finite existence cannot be spoken of in the literal terms of a finite existent without absurdity. If God is simply and literally a being, He cannot be the source of being. If, then, it is to retain any intellectual integrity at all, theology must recognize the paradoxical and analogical character of its language, and must admit that when it speaks of God's deeds, it is speaking "mythically." To many people this denial of literal language and literal truth, and this assertion of the mythical character of our religious language, seems a retreat from the solid ground of religious certainty. In this they are wrong. Literal language about God is less religious and less true than mythical. Its reference is solely to the plane of finite fact, not to the ultimate dimensions and depths of existence. Thus it implies that God is neither transcendent nor holy, but merely a finite being within the general universe—and such an implication reflects neither good sense nor good piety.

2. The second reason that the paradoxical-analogical language of myth is most appropriate for theology is that such language preserves both the religious relevance and the religious validity of the concepts of theology. If the "myth" of creation is taken to be literally and simply "true," that is, true in the sense that a description of any objective fact is true, then it loses all its religious character. For religious truth is truth in which the whole existence of every man is unconditionally involved. It is, in a literal sense, true to say that in 1955 an eclipse of the sun occurred which was visible in the United States; this is an objective, cosmological fact of interest to astronomers and

to those fortunate people who were able to view that event. But the relevance and so the area of human concern for such a cosmological event is circumscribed in two ways: (a) only a certain number of people are interested in it, and (b) their interest is intellectual and aesthetic, a matter of curiosity and mild wonder. Now if the idea of creation represents in this sense a literal and objective truth about the origin of the world, a homely description about the originating process of the world system, then it has no religious character. Such a description may point to an interesting fact which satisfies our inquiries about the first days of the world, but it has no relevance to our lives beyond that flash of momentary curiosity. As an objective truth about the world's beginning, it has no deep reverberating bearing on our own existence and destiny; it is not a truth about which all men are ultimately concerned. And, as we have seen, as an accurate scientific account of the coming-to-be of the world, this idea is manifestly untrue. In so far, therefore, as religious concepts are taken to represent literal truths, they are scientifically and philosophically untrue, and religiously irrelevant. Paradoxically, a myth can only be true as a *religious* affirmation, if it is untrue as a literal description of fact. As literal truths, myths are "prescientific," and must be discarded—but it is precisely at this point that they have no relevance for religion.

On the other hand, as an expression of the relation of all events, and therefore of my own life, to the Source and Ruler of all existence, the idea of creation truly expresses the deepest relation of my being. On this relation not only my existence, but also its essential goodness, its meaning, and its vocation or purpose, directly depend. As we have seen continually, the most crucial questions about the meaning and destiny of our own contingent and temporal existence drive us back to this question of our ultimate origins; and from our answers to these existential questions stem our most important attitudes toward life. It is its crucial importance to our own existence that gives to the idea of creation its religious character, i.e., that creation points to God, to the transcendent ground of *all* facts and so to the transcendent source of my own present existence, rather than merely to a past, objective fact long before my existence. It is, therefore, solely its reference to the transcendent that gives the doctrine of creation its universal relevance and ultimate significance; it is the fact that it deals with the dimension of depth in *our* existence that makes it religious. But the ground of all events cannot be literally described. The Lord who creates, rules, and claims all of us who are His creatures cannot be brought into the clarity, and ultimate irrelevance, of objective, cosmological fact. It is, therefore, only by analogy and paradox, not by literal language, that we can speak of God as *our* Creator and Lord. And to speak of Him in any other terms, as a mere actor of a far-off deed, is to misunderstand both what creation means and who we are. For it is only when *we* can say "Lord" to our Creator that we really understand Him as the Maker of heaven and earth. And it is only when in our own existence we can affirm the meaning of our life in obedience and commitment to Him that we understand what it is to be created by God. The doctrine of creation, therefore, becomes a religious conception only as "myth," which expresses the meaning of our own existence as dependent upon God, a meaning known only in faith, lived only in commitment and obedience, and understood only through symbol. Thus it is the paradoxical and analogical language of myth, distinguishing it from all literal and therefore objective cosmological fact, that grounds the relevance of the idea of creation to our own existence. As a concept expressing the deepest dimensions of our existence, and not just a past fact, the idea of creation preserves its own deeply religious character as concerned both with the God who transcends and rules us and with our own questions of meaning. Mythical language expresses and preserves, then, that permanent truth in religious concepts which literal, scientific language had lost.[15]

Finally, it is only in this context of existential question and religious answer, expressed in the language of myth, that the theological doctrine of creation can in any sense be validated. It is plain that this idea cannot be proved true by the kind of evidence with which science deals; if it could, it would cease to be a relevant religious and theological idea. However, aside from its indirect validation in Christian experience, to which we have already referred, the idea of creation can be confirmed in the same way that any other fundamental viewpoint concerning the ultimate nature of reality is confirmed. Such viewpoints can never be simply proved by "evidence," for they themselves involve the more basic decision as to what sort of evidence is relevant. They can only be validated by their

[15] Much of the argument with Rudolf Bultmann over the place of "myth" in Christian theology is a semantic problem related to our present discussion. Apparently for Bultmann "myth" means the kind of primitive and imaginary description of objective, cosmological fact which we have maintained to be both untrue and unreligious. In this sense of the word, theology must be "demythologized." But if myth means speaking of the ultimate source and Lord of existence in the dramatic and historical language of personal will and action, then Bultmann recognizes that this is essential to theology, and himself uses this language continually. For example, he speaks of "decisive acts of God," "revelatory events," "that the unseen reality confronts us as love," and finally that "God steps in and acts" ("New Testament and Mythology" in *Kerygma and Myth*, S.P.C.K., pp. 13, 14, 19, and 31 respectively). The fundamental point of his essay is that "faith needs to be emancipated from its association with a world view expressed in objective terms, whether it be a mythical or a scientific one" (*Kerygma and Myth*, p. 210). This is exactly the function of religious myth as we understand it, an expression in language of our relation to God in existential faith, a relation that transcends the objective relations between finite things, and so which is of ultimate concern to every man. Possibly if Bultmann recognized that *his own* language about God was also "myth," or at least analogical and paradoxical language, his discussion would be immensely clarified.

ability to provide a meaningful context for those basic intuitions which are taken to be the ultimate certainties of our experience. In this regard, the idea of creation, and the faith of which it is a part, makes more sense of our experience of being contingent, temporal creatures than does any other alternative viewpoint. For, as we have seen, in its scope the experiences of contingency, of freedom, of responsibility, and of sin are made intelligible; and in its terms we are able to affirm at once the potential goodness of individual and historical life, the reality of its evil, and its certain promise of renewal. In no other ultimate scheme of things do all these certainties of our experience find an intelligible place. In every alternative view of existence, either the freedom, the responsibility, the evil, or the promise of existence is denied. Thus when men cease to look for scientific evidence for a religious affirmation, and instead look into the question of the meaning and purpose of their own existence as contingent, free, and responsible persons, they can find this "myth" validated over and over again as providing that general framework within which our human existence can be most fully and coherently understood. Since it is relevant to our existential questions of meaning and purpose, the myth of creation gives a religious, not a scientific or philosophical, answer: that the God who created us is our Lord and Redeemer. And so again, the language in which this idea is expressed must be language appropriate, not to a description of a finite, objective fact, validatable by scientific evidence, but the language appropriate to the transcendent Source and Ruler of our own immediate existence as it is experienced in our life of contingent freedom and of responsible decision. And such language, as we have seen, is the pardoxical-analogical language of "myth," which, by its form, deals with the relation of finitude to its source, not the relations of finite things to each other.

3. Turning now from the question of the importance of the nonliteral, analogical language of myth, let us see those reasons why the personal, historical, and dramatic

speech of myth, rather than the abstract language of philosophy, is the essential language for theology. First of all, this form of language alone can express the dialectical tensions or paradoxes within the Christian understanding of God without serious religious loss. As we have seen, the central tension or paradox in this understanding is that which exists between God as the eternal, transcendent source of finite being, and God as active, dynamic, and related to finite being; between God as the origin of existence, and God as He who confronts us as a personal Father. The language of myth expresses this dialectical understanding of Christian faith most adequately because of the paradoxical relation of its linguistic form to its intellectual content. While the form of mythical language is temporal, historical, and personal—and so expresses the dynamic, personal relatedness of God—the content of the myth points beyond the realm of finite things to the transcendent, and so implies and expresses the ontological self-sufficiency and absoluteness of God. Through this paradox of form and content, mythical language communicates the paradoxical understanding of God so essential to the life of faith.

Let us examine this point in more detail. The theological myth of creation states that "before all time, God, in an act of purposive freedom, created out of nothing the world and time." The form of the myth is in temporal language: it speaks of "before"; it uses the human analogy of "create," "make," or "fashion"; it points to a free act, and any such action assumes a context of space and time, and a natural environment; and it affirms a purpose or goal to be realized, presumably in the future. The linguistic terms of the myth are historical and dramatic, for it is a "story" about a personal agent, set in the temporal categories of action over a period, of sequence, and of purpose. On the other hand, the intellectual content of the myth points beyond the world of finite things and of time. It defines the analogical word "create" as "out of nothing." As we have seen, this implies that this act transcends because it defies all the intraworldly examples of creation; and it implies as well that the Creator transcends because He originates all of creaturely reality. Likewise, the myth speaks of the act in which time itself is initiated as a creature of God. Nothing could indicate so clearly the transcendence of God over time as the affirmation that God was "before time" as its Source and Creator.

The same myth, however, that indicates this transcendence of God points equally clearly to God's continual dynamic relatedness to the world and time. For the act of creation *ex nihilo* implies the most intimate positive and purposive relation of the Creator to His absolutely dependent yet real creation. This relatedness to the changing world the form of the myth expresses by speaking of the transcendent God in the language of temporal activity. His self-sufficiency is not defined in the static language of substance, but by naming Him the Creator and Lord; and His transcendent eternity is not defined as the negation of time, but paradoxically as "before" time, i.e., as a reality beyond the temporal and yet related to it. Myth, therefore, expresses the paradox of both God's transcendence over time and the world and His dynamic relation to them. For while the analogical language of myth is the language of persons in time, its content points inescapably to the mystery of eternity, being, and love, from which the world and time come. Through this paradox of temporal form and transcendent content, the myth communicates both the transcendence over time and creation and the positive relation to them that characterize God as He is known in revelation. To transform this mythical language into the impersonal, nonparadoxical language of philosophy would be to enclose God within the world or to remove Him from it; and surely it would be to lose His "personal" character as encountered in faith. This is the one form in which the dialectical understanding of God in Christian faith can find accurate expression.

4. A fourth reason for the personal historical language of myth is that in biblical faith God is known through His revelation of Himself in historical events: in His dealings with the Israelite people, in the event of the Incarnation, and in His presence in the Church through the Holy Spirit. Thus a theology that is true to the basic character of the Christian religion is a theology of "recital," a theology that bases its knowledge of God and its descriptions of Him on what He has done in history.[16] Having encountered and known God through events, Christian theology describes Him in terms of activities and deeds. Now the God who is known in and through these historical events is realized to be also a God who transcends history and time. Nevertheless, because, for Christians and Jews alike, all that is known of God is an inference from our knowledge of Him as the living God of history, that very transcendence itself continues to be thought of in the terms of historical deeds, and to be described in the categories of action, purpose, and will. In all language about the transcendent we must proceed from the known to the unknown: in Christian faith the "known of God" is His dramatic activity in history, and so the "unknown" of the divine is expressed through these personal and dramatic symbols. Thus when Christians seek to describe God in His transcendence over history, they use the language of time and of persons acting in time to do so. Myth is this language, the historical language of revelation, encounter, and faith, paradoxically used to describe the transcendent dimension which revelation reveals.

[16] As G. E. Wright has so well said: "It [biblical theology] is fundamentally an interpretation of history, a confessional recital of historical events as the acts of God, events which lead backwards to the beginning of history and forward to its end . . . The being and attributes of God are nowhere systematically presented but are inferences from events . . . Consequently not even the nature of God can be portrayed abstractly. He can only be described *in relation to* the historical process . . ." G. E. Wright, *op. cit.*, pp. 57–58.

5. Finally, the main content of our most immediate and certain knowledge of God is of His personal relationship to us as our Lord and Father. As witnessed throughout Christian history, in their deepest and most transforming experiences of God, Christians have found themselves encountering, not an impersonal substance, but a personal Lord who lays an absolute claim on their life, who judges them with absolute righteousness, and who rescues them with an unconditional love. Because this encounter with God in Christian experience transforms men at the personal center of their being if it heals them at all, it can be expressed only in the language of personal life, in the language of responsibility, of judgment, and of love. The core of the Christian idea of God, therefore, is that of a God who meets us in personal fellowship in Jesus Christ: here we know God first, and so from this point outward we think of Him. For this reason, when we try to understand the other activities of God, such as His creative or His providential activity, it is natural and necessary that we think and speak of Him as we know Him most deeply and immediately. And so we speak of God as we would of a historical person: we refer to His "purpose" in creation, we say He "wills" to create, and that He "loves" His creatures. This is not to say that He who is "up there" is "like us." It is rather to say that in the personal encounter with God in Christ, we know His majestic otherness as a personal judgment and love, and so when we come to speak of that transcendence we use personal analogies. And as we have repeatedly seen, this personal character in God is the basis for the meaning and significance of our finite, temporal existence. Our life can be filled with purpose and hope because it has not been merely processed into being like an industrial product, but has been created for a loving purpose by our Father's gracious will. Thus, despite all of its profound ontological and philosophical implications, which require that metaphysical language be continually used in theology, even the doctrine of creation is finally to be conceived most truly in terms of personal and

dramatic analogies. For this reason, the simple "myth" that "God out of the freedom of his love created the world from nothing because it was good" expresses on the profoundest level the Christian understanding of God and so of the meaning of our existence. In this sense, this book on creation has been an explication of the *meaning* of the theological myth of creation, elaborating its many implications, religious, metaphysical, and existential. Since we have not transcended or "gone beyond" this myth, but merely explored its content, the myth itself remains the profoundest expression of all we have said.

Two Final Queries

In outlining the mythical and analogical nature of our theological language, we have emphasized the inescapable paradoxes within the idea of God. This discussion, however, leaves us with two final queries. First, if the idea of God is filled with conflicting tensions, is there any unity to this conception, or is it just a jumble of opposites whose resolution is quite unknown? And secondly, if all our knowledge of God is in terms of analogies, can we be said to possess any significant knowledge of God at all? Or do our ideas of God, like tiny finite beams, barely rise into the darkness of an infinite night, so that the mystery of our origins remains as dark as ever? Is there no knowledge of God that reaches to His ultimate nature, that is not a mere human analogy paradoxically applied to an unfathomed abyss?

This is a question which must be answered. Theology can defend itself against the criticism of science and common sense by saying its language is not literal but analogical; and it can defend itself against the criticisms of philosophical logic by showing why its language must be paradoxical. But it cannot rest there. For a knowledge of God that is *merely* analogical and paradoxical is no knowledge at all. For example, we say God "exists" and "creates"

—but not as anything else exists and creates; we say God is "personal" and "free"—but not as we humans are personal and free. Until we know in what sense these words apply to God, however, they are useless to us. Without some knowledge of how they are to be understood in relation to God, they are merely feeble human cries, thrown up against an infinite mystery. For this reason Christian theologians have recognized that if we are to speak intelligibly about God we must possess some direct and unsymbolic knowledge of Him.

There has, however, been disagreement about what this unsymbolic and direct knowledge of God is. One tradition has maintained that we speak of God most directly when we understand Him as the unconditioned source of our being, as the first cause of being, as being itself, or pure being. Since, according to this view, this is the closest and most direct knowledge man can have, all else that we say about God is said with this basic idea in mind. Personal words, such as judgment, love, forgiveness, etc., are hung like hats on the stand of this one ontological definition of God.[17] Now clearly we have agreed in part with this

[17] Two great examples of this impressive "ontological" tradition spring to mind. The first is Thomas Aquinas, who, having proved that God is the first cause of being, declared that the fundamental name of God is "He Who Is," "Pure Being or Actuality," and that all religious or biblical words applied to God are symbols to be interpreted according to the analogical relation between contingent being and necessary, self-sufficient being.

The greatest modern representative of this ontological tradition, Tillich, does not, as did Thomas, reach the conception of Being Itself by means of a cosmological proof. Rather for him the notion that God is Being Itself is the direct implication of God's known transcendence to the finite, and so of the certain statement that all the words we use of him are analogical. Having asked whether there is any point at which a nonsymbolic assertion about God is possible, he answers: "There is such a point, namely, the statement that everything we say about God is symbolic. Such a statement is an assertion about God which itself is not symbolic." Tillich, op. cit., Volume II, p. 9. That is to say, if all language about God is symbolic, this implies directly the transcendence of God, and so His status as Being Itself.

tradition. With them we have emphasized the importance of understanding God as the source of our being, and so of describing Him in the philosophical terms of ontology: of saying He is self-sufficient, eternal, unconditioned, etc. If God is to be called Creator, then He must be thought about in these metaphysical and philosophical terms. But for several reasons we do not feel that this is our most direct or most significant knowledge of God.

This metaphysical language about God, perhaps more than other language, is itself symbolic and analogical in character. It uses as its fundamental categories concepts

---

Hence the symbols "Pure Being," and "Ground of Being" are the most direct knowledge of God we possess.

We would agree that the one absolutely nonsymbolic statement about God is the general principle of negative theology "not this and not that"—i.e., everything we say of God is to be negated as well as affirmed. But we should note that this statement is fundamentally negative, not affirmative: it says "no" to literal knowledge. It does not affirm even the transcendent being of God, for this is itself an inference, and must be expressed by symbol; it merely denies His likeness to creatures. In this statement, therefore, the category of being is not involved at all—in such a mere negation, the "being" or "reality" of the divine is still in doubt, as in the "negative" form of Mahayana Buddhism represented by Nagarjuna. Thus the categories of ontology cannot be derived from this unsymbolic but essentially negative statement, any more than can the categories of history and persons. Both are unrelated to this negative assertion, and both are symbolic, drawn from different areas of our finite experience.

The reason, then, that Tillich chose the ontological categories as basic seems not to be that they are implied by this statement, but rather that his experience of renewal is fundamentally the experience of ontological renewal, of "new being"—rather than the more personal experience of mercy and forgiveness. And on the basis of that experience, he thinks of God as the source of that experience, as the "Ground of Being." Thus the basis for his central language about God is the same as that here advanced, namely that we think of God ultimately in the terms where we know him most directly. Only for Tillich that experience of revelation is the essentially ontological experience of alienation overcome by "new being" rather than the essentially personal experience of guilt overcome by forgiveness and love.

derived from a philosophical analysis of natural finite existence and then referred analogically to God as the infinite ground of that existence. The *direct* knowledge here is of the finite being which alone the metaphysician can analyze; it is not of God, for a transcendent God cannot be the direct object of metaphysical inquiry. The concept of being is then applied to God as an indirect symbol of this directly experienced finite being. This is indicated by the fact that all such systems refer to God as *pure* being, *ground* of being, being *itself*, or *first cause* of being, showing by each of these qualifying words that the ordinary, garden-variety concept of being has been analogically transformed when it is applied to the transcendent. Our ontological concepts of God's being are, therefore, as much inferences, symbols, and analogies as any other of our ideas about God. Moreover, in this metaphysical tradition, the knowledge of God in historical revelation and in our encounter with God in our personal life, is subordinated to this analogical knowledge of God in natural philosophy, and this we feel is untrue to the essence of the Christian understanding of God.

As we have indicated, the point where God is most directly known is in historical revelation, and especially in the person of Jesus Christ. In Christ, God is not known as He is in Himself, it is true. What Christians have found is the love and the power of God poured, so to speak, into the finite, which received it and revealed it. Jesus the Christ is "transparent" to the transcendent judgment and the unconditioned love of God, and indirectly, as we have seen, to the almighty power of God. The result is that all who receive Him in faith can now experience and know with overwhelming immediacy the nature of God as holy love united with holy power. In the Word of God Incarnate, therefore, Christians confront God directly; through Him they stand "*coram Deo*," in the presence of God. Thus the personal recreative love of God in Christ, not the ontological power of God in general existence, is the one unsymbolic and direct idea of God that Christians possess.

A Christian's idea of God, therefore, is not a mere jumble of contradictory elements, some philosophical and some religious. It is centered about the love of God as that is known in Jesus Christ, a love that has created us for fellowship with God, and then recreated us into new life when we had fallen away from that fellowship. And all else that Christians must say about God—about His judgment on ourselves and on others, about His purposes for us all, about His providential will for history, and even about His creation and preservation of the being of the world—should be united to and expressive of this central concept of love. We should, it is true, never cease to think about God in such philosophical terms as the unconditioned ground of our being and the eternal source of time. The central issue for faith and its relationship to philosophy is not that we refuse to think about God, or even about His metaphysical relations, in so far as we are able. The important point for a theology that wishes to retain the integrity of our faith is that we refuse to think about God in any way that might prevent the Gospel of judgment and of mercy, of revelation and salvation, of the covenant and Christ, from coming to us in the experience of faith. The judgment and especially the love of God in Christ are the sources and the continuing grounds of our relation to God in faith. Correspondingly, it is this love and the personal terms that are expressive of it that are the center of our theological efforts to understand God. God is first love and then being for us. For as Christians we know God as the source of our existence only when we first know him to be the love that will not let us go.

BIBLICAL REFERENCES

INDEX

Absolute
  of philosophy, 101f, 105, 237
Absolute Beginning, 310ff
  how known, 311f
  as myth not fact, 317f
American culture (*see also* Western culture)
  view of meaning, 165ff
Analogy
  and creation, 53f, 67ff, 323f
  its difficulties, 102f, 356f
  its knowledge of God, 53, 67, 99ff, 323ff, 356f
  and myth, 342f
  and ontology, 358f
  and paradox, 336f
  of persons, 320
Anthropomorphism, 10, 319ff, 355f
Anxiety
  conquered in faith, 230f
  of contingency, 6–7, 168ff
  of temporality, 289ff
Apostles' Creed, 251
Arians, 60n, 250
Aristotle, 42, 45, 199, 296, 297, 298n, 300
Aseity, of God, 87
  and God's freedom, 109
Athanasius, 53, 53n, 97, 250n, 267, 284
Atonement, 264
Augustine, 41, 49, 60, 60n, 69n, 78, 78n, 100n, 165n, 198n, 220, 220n, 222n, 235, 244, 245n, 248, 257n, 261, 262n, 301–5, 301n, 339f
Aulén, G., 86n, 98n, 108n, 341n

Babylonian, creation myths, 27
Bad Fortune, 167
Baillie, D. M., 337n
Baillie, J., 327n
Barth, K., 97
Beckett, S., 176n
Behaviorism, and purpose, 73f
Being
  and creation, 52
  and God, 30f, 52, 82, 85ff, 115, 357ff
  as ontological question, 18, 30f
Bible
  and revelation, 27f, 325ff
Biblical faith
  and creation, 330ff
  and evolution, 209
  its idea of God, 113ff
  importance of creation to, 4ff, 24ff, 44ff, 57, 58ff, 91f, 96, 109ff, 218ff, 228ff, 249ff, 278ff, 304, 328f
  and ontology, 86ff, 92, 96, 103f, 109ff, 142, 228f, 355ff
  and paradox, 340f